CLIVE BARKER'S
NEXT TESTAMENT

VOLUME THREE

PRAISE FOR
CLIVE BARKER'S NEXT TESTAMENT

"Worship at the altar of your new God of horror Wick, resurrected to life by Clive Barker and Mark Miller, and pray for mercy. Next Testament will blow your mind, shake your faith, and steal your soul and you'll keep coming back for more."
— **Jessica Dwyer**, *HorrorHound*

"What if the Old Testament God—in all his insane and genocidal glory—returned to the modern world for a little fun? This is a smart, hilarious, and stunningly visualized apocalypse—and probably the only place you'll ever get to see members of the Trinity punching each other."
— **Issac Marion**

"This is a masterpiece that will gain prominent significance with comic book and horror fans as years go by."
— **Bloody Disgusting**

"Next Testament is violent, bloody, contemplative fiction."
— **Christopher Golden**

"The overlord of sublime horror, Clive Barker, is at his shining finest in this series. When he's dealing with gods and monsters, Barker always delivers. Like a song, Haemi Jang's artwork is a perfectly lyrical compliment to Barker and Miller's melody."
— **Steve Johnson**, *Special Effects/Makeup Artist*
War of the Worlds
Lord of Illusions
Big Trouble in Little China

"Clive Barker's Next Testament reminds me—as if I needed the reminder—of the blazing scope of Mr. Barker's imagination. I've been reading him since the Books of Blood tore my fragile teenage mind asunder two decades ago, and I remain in awe of the seemingly limitless span of his creativity. He sees things the rest of us cannot—doorways hidden in the ordinary fabric of things, places where the world bends on strange and startling angles. He does what the very best writers do, which is to say he makes readers see our quotidian world in a totally new way. And if his vision is occasionally harsh (and yes, it is) or brutal, or bloody, there remains an unaccountable beauty in it. It simply blew me away."
— **Nick Cutter**

"Two people genuinely in love find out there doesn't have to be a Devil because God is already worse. Clive Barker and Mark Miller deliver an interesting new take on apocalypse as humanity is not only threatened with destruction but also criticized for becoming banal. An interesting mix of social commentary, perversion, death and hope."
— **Alan Kistler,**
The Game of Thrones Cookbook
Doctor Who a History
Star Trek and History

"So it is really no surprise that CLIVE BARKER'S NEXT TESTAMENT would end well, but just how well was this series going to end? Perfectly."
— **Samantha Roehrig,** *Comic Bastards*

"This feels like Clive Barker by way of 90's Vertigo, and that's a fantastic thing."
— **Big Comic Page**

CLIVE BARKER'S NEXT TESTAMENT Volume Three, August 2015. Published by BOOM! Studios, a division of Boom
Entertainment, Inc. Clive Barker's Next Testament is ™ & © 2015 Boom Entertainment, Inc. and Clive Barker. Originally published
in single magazine form as CLIVE BARKER'S NEXT TESTAMENT No. 9-12. ™ & © 2014 Boom Entertainment, Inc and Clive
Barker. All rights reserved. BOOM! Studios™ and the BOOM! Studios logo are trademarks of Boom Entertainment, Inc., registered
in various countries and categories. All characters, events, and institutions depicted herein are fictional. Any similarity between any
of the names, characters, persons, events, and/or institutions in this publication to actual names, characters, and persons, whether
living or dead, events, and/or institutions is unintended and purely coincidental. BOOM! Studios does not read or accept unsolicited
submissions of ideas, stories, or artwork.

A catalog record of this book is available from OCLC and from the BOOM! Studios website, www.boom-studios.com, on the
Librarians Page.

BOOM! Studios, 5670 Wilshire Boulevard, Suite 450, Los Angeles, CA 90036-5679. Printed in China. First Printing.

ISBN: 978-1-60886-722-6, eISBN: 978-1-61398-393-5

WRITTEN BY
CLIVE BARKER
& MARK MILLER

ILLUSTRATED BY
HAEMI JANG

COLORS BY
VLADIMIR POPOV
CHAPTERS 9-11
HAEMI JANG
CHAPTER 12

LETTERS BY
STEVE WANDS

COVER BY
GOÑI MONTES

DESIGNER
KARA LEOPARD

ASSISTANT EDITOR
CHRIS ROSA

EDITOR
IAN BRILL

SPECIAL THANKS TO RON MCKENZIE, JESSICA DWYER, ERIC WEBB, ANNE SIBBALD, CHRISTIAN FRANCIS, BEN MEARES, AND STEFANIE MILLER

INTRODUCTION BY THOMAS F. MONTELEONE

There is an apocryphal story about Mark Twain that goes something like this...

In his later years he was giving a lecture and ended the session with a Q&A from the audience. A woman made a reference to the author's irreverent and often very humorous collection of essays, "Letters from the Earth," in which Twain skewers some of the Bible's more well-known stories and turns them on the spit of his sarcastic wit. She asked him, based on that piece of work, if he did indeed believe in God.

Supposedly Twain considered the question for a moment before surprising his audience with the following reply: "Madame, I believe that if God exists, then he is surely a malign thug."
I'm willing to bet Clive Barker is familiar with that quote; and in truth, I wouldn't have been surprised to see the line or a suitable variant appear in the dialogue of Next Testament's characters.

And speaking of characters, I think that's what this series is really all about. The religious (and dare I say mythic?) aspects of the larger narrative are familiar enough templates upon which Barker and co-writer Mark Miller hangs the elements of their story. We see very few familiar faces or stock characters in these pages. Everyone has a backstory and motivations about which we will need to know more before passing judgment. We inherently understand the etiology the writer employs and we are just fine with the initial buy-in.

But after we've been given our chips, we realize this is not a game we've played before.

When the story opens, we are led to believe we are meeting the Gandalf or the Obi-Wan of our epic tale in the figure of Julian. He is a mover and a shaker and he is the actuator of the entire story that unfolds. But our writers know that to follow the classic archetype will make his epic too . . . too comfortable, too predictable. And so, we quickly learn that Julian is more savvy and relentless for his own (and ultimately all of humankind's) good. In his zeal to complete the circle of his dreams and his unconscious beliefs, he unleashes the most primal of all X-factors into our world—a being who calls himself by the odd nomer of "Wick."

And just who this is guy?

Well, following the not-so-obtuse clues of the tripartite orobourisian symbology and melding it with the blatant and not terribly oblique references to the Trinity, we have little choice but to accept whom he tells us he is. Wick is that persona previously mis-portrayed in a plethora of Renaissance imaginings as the white-bearded patriarch who coasts upon a majestic bank of clouds as He benignly regards all that comprises His Creation.

In the first three parts of Next Testament we are forced to accept a consciousness, an entity that is beyond our capacity to truly understand. What at turns appears to be complete ignorance of an attribute of the human condition becomes instantly transformed into a cruel recognition that can only be explicated by the highest irony. Wick makes a mockery of the usually accepted formulae for how to appease and worship any worthy deity. He seems to delight in the exposition of such human folly. I mean, who would really want a Golden Calf in his or her image. . . even a great pyramid is revealed to be something silly and not necessary.

I suspect what Barker and Miller are doing here is taking the whole cast of Joseph Campbell's mythic archetypes and turning them inside-out. Indeed Wick appears not at all like the Creator of accepted dogma, but quite the antipodal conceit. He draws no joy or satisfaction from the world he forced into being . . . only from its utter devastation.

Which says what about this kind of god? If he sees only imperfection in the things he has created, then what does that say about himself? Can Wick handle the idea that he is equally imperfect and therefore as flawed and despicable as his mere humans?

Just as any immature child will crumple up the scratch paper of his crayoned attempts to capture reality, Wick consoles himself with the idea of just starting over.

I'm not going to get railed out of town for any major spoilers, but I honestly don't think I'm giving much away by reminding you at this point we are still missing the presence of those who should be considered Major Pieces on the Cosmic Game Board. Surely you've been wondering and anticipating with the rest of us. And that's why the pages to follow will unfold with such power and wonder.

Enough said on that particular denouement. I would be remiss if I didn't at least shine a thin beam on the subtext of the entire narrative that persists like the steadiest beat of an engine that will not be stilled.

Julian's son, Tristan, by the unerring force of his belief in himself and his one true love, he refuses to allow the sins of his father to be transferred to his own head. Throughout the saga, the spiritual gyroscope that keeps the tale from spinning off into a perhaps-deserved oblivion is the persevering quest for truth in the personae of Tristan and Elspeth. When we consider the story of the original Tristan, and that Elspeth derives from the Scottish for "chosen by God," let's just say the pair are well-named.

To say much more would be pressing my luck, because I believe I've said more than enough to make you anxious to jump into this concluding book of wonders, terrors, and revelations. Regardless of your own belief system or weltanschauung, Clive Barker and Mark Miller promise an unraveling that will challenge you, and move you to do what the Jesuit theologian-philosopher Tielhard de Chardin urged we do always: ask the next question.

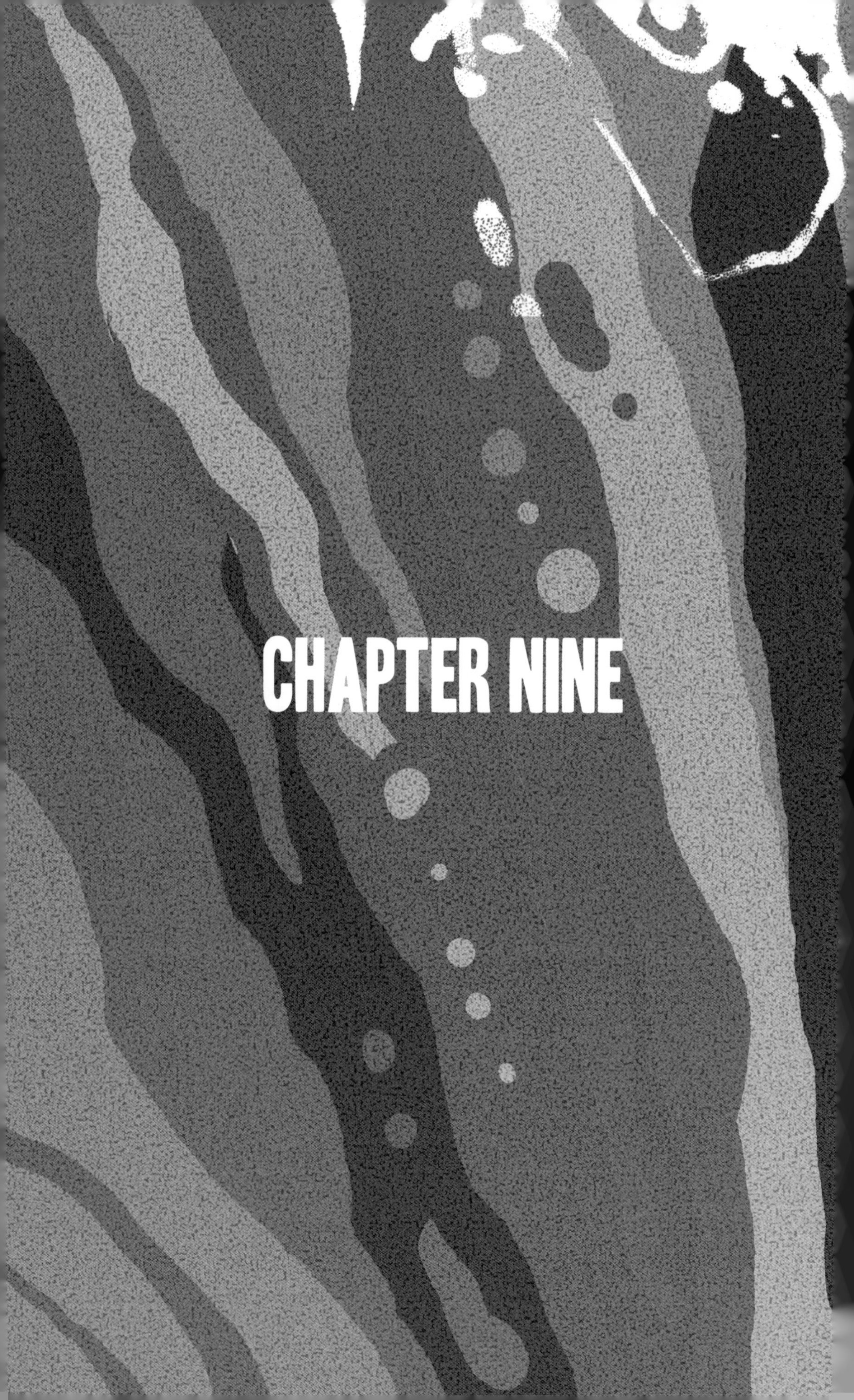

CHAPTER NINE

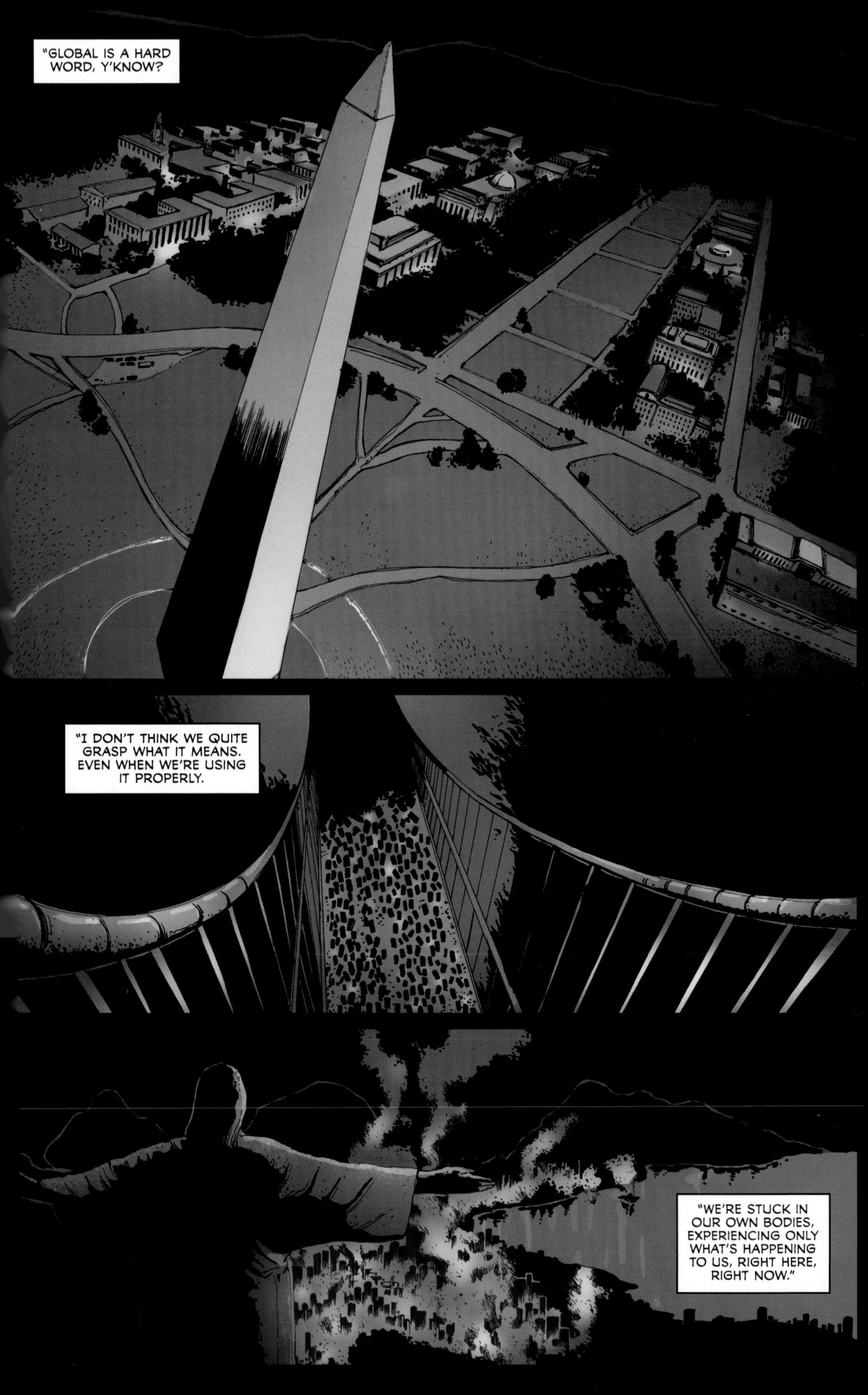
"GLOBAL IS A HARD WORD, Y'KNOW?
"I DON'T THINK WE QUITE GRASP WHAT IT MEANS. EVEN WHEN WE'RE USING IT PROPERLY.
"WE'RE STUCK IN OUR OWN BODIES, EXPERIENCING ONLY WHAT'S HAPPENING TO US, RIGHT HERE, RIGHT NOW."

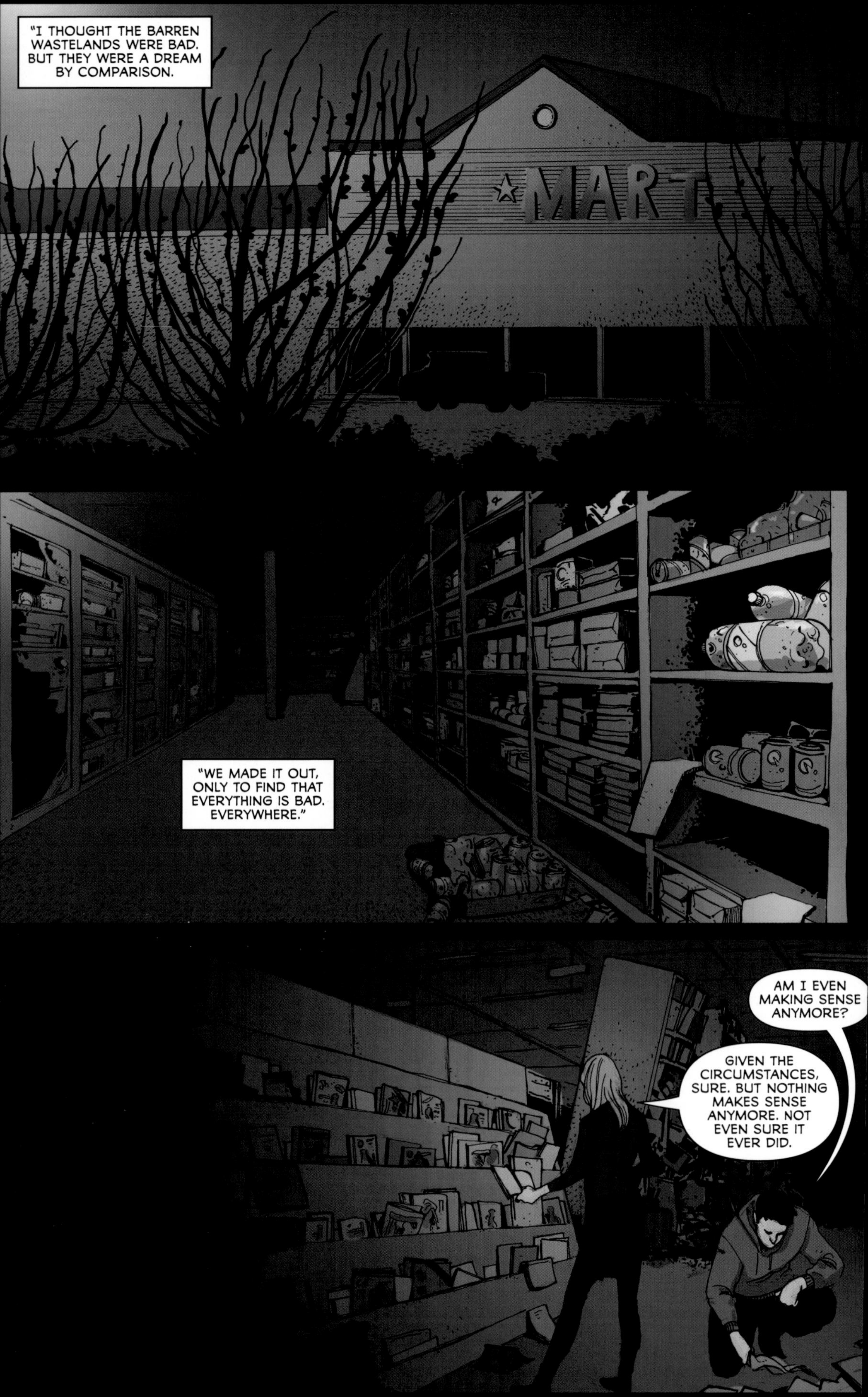
"I THOUGHT THE BARREN WASTELANDS WERE BAD. BUT THEY WERE A DREAM BY COMPARISON.
MART
"WE MADE IT OUT, ONLY TO FIND THAT EVERYTHING IS BAD. EVERYWHERE."
AM I EVEN MAKING SENSE ANYMORE?
GIVEN THE CIRCUMSTANCES, SURE. BUT NOTHING MAKES SENSE ANYMORE. NOT EVEN SURE IT EVER DID.

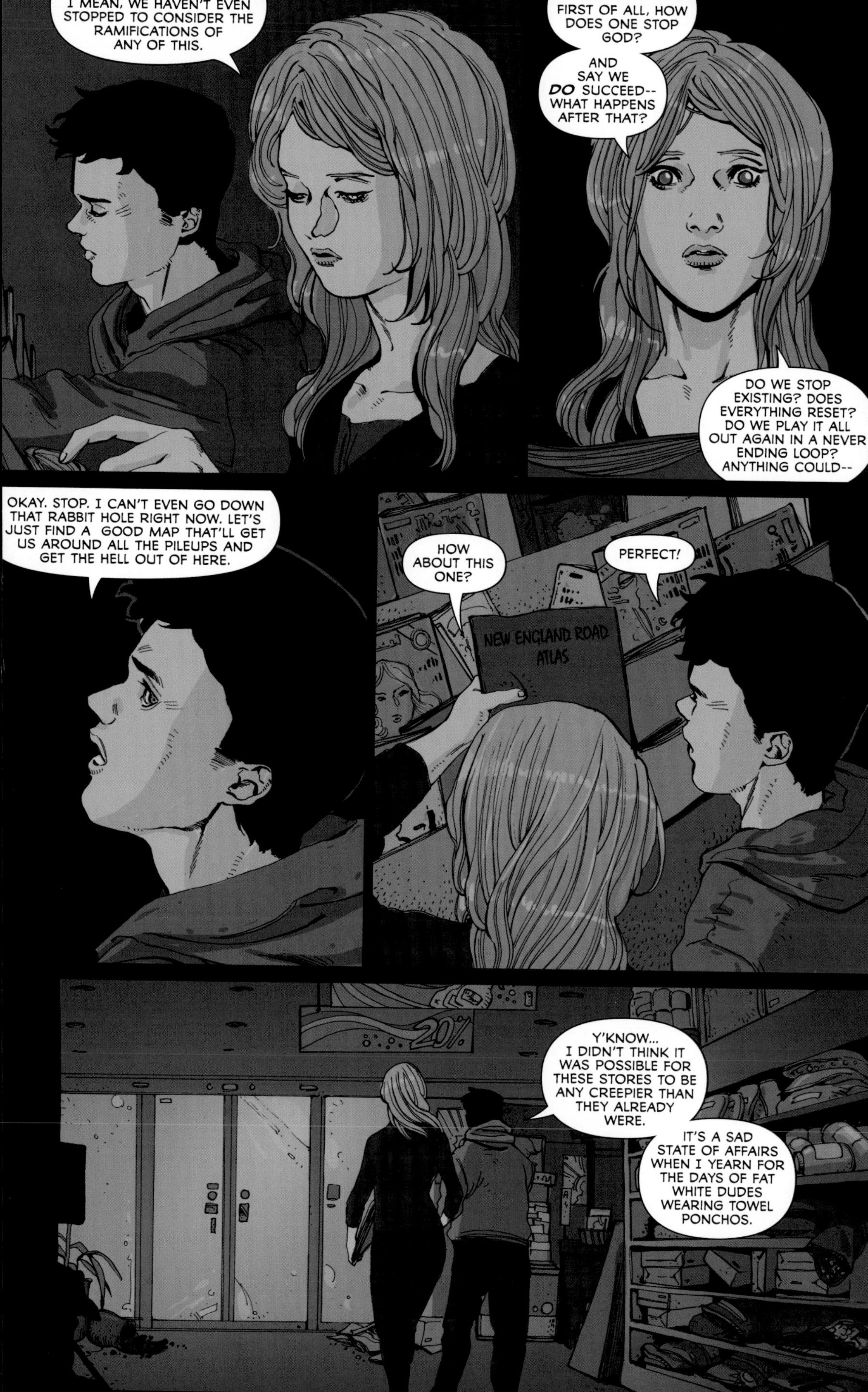
I MEAN, WE HAVEN'T EVEN STOPPED TO CONSIDER THE RAMIFICATIONS OF ANY OF THIS.
FIRST OF ALL, HOW DOES ONE STOP GOD?
AND SAY WE *DO* SUCCEED-- WHAT HAPPENS AFTER THAT?
DO WE STOP EXISTING? DOES EVERYTHING RESET? DO WE PLAY IT ALL OUT AGAIN IN A NEVER ENDING LOOP? ANYTHING COULD--
OKAY. STOP. I CAN'T EVEN GO DOWN THAT RABBIT HOLE RIGHT NOW. LET'S JUST FIND A GOOD MAP THAT'LL GET US AROUND ALL THE PILEUPS AND GET THE HELL OUT OF HERE.
HOW ABOUT THIS ONE?
NEW ENGLAND ROAD ATLAS
PERFECT!
20%
Y'KNOW... I DIDN'T THINK IT WAS POSSIBLE FOR THESE STORES TO BE ANY CREEPIER THAN THEY ALREADY WERE.
IT'S A SAD STATE OF AFFAIRS WHEN I YEARN FOR THE DAYS OF FAT WHITE DUDES WEARING TOWEL PONCHOS.

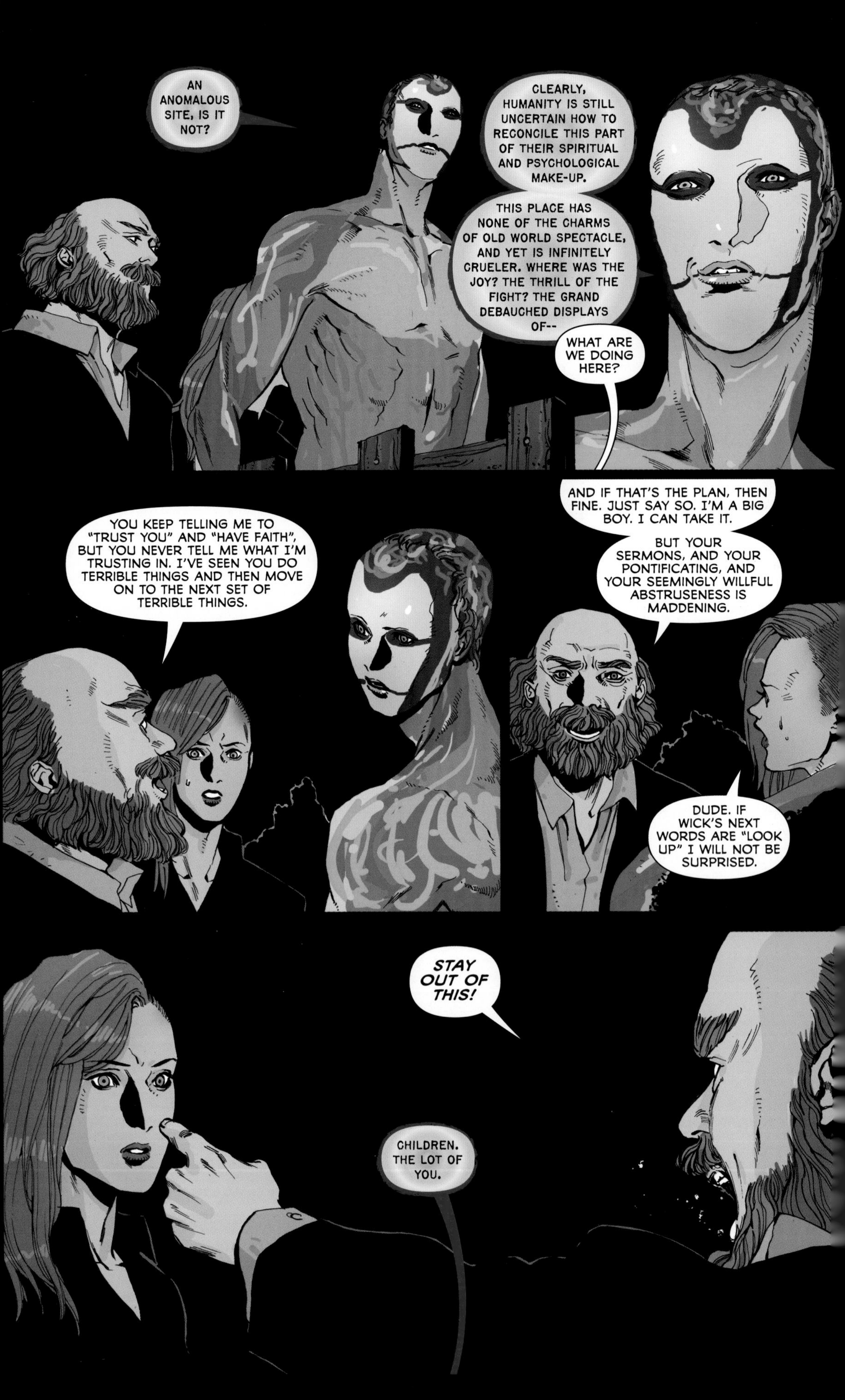
AN ANOMALOUS SITE, IS IT NOT?
CLEARLY, HUMANITY IS STILL UNCERTAIN HOW TO RECONCILE THIS PART OF THEIR SPIRITUAL AND PSYCHOLOGICAL MAKE-UP.
THIS PLACE HAS NONE OF THE CHARMS OF OLD WORLD SPECTACLE, AND YET IS INFINITELY CRUELER. WHERE WAS THE JOY? THE THRILL OF THE FIGHT? THE GRAND DEBAUCHED DISPLAYS OF--
WHAT ARE WE DOING HERE?
YOU KEEP TELLING ME TO "TRUST YOU" AND "HAVE FAITH", BUT YOU NEVER TELL ME WHAT I'M TRUSTING IN. I'VE SEEN YOU DO TERRIBLE THINGS AND THEN MOVE ON TO THE NEXT SET OF TERRIBLE THINGS.
AND IF THAT'S THE PLAN, THEN FINE. JUST SAY SO. I'M A BIG BOY. I CAN TAKE IT.
BUT YOUR SERMONS, AND YOUR PONTIFICATING, AND YOUR SEEMINGLY WILLFUL ABSTRUSENESS IS MADDENING.
DUDE. IF WICK'S NEXT WORDS ARE "LOOK UP" I WILL NOT BE SURPRISED.
STAY OUT OF THIS!
CHILDREN. THE LOT OF YOU.

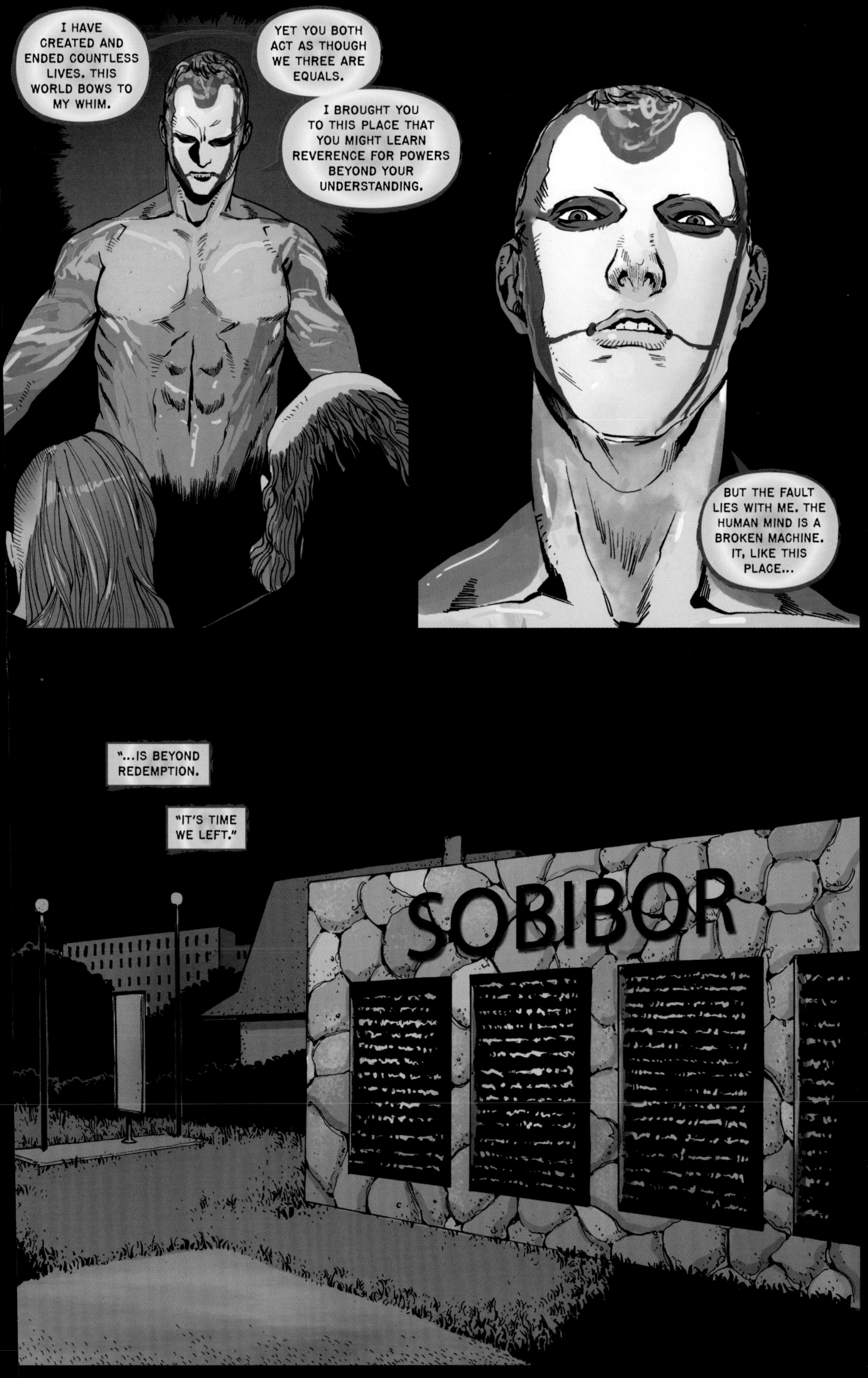
I HAVE CREATED AND ENDED COUNTLESS LIVES. THIS WORLD BOWS TO MY WHIM.
YET YOU BOTH ACT AS THOUGH WE THREE ARE EQUALS.
I BROUGHT YOU TO THIS PLACE THAT YOU MIGHT LEARN REVERENCE FOR POWERS BEYOND YOUR UNDERSTANDING.
BUT THE FAULT LIES WITH ME. THE HUMAN MIND IS A BROKEN MACHINE. IT, LIKE THIS PLACE...
"...IS BEYOND REDEMPTION.
"IT'S TIME WE LEFT."
SOBIBOR

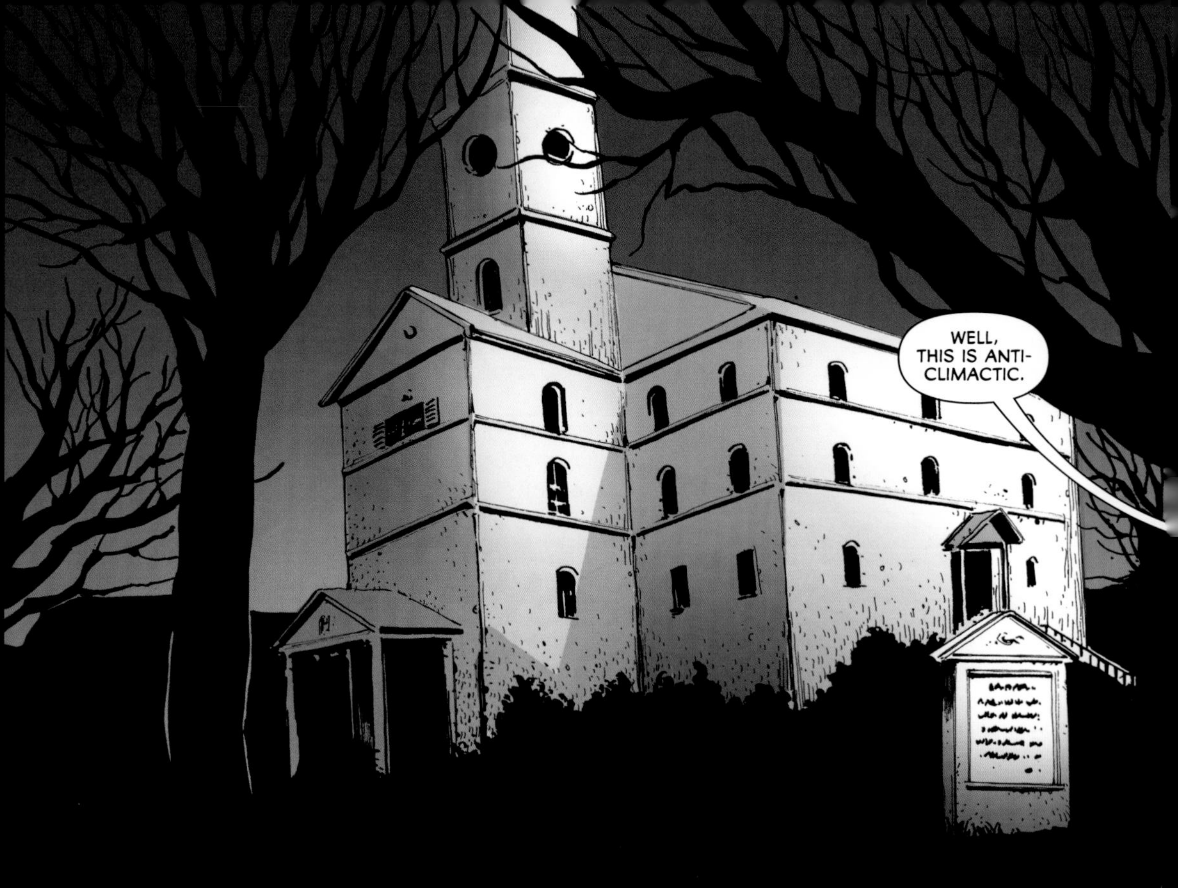
WELL, THIS IS ANTI-CLIMACTIC.

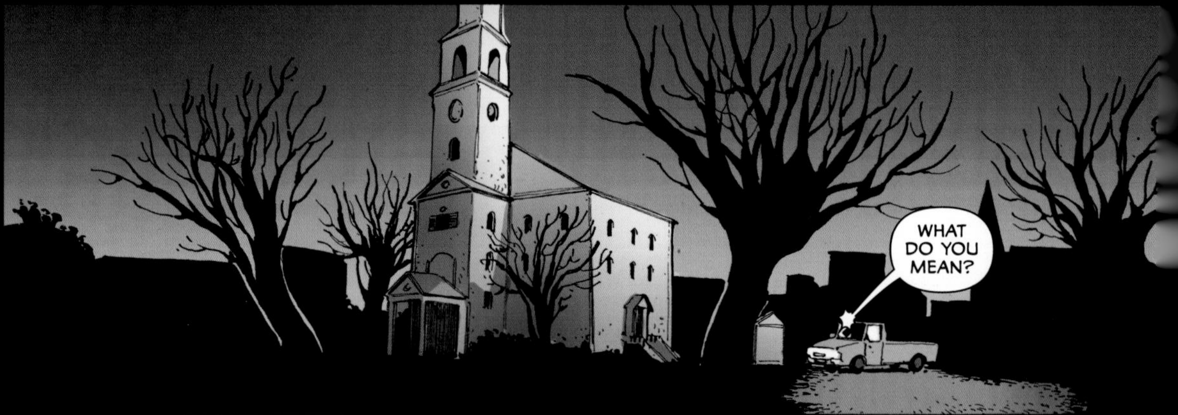
WHAT DO YOU MEAN?

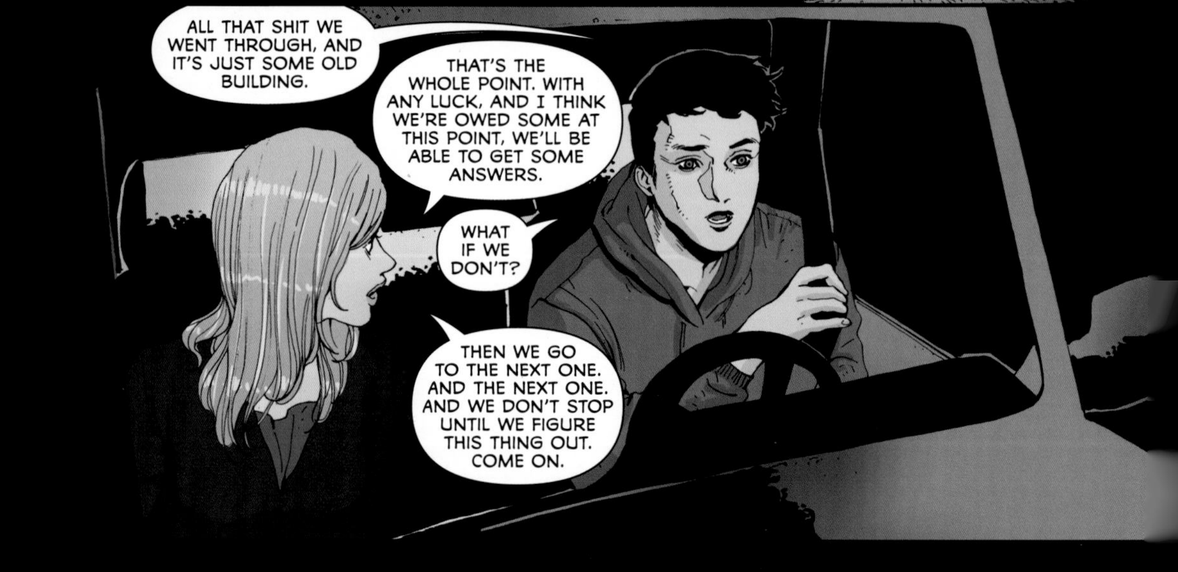
ALL THAT SHIT WE WENT THROUGH, AND IT'S JUST SOME OLD BUILDING.
THAT'S THE WHOLE POINT. WITH ANY LUCK, AND I THINK WE'RE OWED SOME AT THIS POINT, WE'LL BE ABLE TO GET SOME ANSWERS.
WHAT IF WE DON'T?
THEN WE GO TO THE NEXT ONE. AND THE NEXT ONE. AND WE DON'T STOP UNTIL WE FIGURE THIS THING OUT. COME ON.

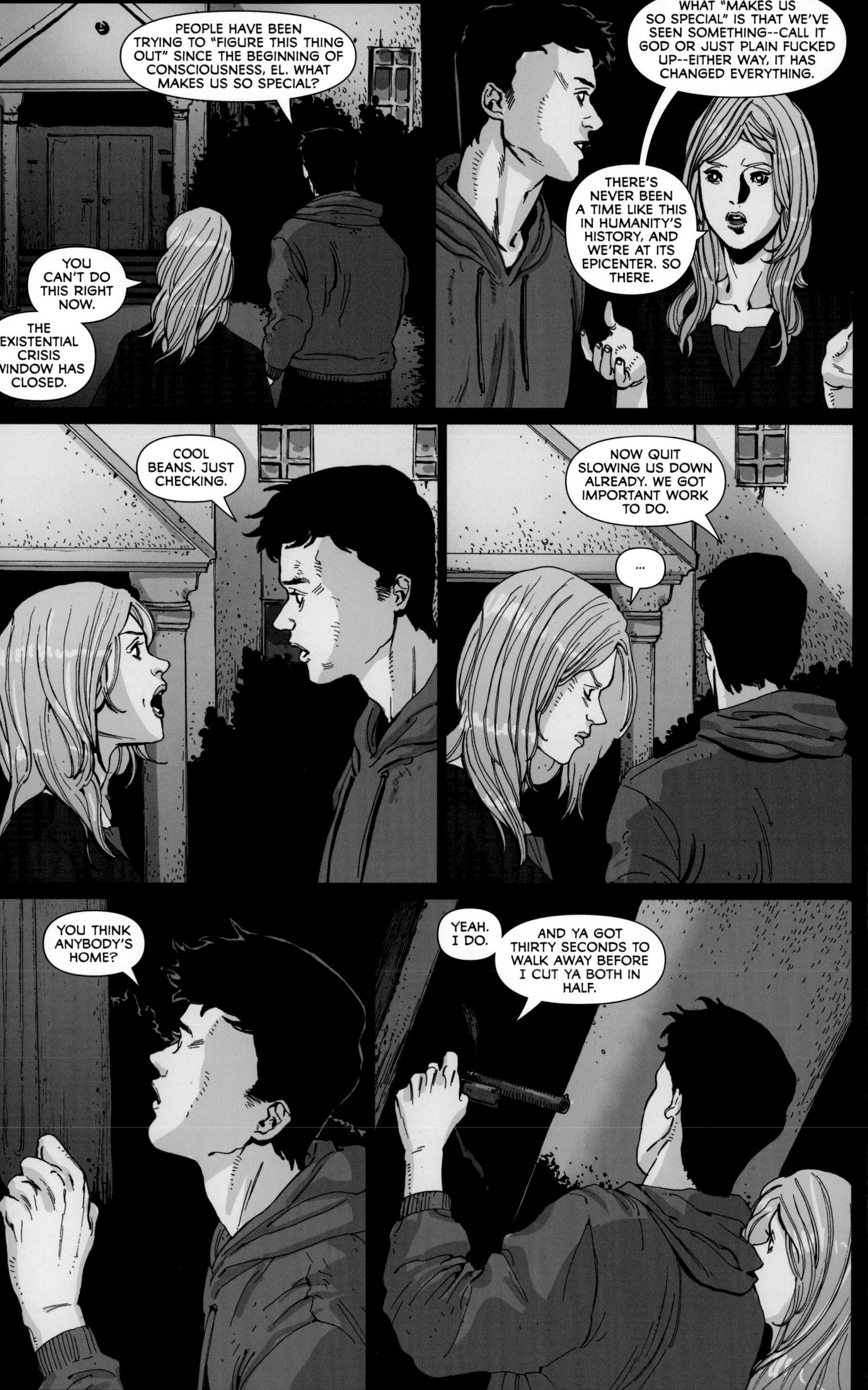
PEOPLE HAVE BEEN TRYING TO "FIGURE THIS THING OUT" SINCE THE BEGINNING OF CONSCIOUSNESS, EL. WHAT MAKES US SO SPECIAL?
YOU CAN'T DO THIS RIGHT NOW.
THE EXISTENTIAL CRISIS WINDOW HAS CLOSED.
WHAT "MAKES US SO SPECIAL" IS THAT WE'VE SEEN SOMETHING--CALL IT GOD OR JUST PLAIN FUCKED UP--EITHER WAY, IT HAS CHANGED EVERYTHING.
THERE'S NEVER BEEN A TIME LIKE THIS IN HUMANITY'S HISTORY, AND WE'RE AT ITS EPICENTER. SO THERE.
COOL BEANS. JUST CHECKING.
NOW QUIT SLOWING US DOWN ALREADY. WE GOT IMPORTANT WORK TO DO.
...
YOU THINK ANYBODY'S HOME?
YEAH. I DO.
AND YA GOT THIRTY SECONDS TO WALK AWAY BEFORE I CUT YA BOTH IN HALF.

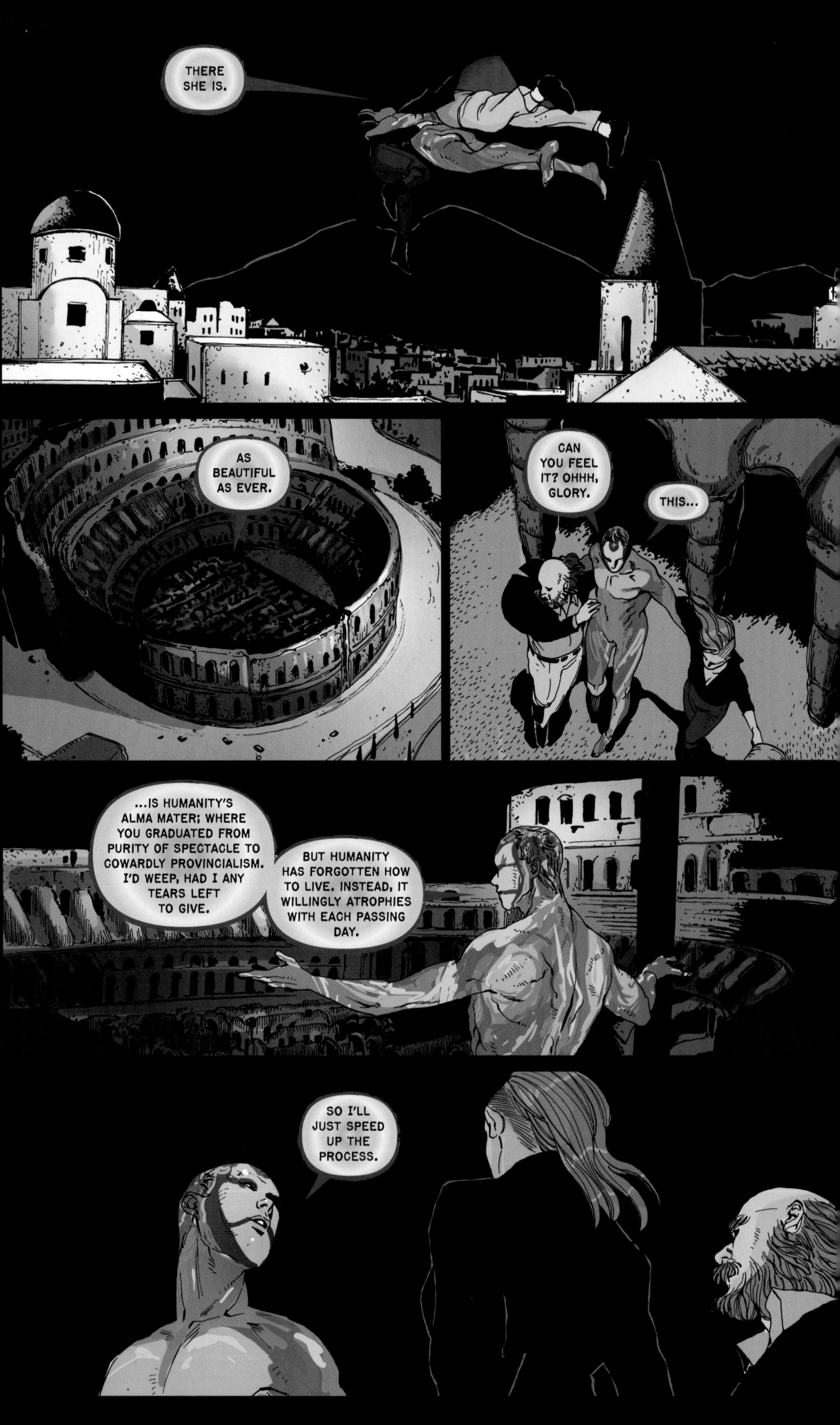
THERE SHE IS.
AS BEAUTIFUL AS EVER.
CAN YOU FEEL IT? OHHH, GLORY.
THIS...
...IS HUMANITY'S ALMA MATER; WHERE YOU GRADUATED FROM PURITY OF SPECTACLE TO COWARDLY PROVINCIALISM. I'D WEEP, HAD I ANY TEARS LEFT TO GIVE.
BUT HUMANITY HAS FORGOTTEN HOW TO LIVE. INSTEAD, IT WILLINGLY ATROPHIES WITH EACH PASSING DAY.
SO I'LL JUST SPEED UP THE PROCESS.

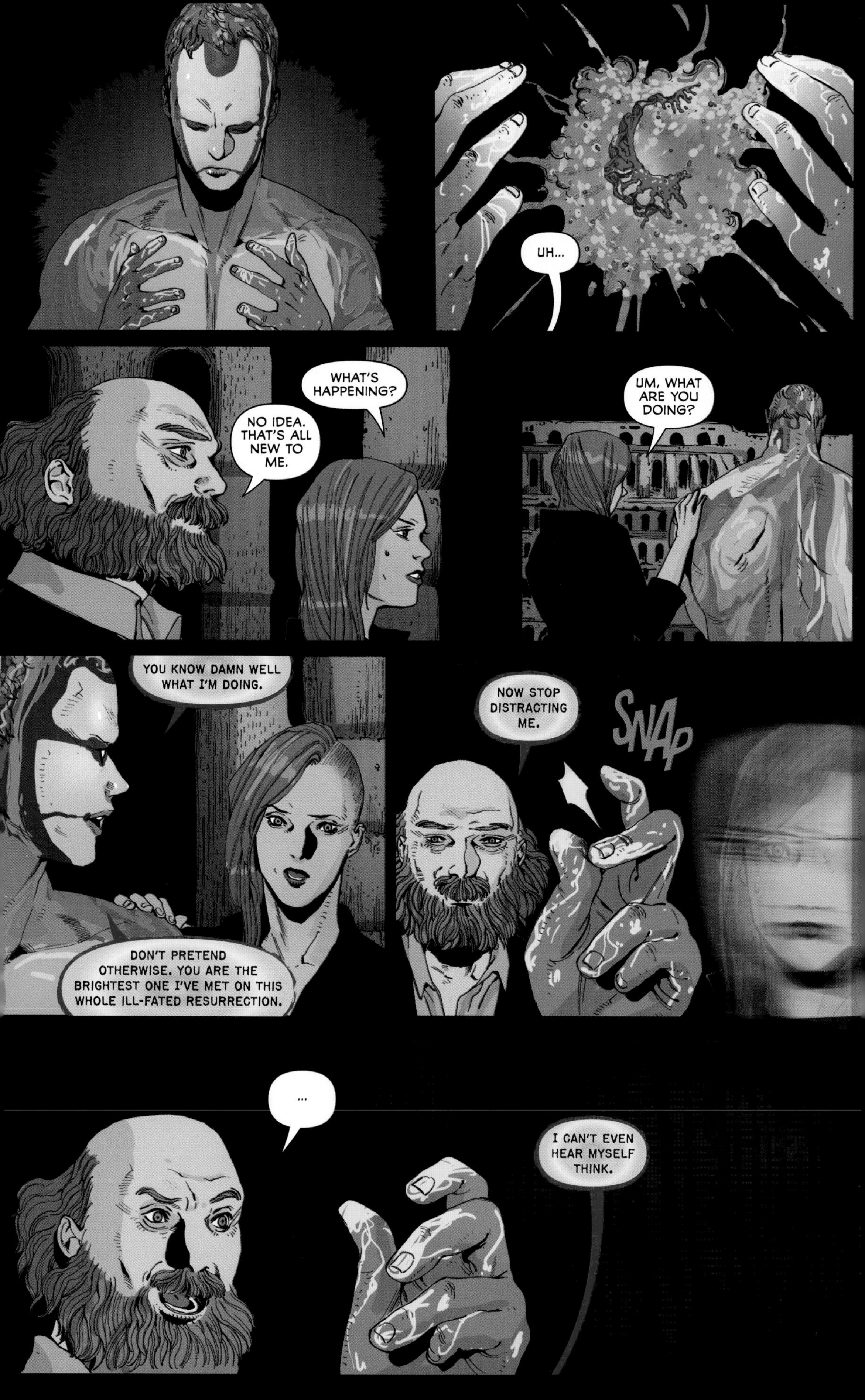
UH...
WHAT'S HAPPENING?
NO IDEA. THAT'S ALL NEW TO ME.
UM, WHAT ARE YOU DOING?
YOU KNOW DAMN WELL WHAT I'M DOING.
DON'T PRETEND OTHERWISE. YOU ARE THE BRIGHTEST ONE I'VE MET ON THIS WHOLE ILL-FATED RESURRECTION.
NOW STOP DISTRACTING ME.
SNAP
...
I CAN'T EVEN HEAR MYSELF THINK.

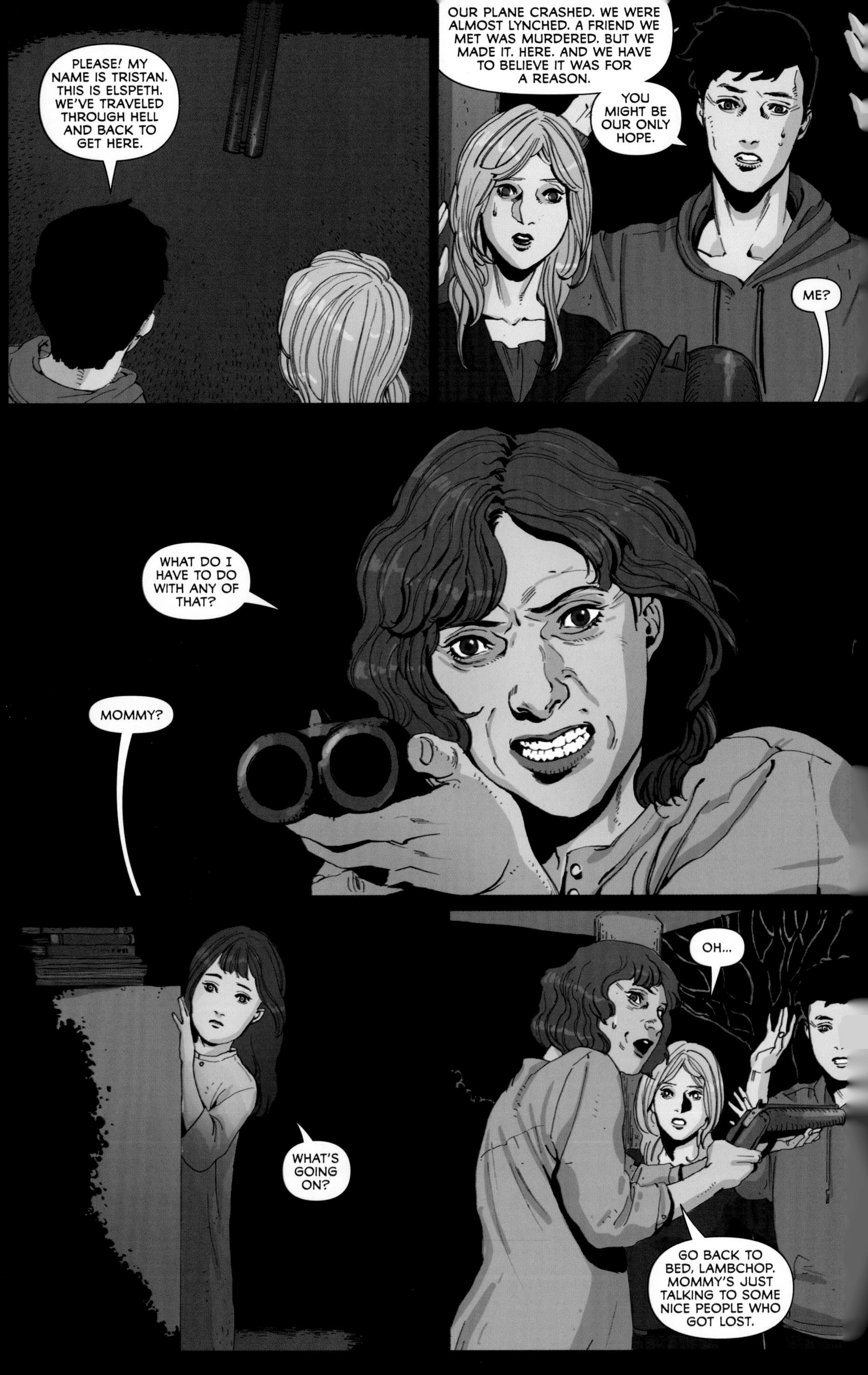
PLEASE! MY NAME IS TRISTAN. THIS IS ELSPETH. WE'VE TRAVELED THROUGH HELL AND BACK TO GET HERE.
OUR PLANE CRASHED. WE WERE ALMOST LYNCHED. A FRIEND WE MET WAS MURDERED. BUT WE MADE IT. HERE. AND WE HAVE TO BELIEVE IT WAS FOR A REASON.
YOU MIGHT BE OUR ONLY HOPE.
ME?
WHAT DO I HAVE TO DO WITH ANY OF THAT?
MOMMY?
WHAT'S GOING ON?
OH...
GO BACK TO BED, LAMBCHOP. MOMMY'S JUST TALKING TO SOME NICE PEOPLE WHO GOT LOST.

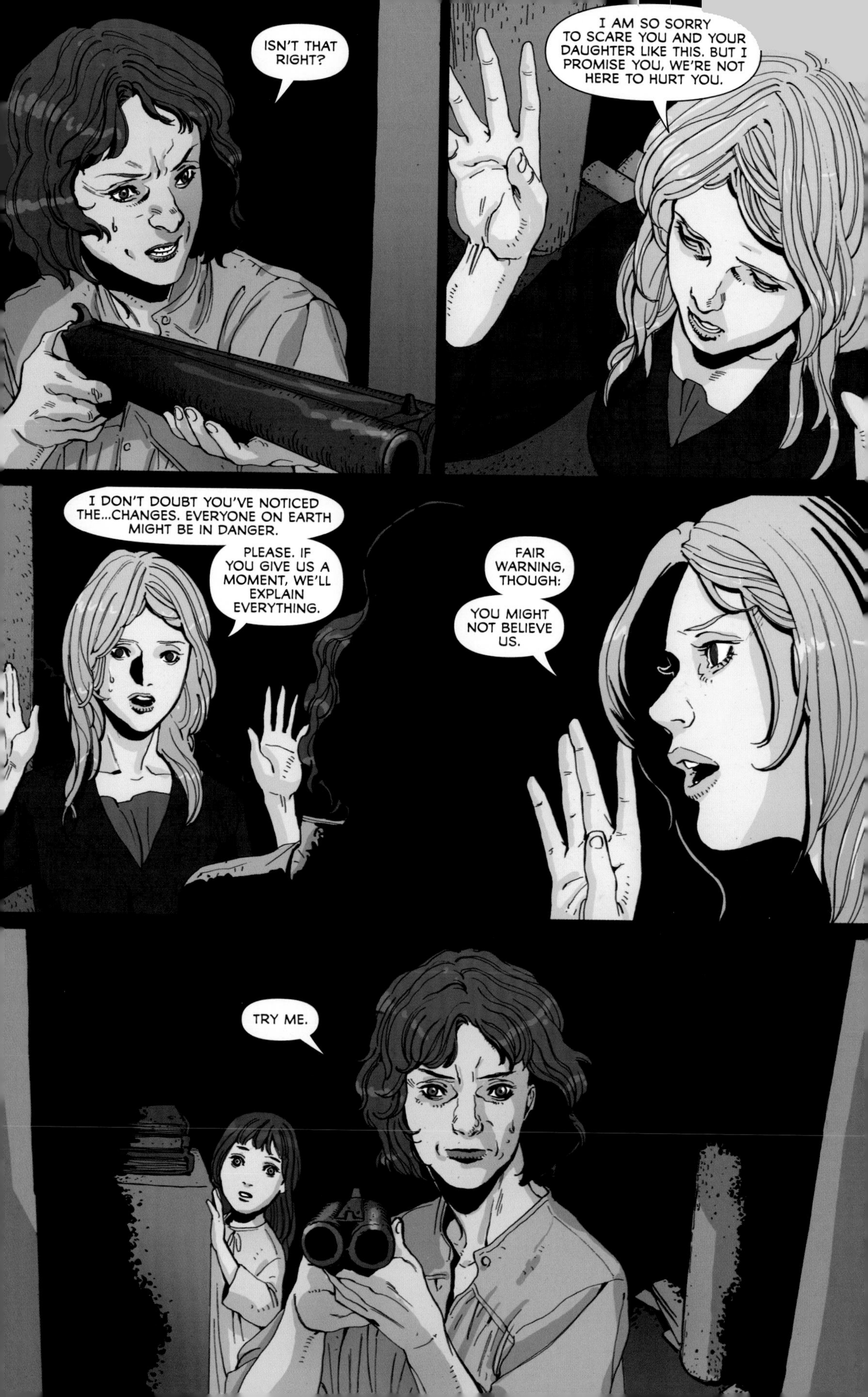
ISN'T THAT RIGHT?
I AM SO SORRY TO SCARE YOU AND YOUR DAUGHTER LIKE THIS. BUT I PROMISE YOU, WE'RE NOT HERE TO HURT YOU.
I DON'T DOUBT YOU'VE NOTICED THE...CHANGES. EVERYONE ON EARTH MIGHT BE IN DANGER.
PLEASE. IF YOU GIVE US A MOMENT, WE'LL EXPLAIN EVERYTHING.
FAIR WARNING, THOUGH:
YOU MIGHT NOT BELIEVE US.
TRY ME.

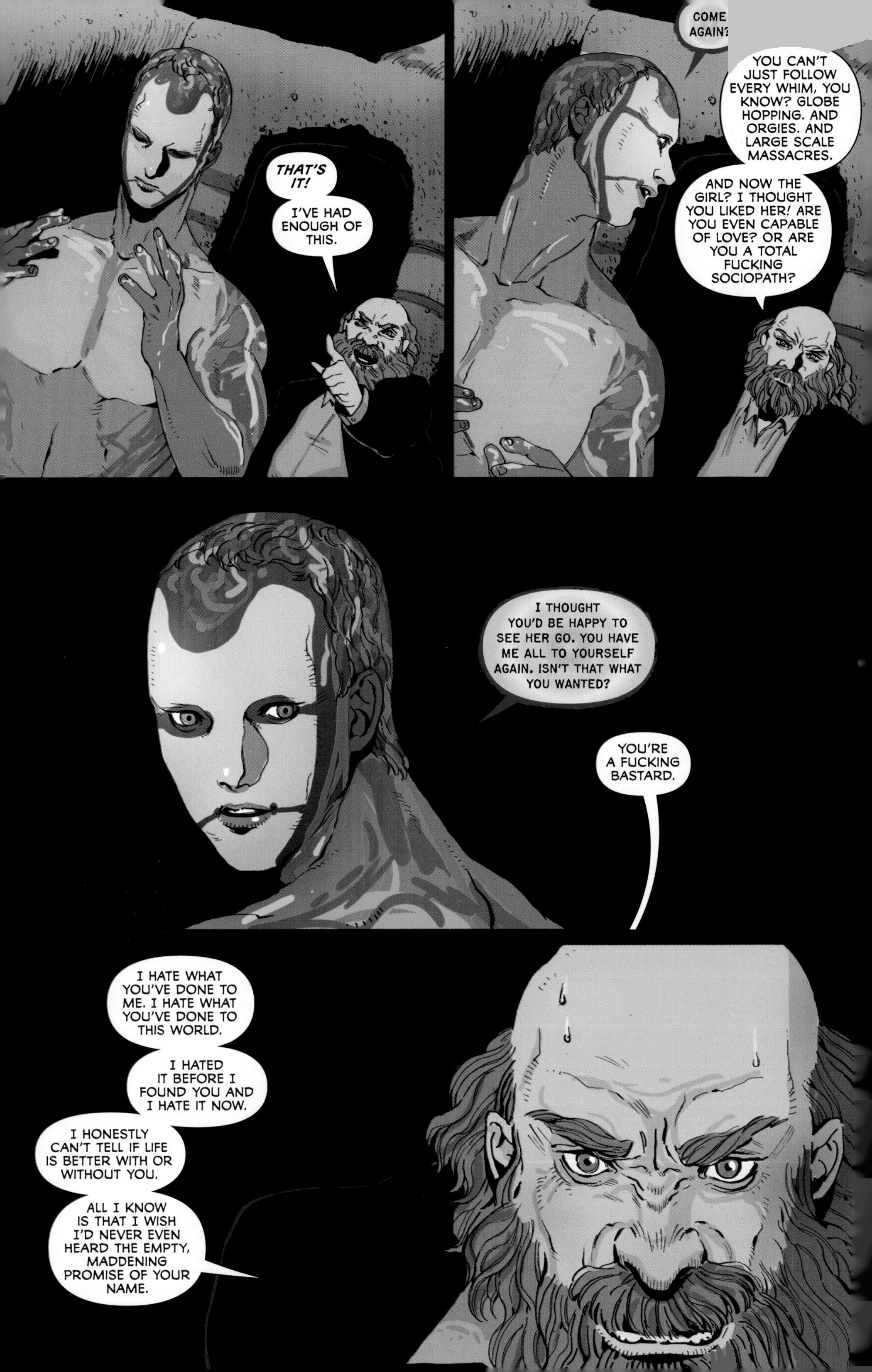
THAT'S IT!
I'VE HAD ENOUGH OF THIS.
COME AGAIN?
YOU CAN'T JUST FOLLOW EVERY WHIM, YOU KNOW? GLOBE HOPPING. AND ORGIES. AND LARGE SCALE MASSACRES.
AND NOW THE GIRL? I THOUGHT YOU LIKED HER! ARE YOU EVEN CAPABLE OF LOVE? OR ARE YOU A TOTAL FUCKING SOCIOPATH?
I THOUGHT YOU'D BE HAPPY TO SEE HER GO. YOU HAVE ME ALL TO YOURSELF AGAIN. ISN'T THAT WHAT YOU WANTED?
YOU'RE A FUCKING BASTARD.
I HATE WHAT YOU'VE DONE TO ME. I HATE WHAT YOU'VE DONE TO THIS WORLD.
I HATED IT BEFORE I FOUND YOU AND I HATE IT NOW.
I HONESTLY CAN'T TELL IF LIFE IS BETTER WITH OR WITHOUT YOU.
ALL I KNOW IS THAT I WISH I'D NEVER EVEN HEARD THE EMPTY, MADDENING PROMISE OF YOUR NAME.

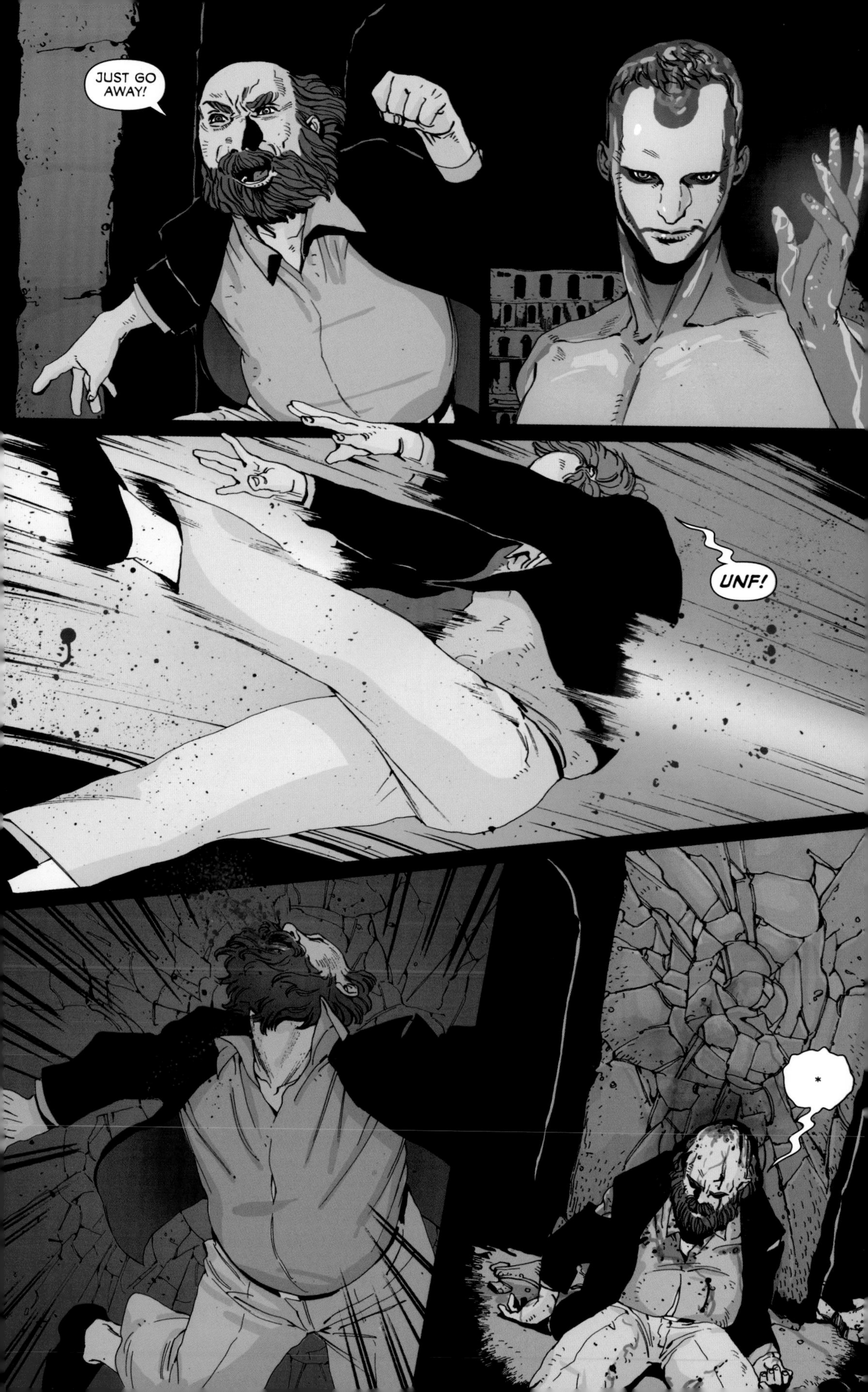
JUST GO AWAY!
UNF!
*

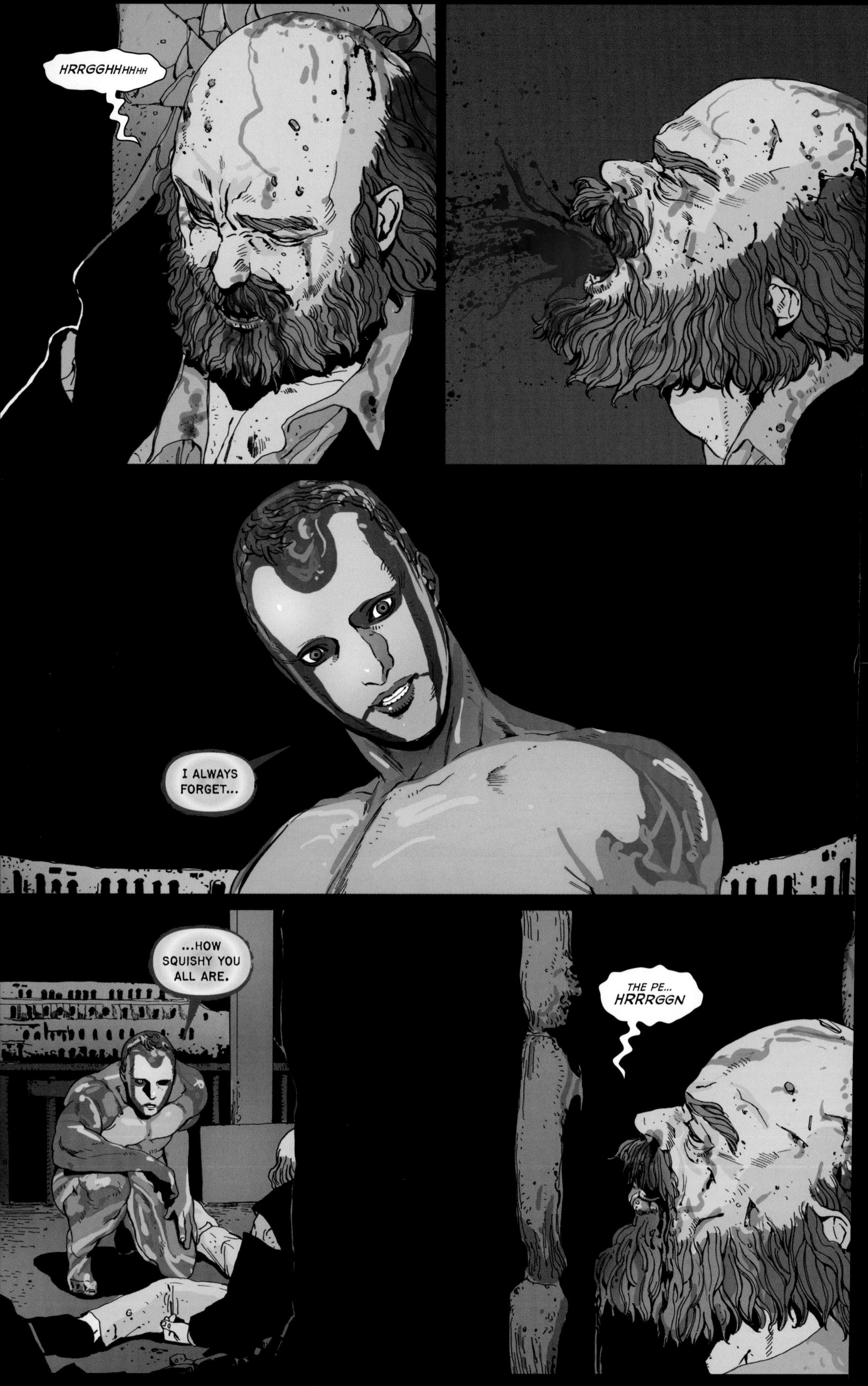
HRRGGHHHHHH
I ALWAYS FORGET...
...HOW SQUISHY YOU ALL ARE.
THE PE... HRRRGGN

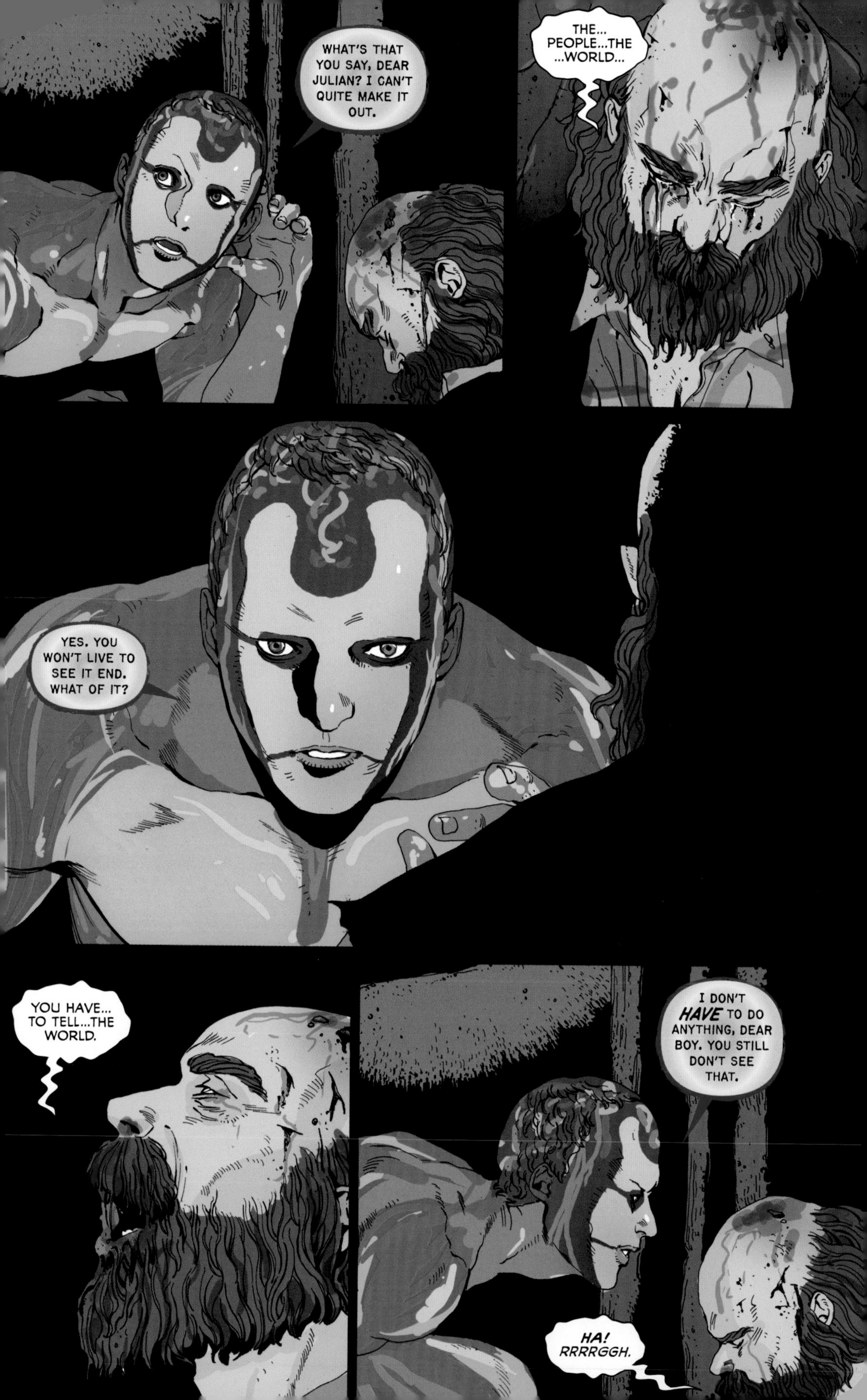
WHAT'S THAT YOU SAY, DEAR JULIAN? I CAN'T QUITE MAKE IT OUT.
THE... PEOPLE...THE ...WORLD...
YES. YOU WON'T LIVE TO SEE IT END. WHAT OF IT?
YOU HAVE... TO TELL...THE WORLD.
I DON'T HAVE TO DO ANYTHING, DEAR BOY. YOU STILL DON'T SEE THAT.
HA! RRRRGGH.

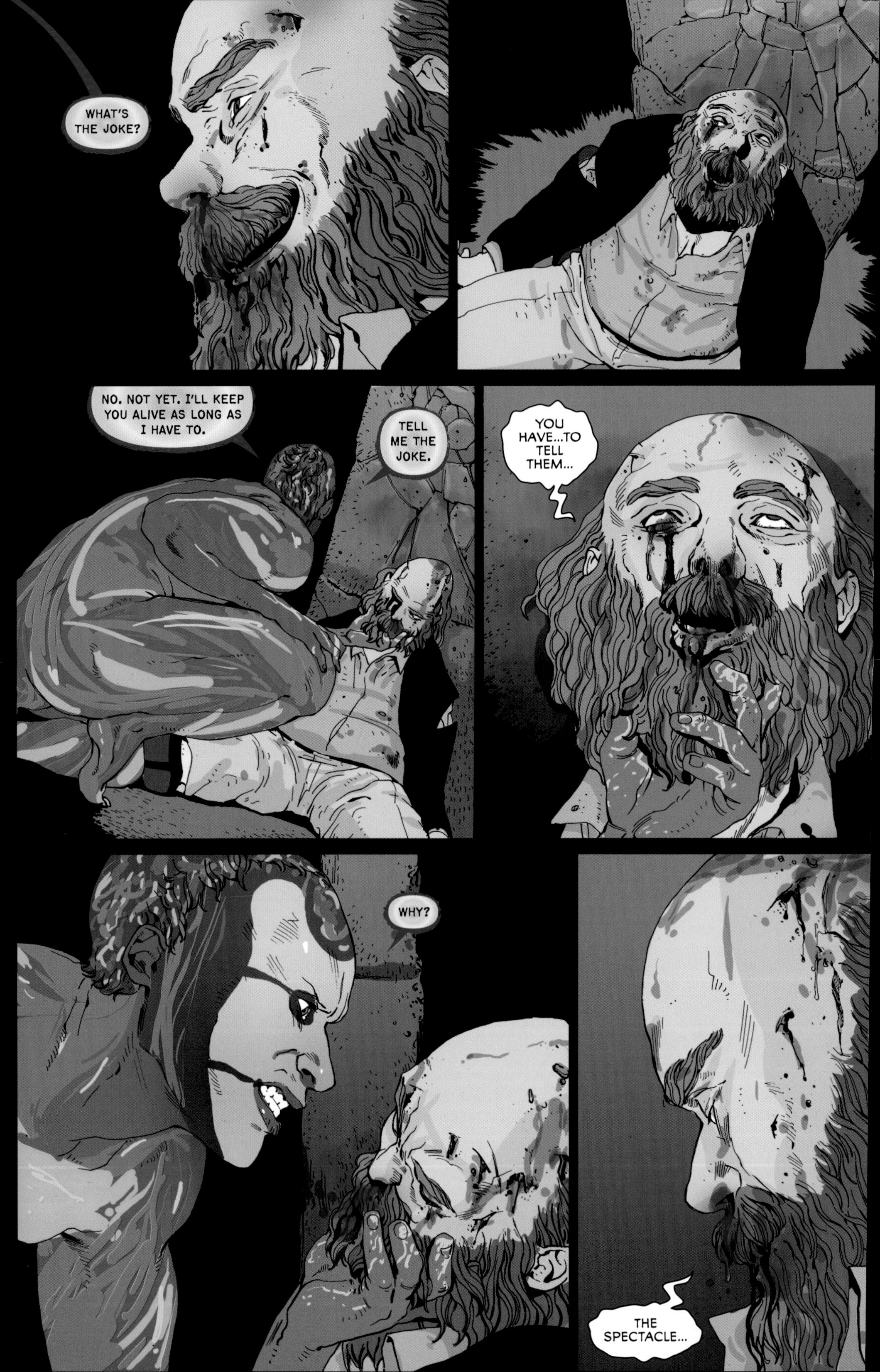
WHAT'S THE JOKE?
NO. NOT YET. I'LL KEEP YOU ALIVE AS LONG AS I HAVE TO.
TELL ME THE JOKE.
YOU HAVE...TO TELL THEM...
WHY?
THE SPECTACLE...

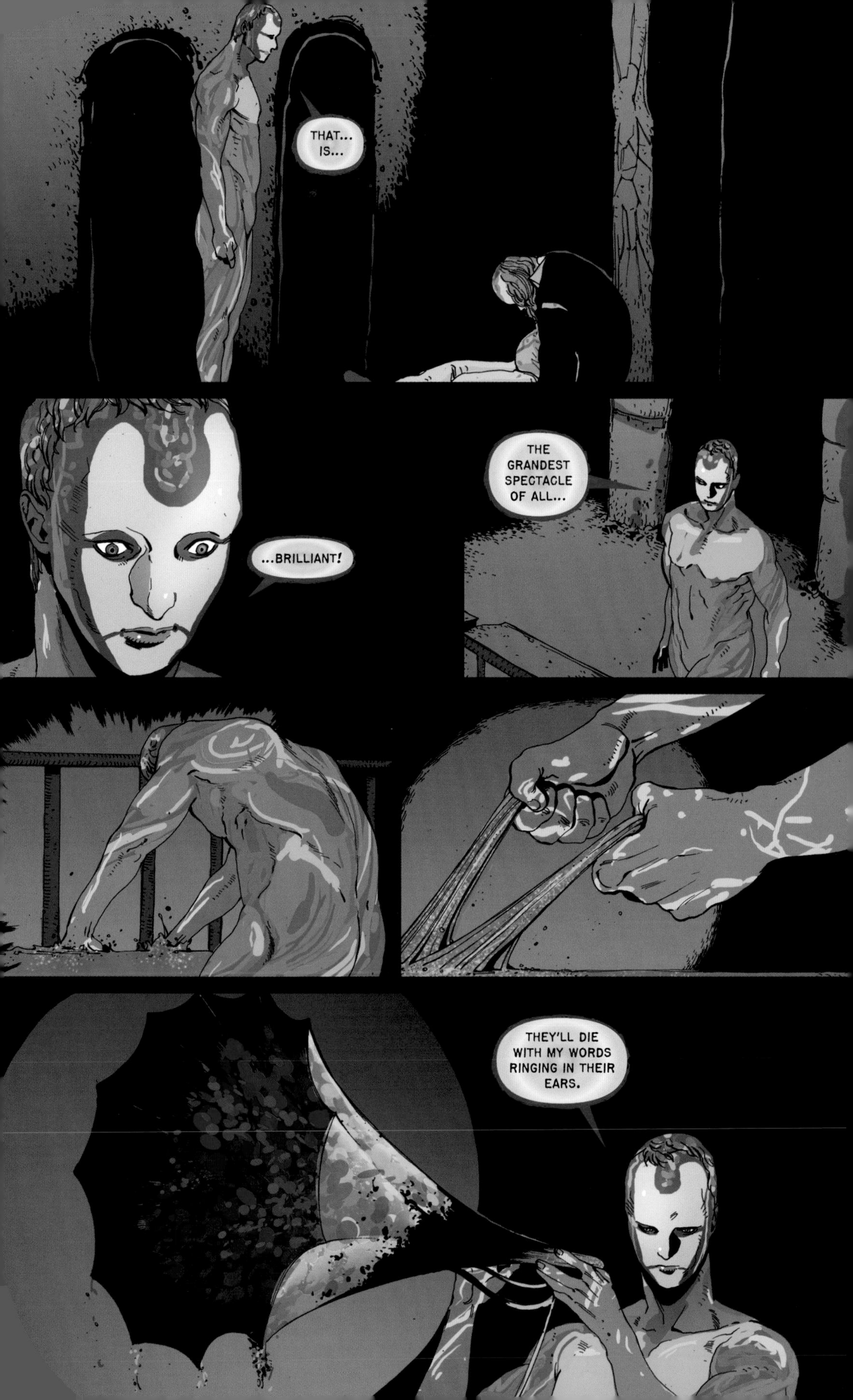
THAT... IS...
THE GRANDEST SPECTACLE OF ALL...
...BRILLIANT!
THEY'LL DIE WITH MY WORDS RINGING IN THEIR EARS.

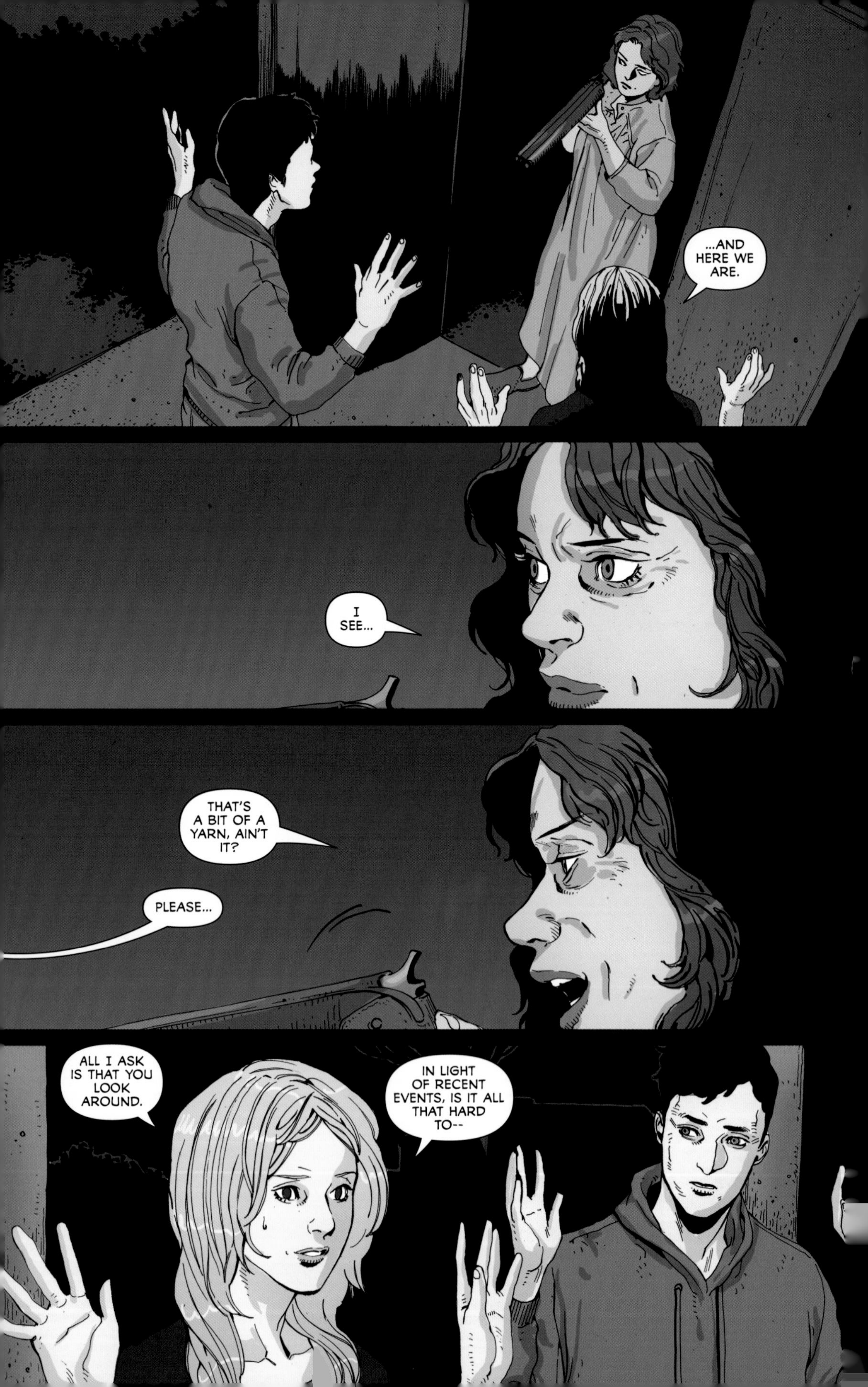
...AND HERE WE ARE.
I SEE...
THAT'S A BIT OF A YARN, AIN'T IT?
PLEASE...
ALL I ASK IS THAT YOU LOOK AROUND.
IN LIGHT OF RECENT EVENTS, IS IT ALL THAT HARD TO--

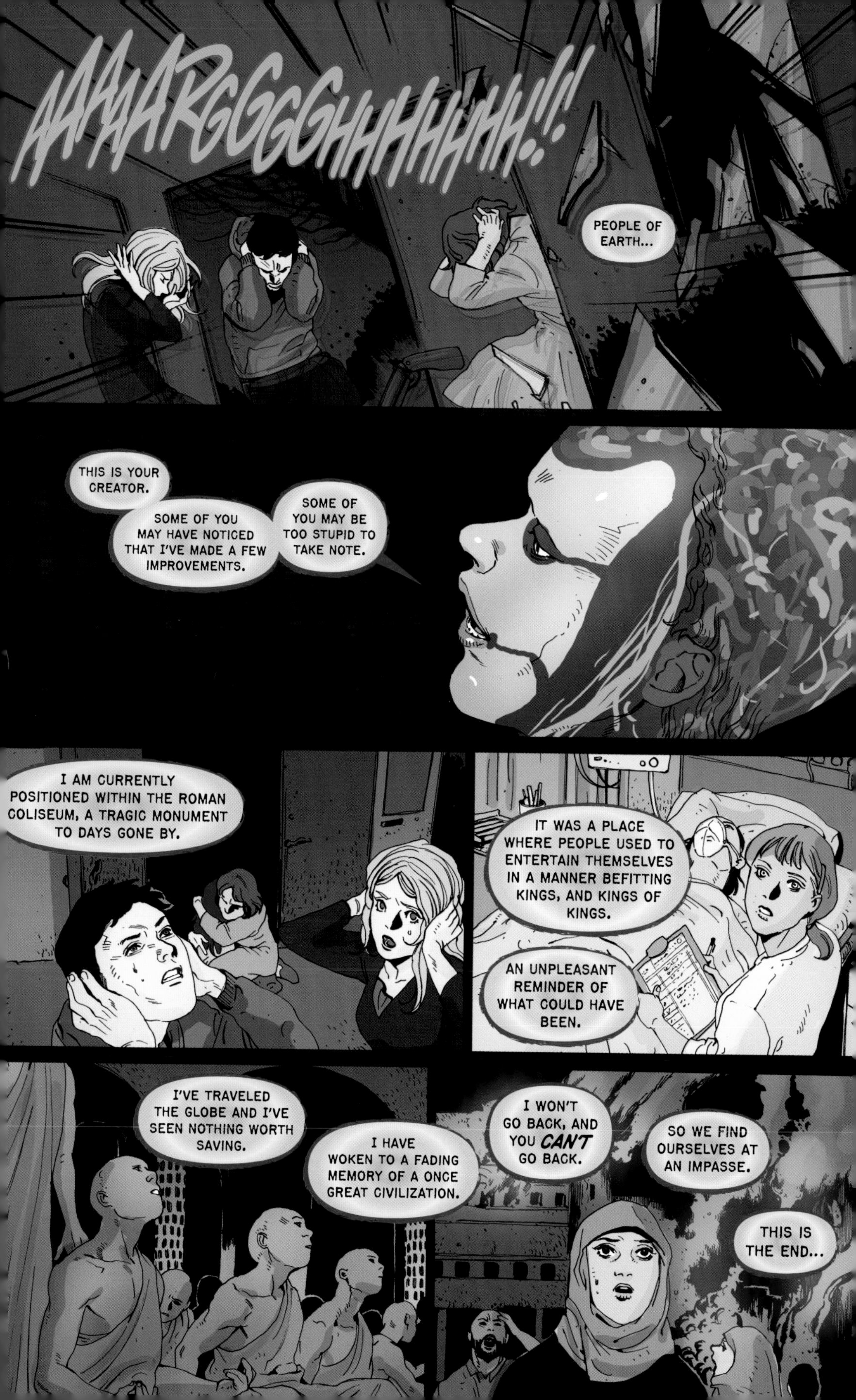
AAAARGGGGHHHHHHH!!!
PEOPLE OF EARTH...
THIS IS YOUR CREATOR.
SOME OF YOU MAY HAVE NOTICED THAT I'VE MADE A FEW IMPROVEMENTS.
SOME OF YOU MAY BE TOO STUPID TO TAKE NOTE.
I AM CURRENTLY POSITIONED WITHIN THE ROMAN COLISEUM, A TRAGIC MONUMENT TO DAYS GONE BY.
IT WAS A PLACE WHERE PEOPLE USED TO ENTERTAIN THEMSELVES IN A MANNER BEFITTING KINGS, AND KINGS OF KINGS.
AN UNPLEASANT REMINDER OF WHAT COULD HAVE BEEN.
I'VE TRAVELED THE GLOBE AND I'VE SEEN NOTHING WORTH SAVING.
I HAVE WOKEN TO A FADING MEMORY OF A ONCE GREAT CIVILIZATION.
I WON'T GO BACK, AND YOU CAN'T GO BACK.
SO WE FIND OURSELVES AT AN IMPASSE.
THIS IS THE END...

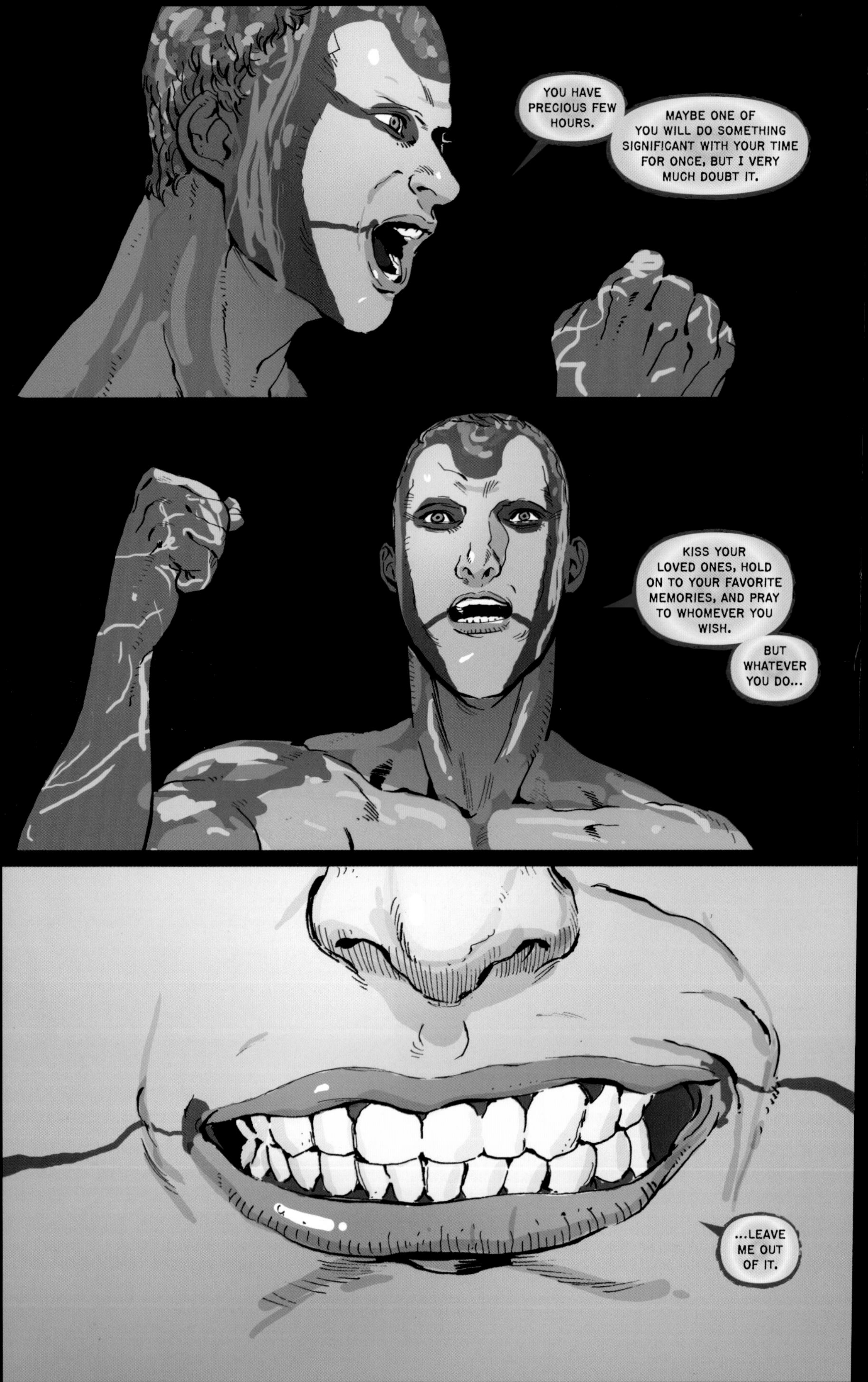
YOU HAVE PRECIOUS FEW HOURS.
MAYBE ONE OF YOU WILL DO SOMETHING SIGNIFICANT WITH YOUR TIME FOR ONCE, BUT I VERY MUCH DOUBT IT.
KISS YOUR LOVED ONES, HOLD ON TO YOUR FAVORITE MEMORIES, AND PRAY TO WHOMEVER YOU WISH.
BUT WHATEVER YOU DO...
...LEAVE ME OUT OF IT.

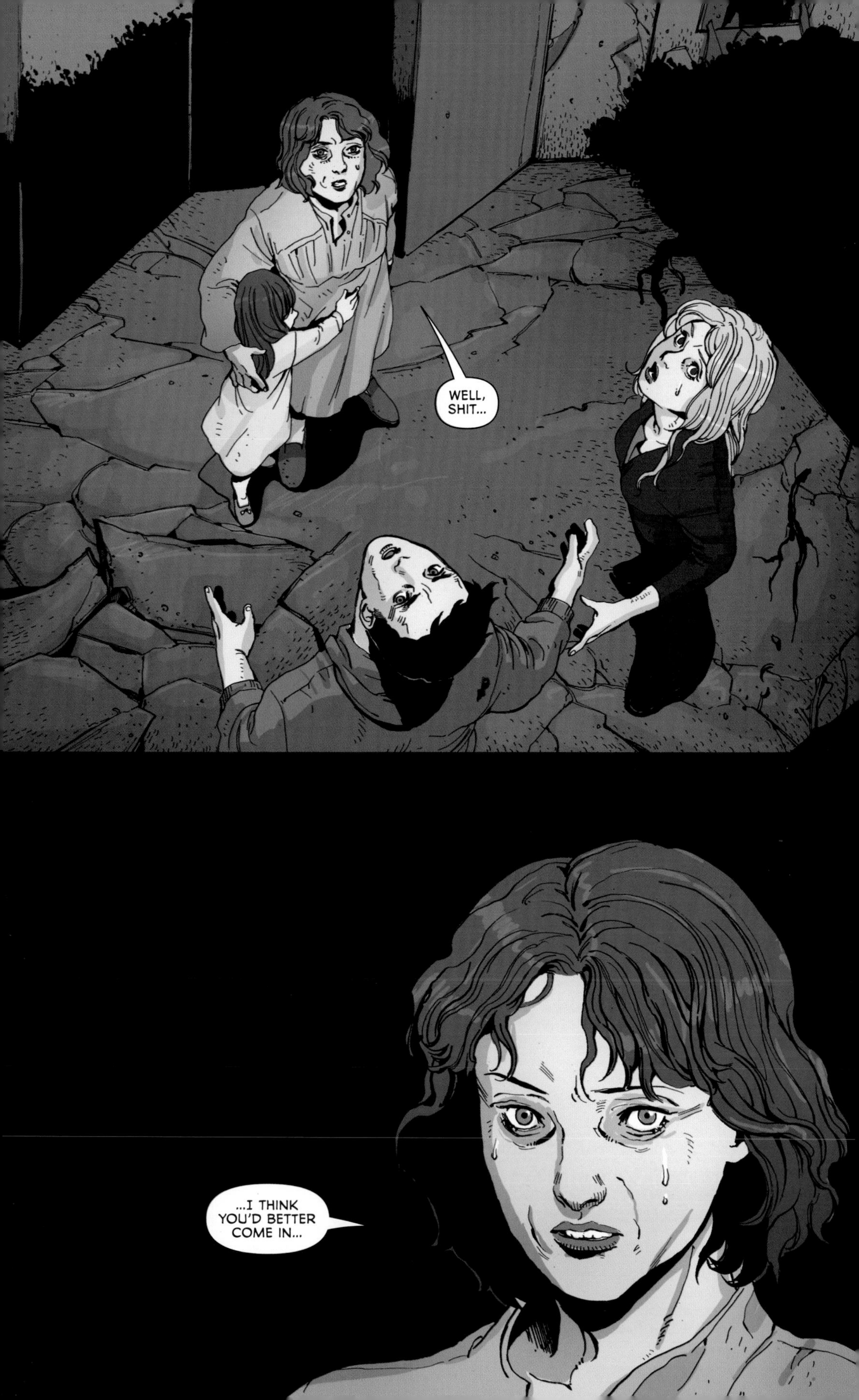
WELL, SHIT...
...I THINK YOU'D BETTER COME IN...

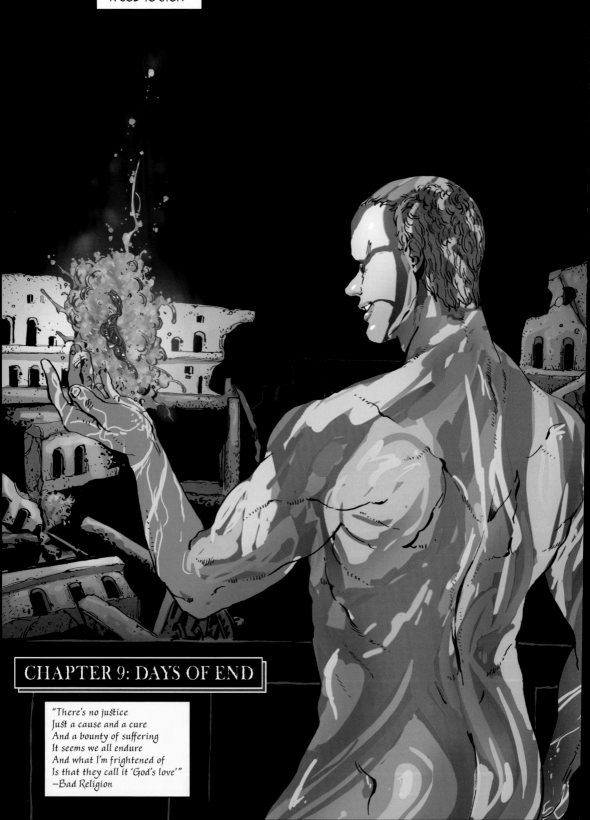

"...IT SEEMS WE HAVE A GOD TO STOP."

CHAPTER 9: DAYS OF END

"There's no justice
Just a cause and a cure
And a bounty of suffering
It seems we all endure
And what I'm frightened of
Is that they call it 'God's love'"
—Bad Religion

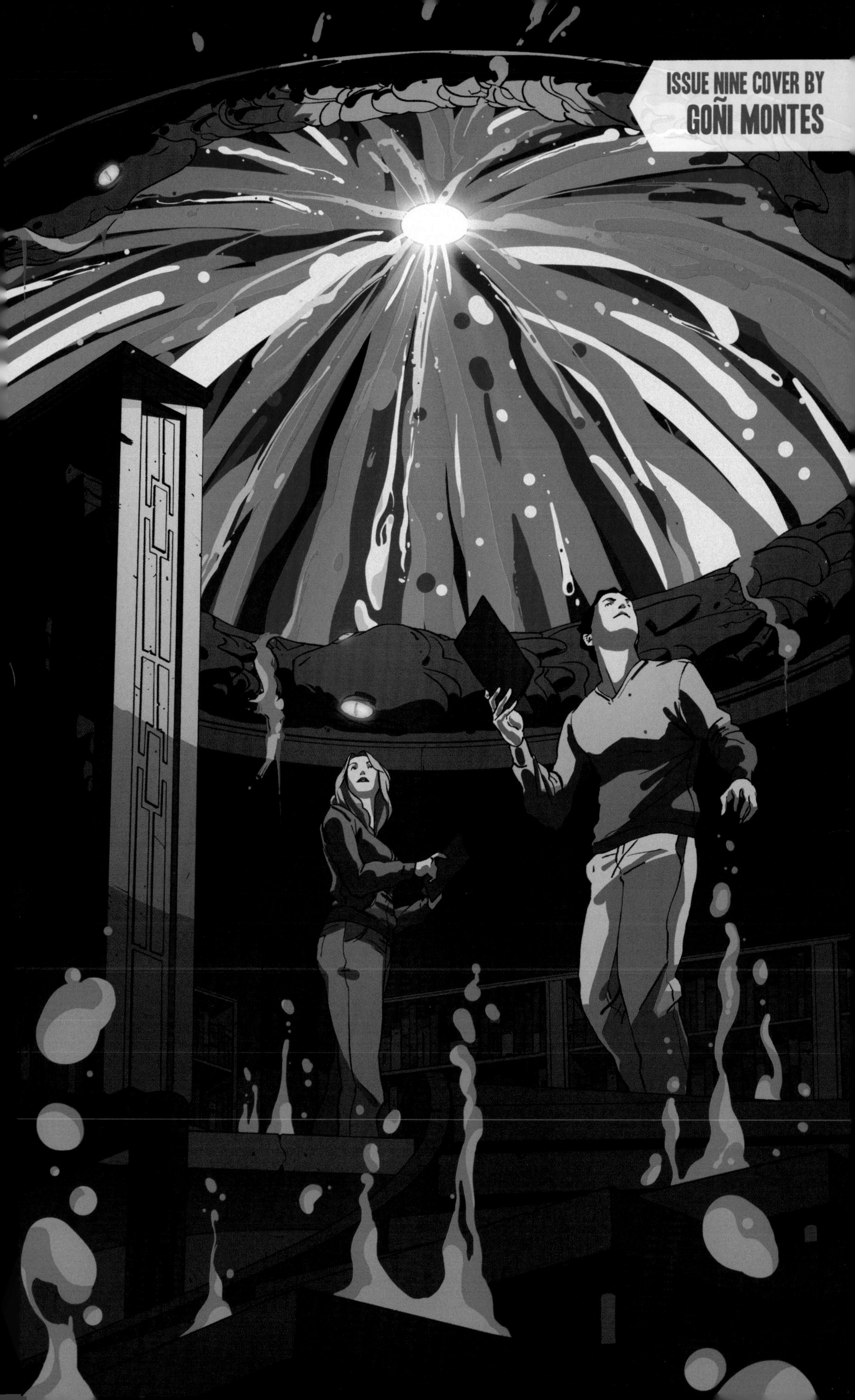

ISSUE NINE COVER BY
GOÑI MONTES

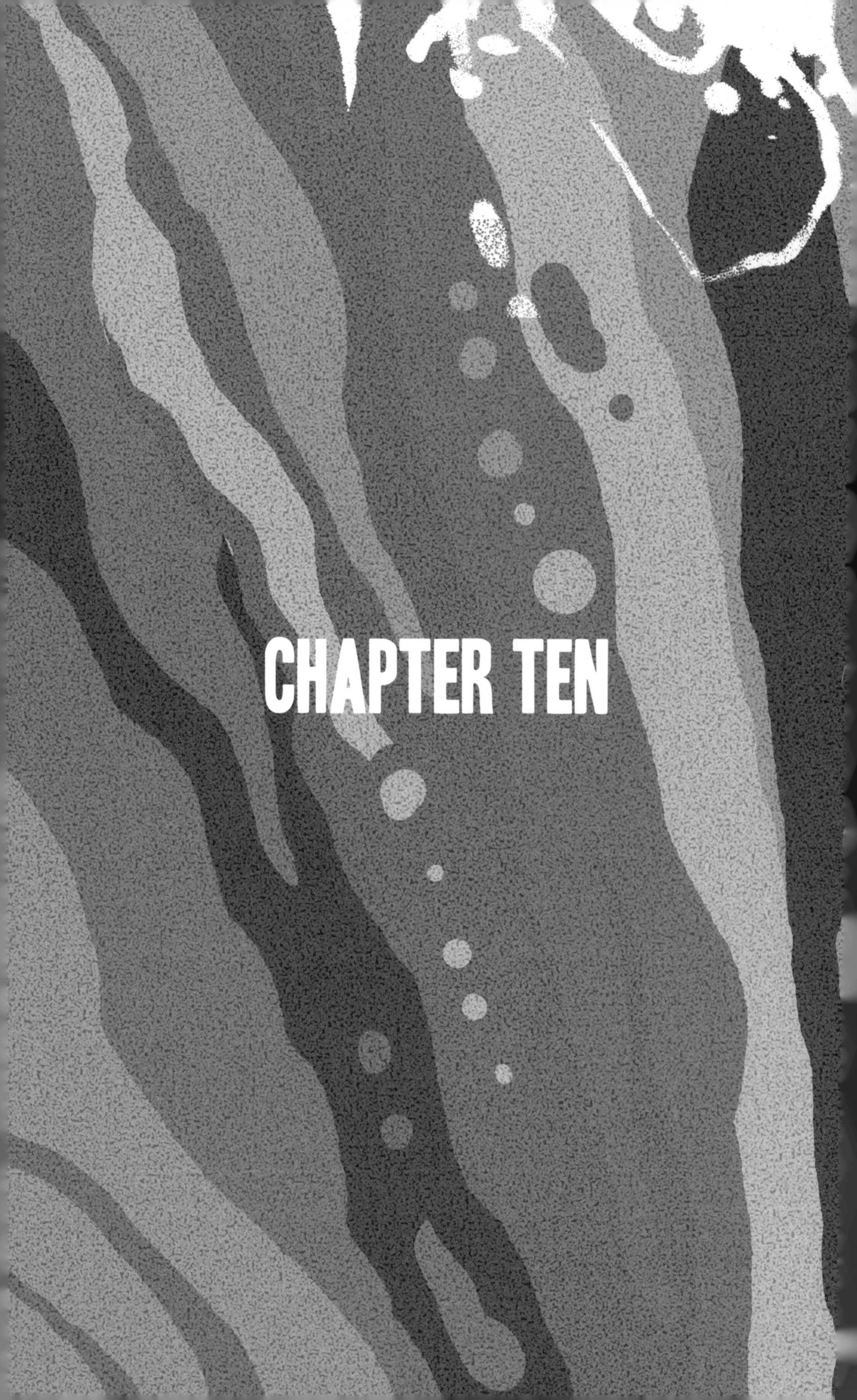

CHAPTER TEN

HAPTER 10: THE RIGHTEOUS AND THE WICKED

"The God of the Old Testament is arguably the most unpleasant character in all fiction: jealous and proud of it; a petty, unjust, unforgiving control-freak; a vindictive, bloodthirsty ethnic cleanser; a misogynistic, homophobic, racist, infanticidal, genocidal, filicidal, pestilential, megalomaniacal, sadomasochistic, capriciously malevolent bully."
—Richard Dawkins

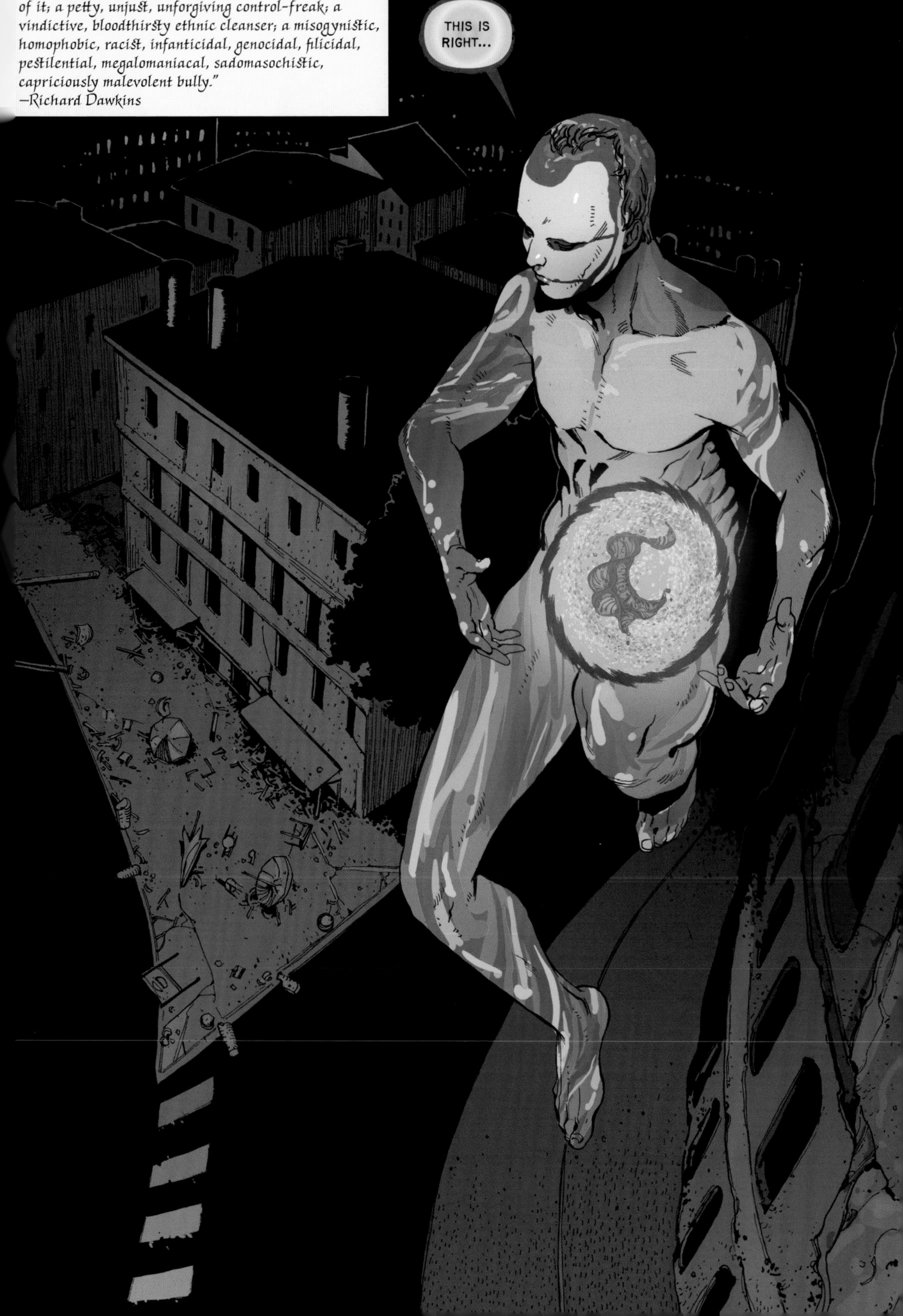
THIS IS RIGHT...

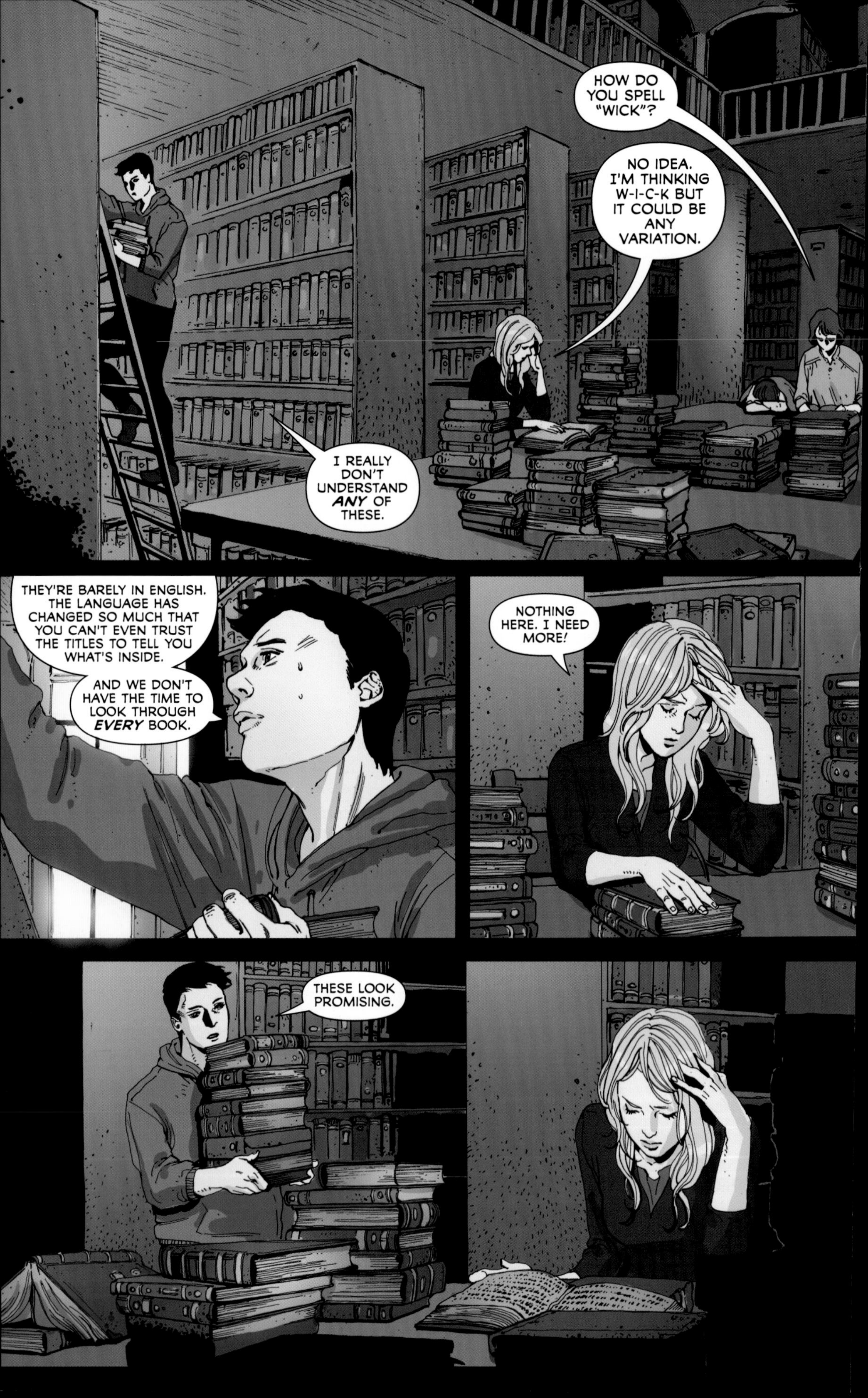
HOW DO YOU SPELL "WICK"?
NO IDEA. I'M THINKING W-I-C-K BUT IT COULD BE ANY VARIATION.
I REALLY DON'T UNDERSTAND *ANY* OF THESE.
THEY'RE BARELY IN ENGLISH. THE LANGUAGE HAS CHANGED SO MUCH THAT YOU CAN'T EVEN TRUST THE TITLES TO TELL YOU WHAT'S INSIDE.
AND WE DON'T HAVE THE TIME TO LOOK THROUGH ***EVERY*** BOOK.
NOTHING HERE. I NEED MORE!
THESE LOOK PROMISING.

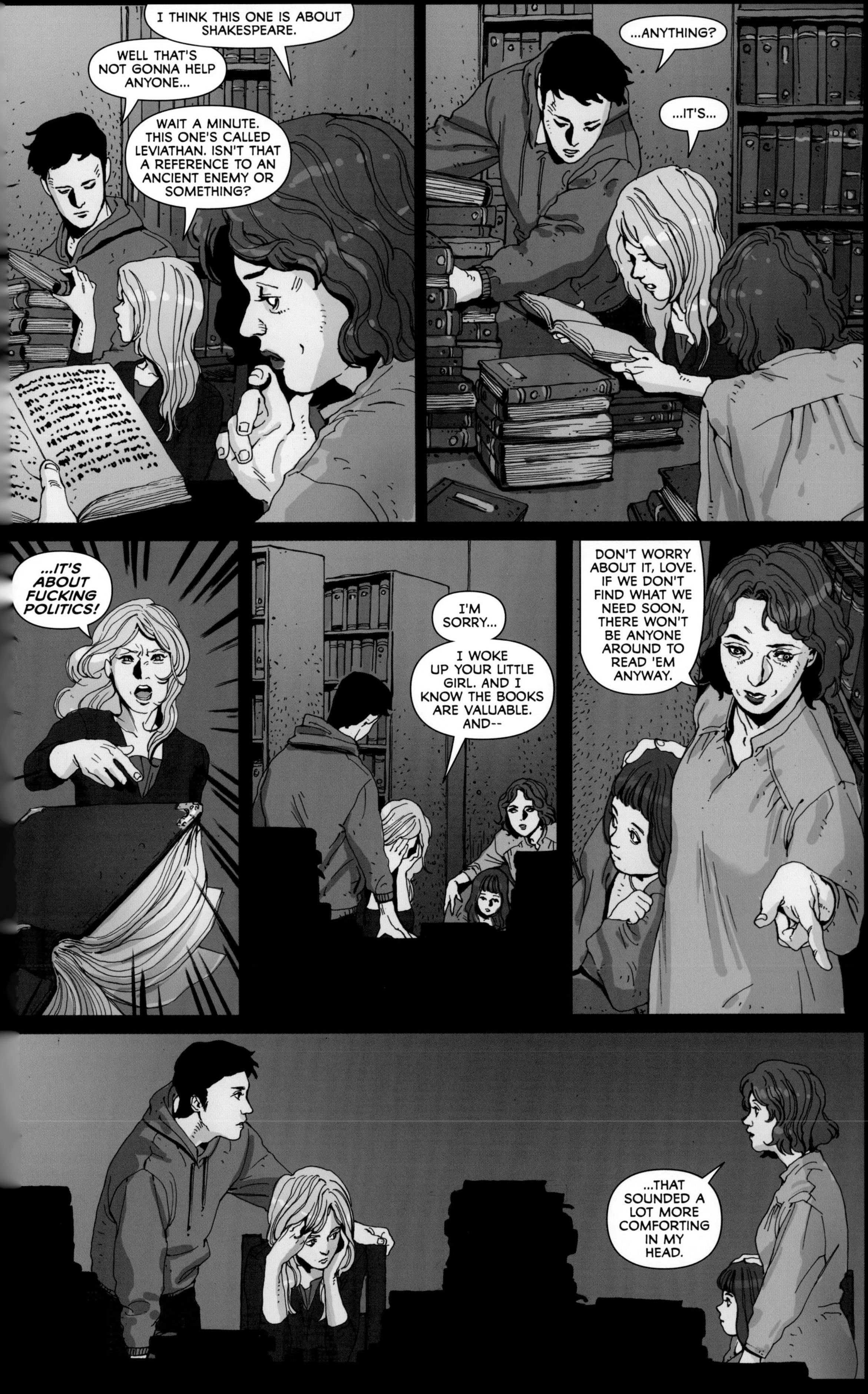
I THINK THIS ONE IS ABOUT SHAKESPEARE.
WELL THAT'S NOT GONNA HELP ANYONE...
WAIT A MINUTE. THIS ONE'S CALLED LEVIATHAN. ISN'T THAT A REFERENCE TO AN ANCIENT ENEMY OR SOMETHING?
...ANYTHING?
...IT'S...
...IT'S ABOUT FUCKING POLITICS!
I'M SORRY...
I WOKE UP YOUR LITTLE GIRL. AND I KNOW THE BOOKS ARE VALUABLE. AND--
DON'T WORRY ABOUT IT, LOVE. IF WE DON'T FIND WHAT WE NEED SOON, THERE WON'T BE ANYONE AROUND TO READ 'EM ANYWAY.
...THAT SOUNDED A LOT MORE COMFORTING IN MY HEAD.

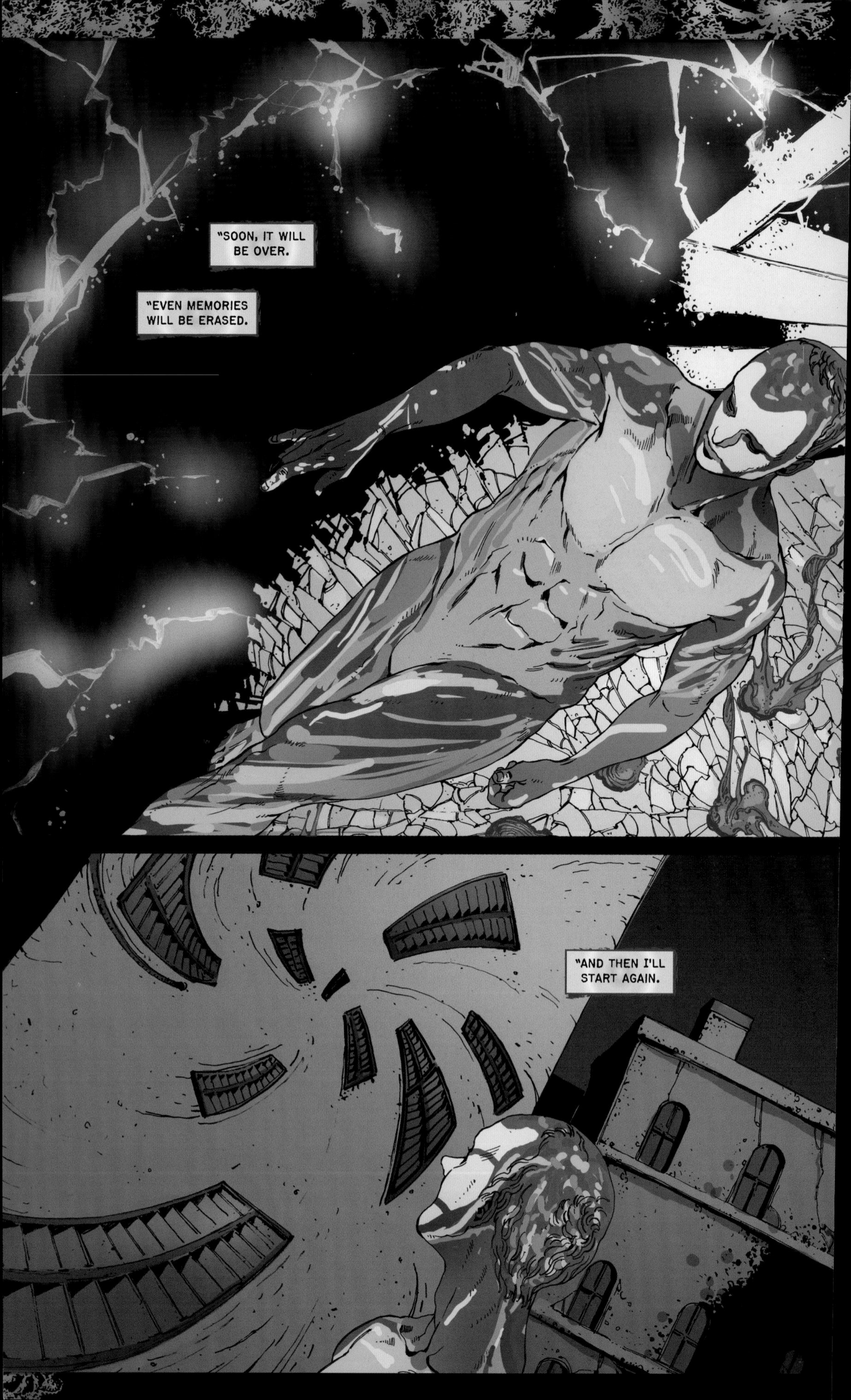
"SOON, IT WILL BE OVER.
"EVEN MEMORIES WILL BE ERASED.
"AND THEN I'LL START AGAIN.

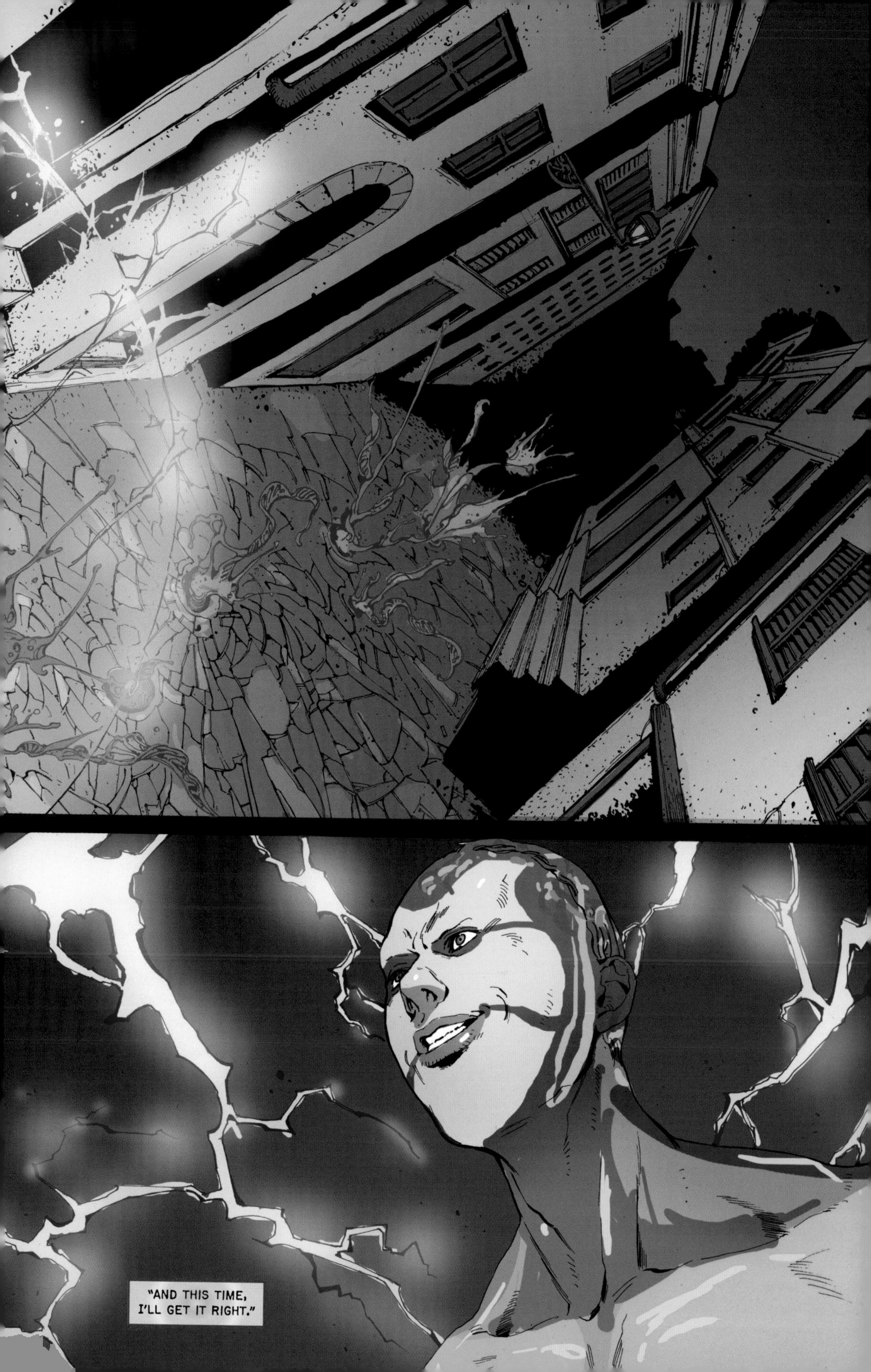
"AND THIS TIME,
I'LL GET IT RIGHT."

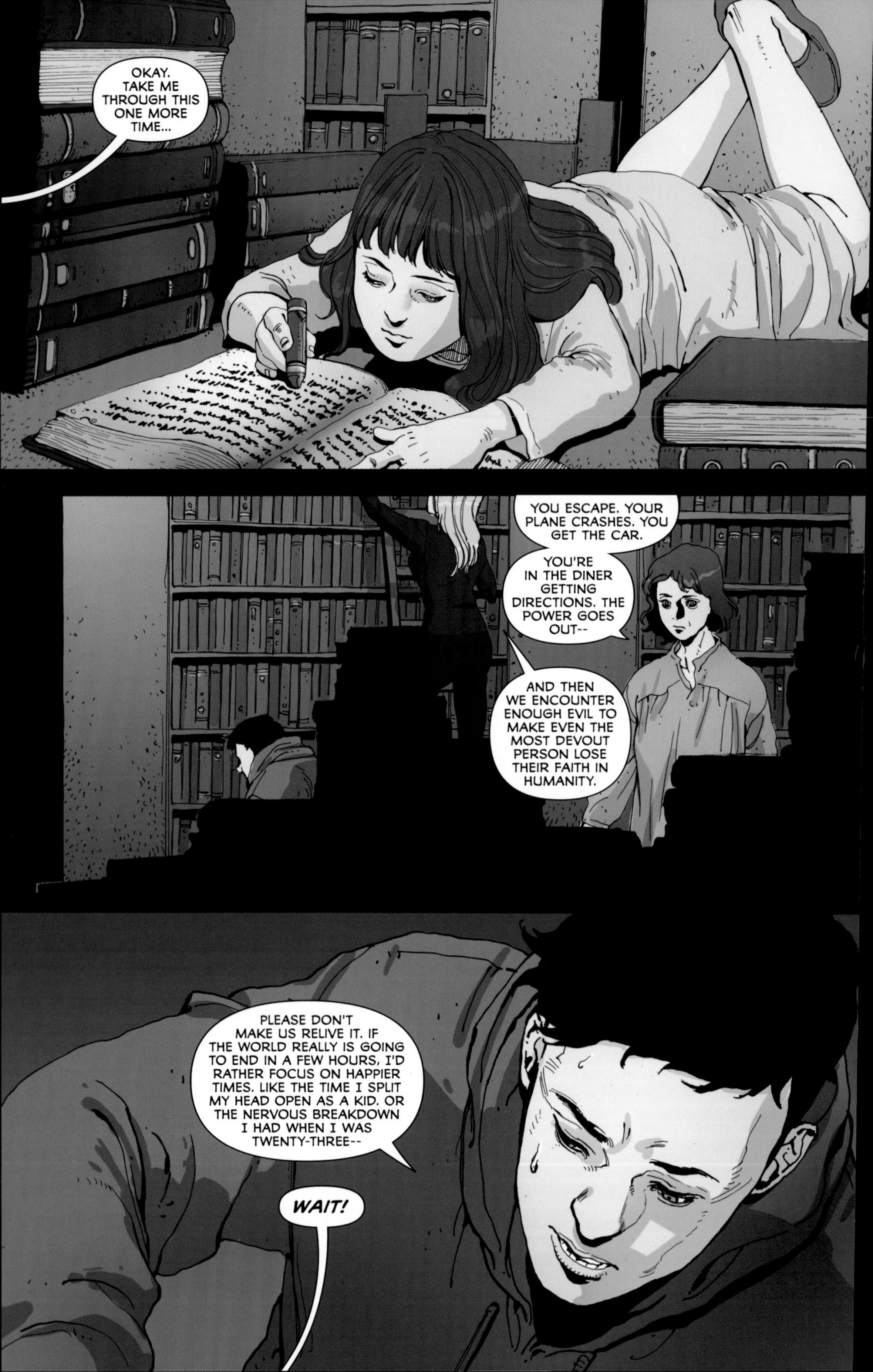
OKAY. TAKE ME THROUGH THIS ONE MORE TIME...
YOU ESCAPE. YOUR PLANE CRASHES. YOU GET THE CAR.
YOU'RE IN THE DINER GETTING DIRECTIONS. THE POWER GOES OUT--
AND THEN WE ENCOUNTER ENOUGH EVIL TO MAKE EVEN THE MOST DEVOUT PERSON LOSE THEIR FAITH IN HUMANITY.
PLEASE DON'T MAKE US RELIVE IT. IF THE WORLD REALLY IS GOING TO END IN A FEW HOURS, I'D RATHER FOCUS ON HAPPIER TIMES. LIKE THE TIME I SPLIT MY HEAD OPEN AS A KID. OR THE NERVOUS BREAKDOWN I HAD WHEN I WAS TWENTY-THREE--
WAIT!

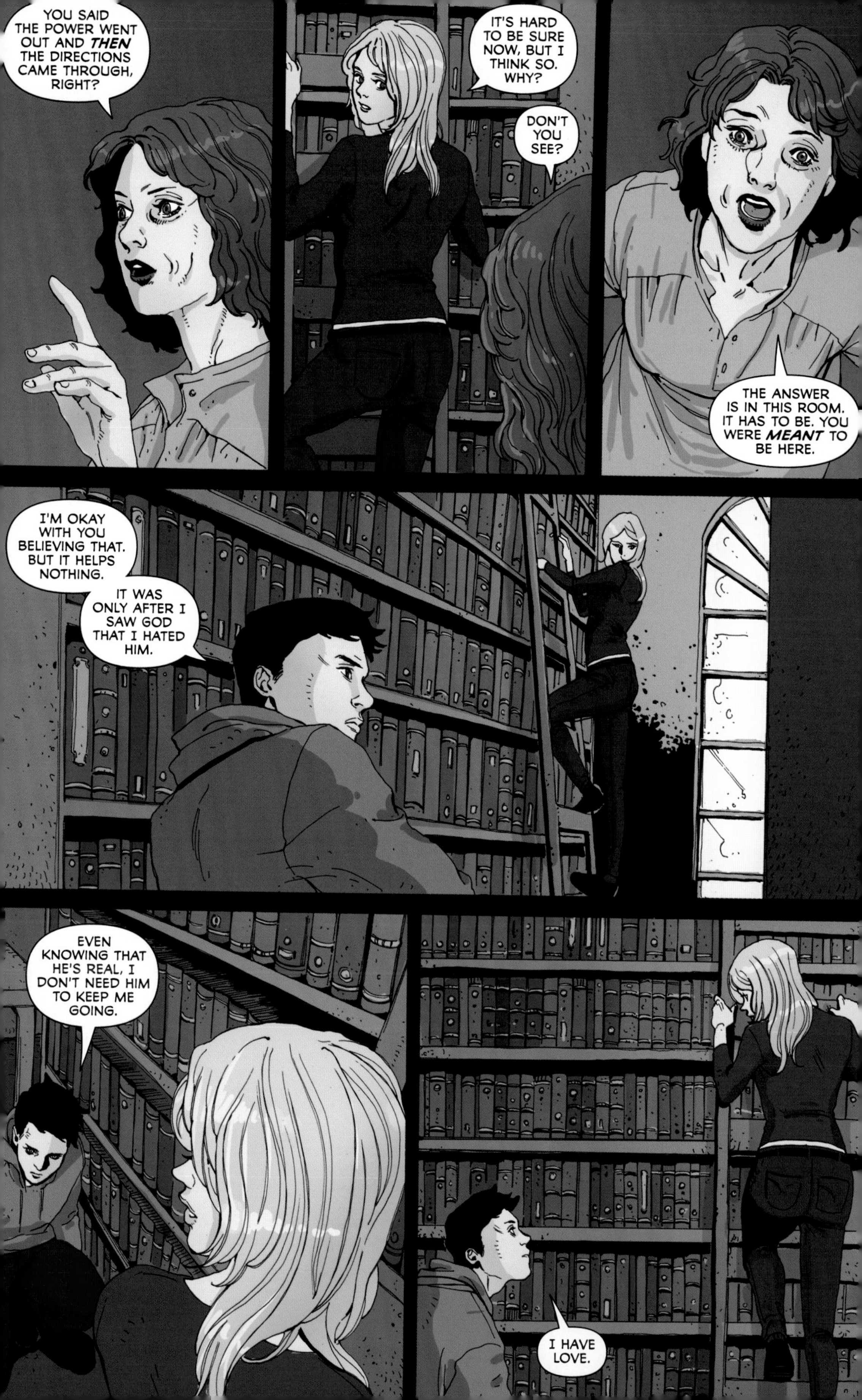
YOU SAID THE POWER WENT OUT AND *THEN* THE DIRECTIONS CAME THROUGH, RIGHT?
IT'S HARD TO BE SURE NOW, BUT I THINK SO. WHY?
DON'T YOU SEE?
THE ANSWER IS IN THIS ROOM. IT HAS TO BE. YOU WERE *MEANT* TO BE HERE.
I'M OKAY WITH YOU BELIEVING THAT. BUT IT HELPS NOTHING.
IT WAS ONLY AFTER I SAW GOD THAT I HATED HIM.
EVEN KNOWING THAT HE'S REAL, I DON'T NEED HIM TO KEEP ME GOING.
I HAVE LOVE.

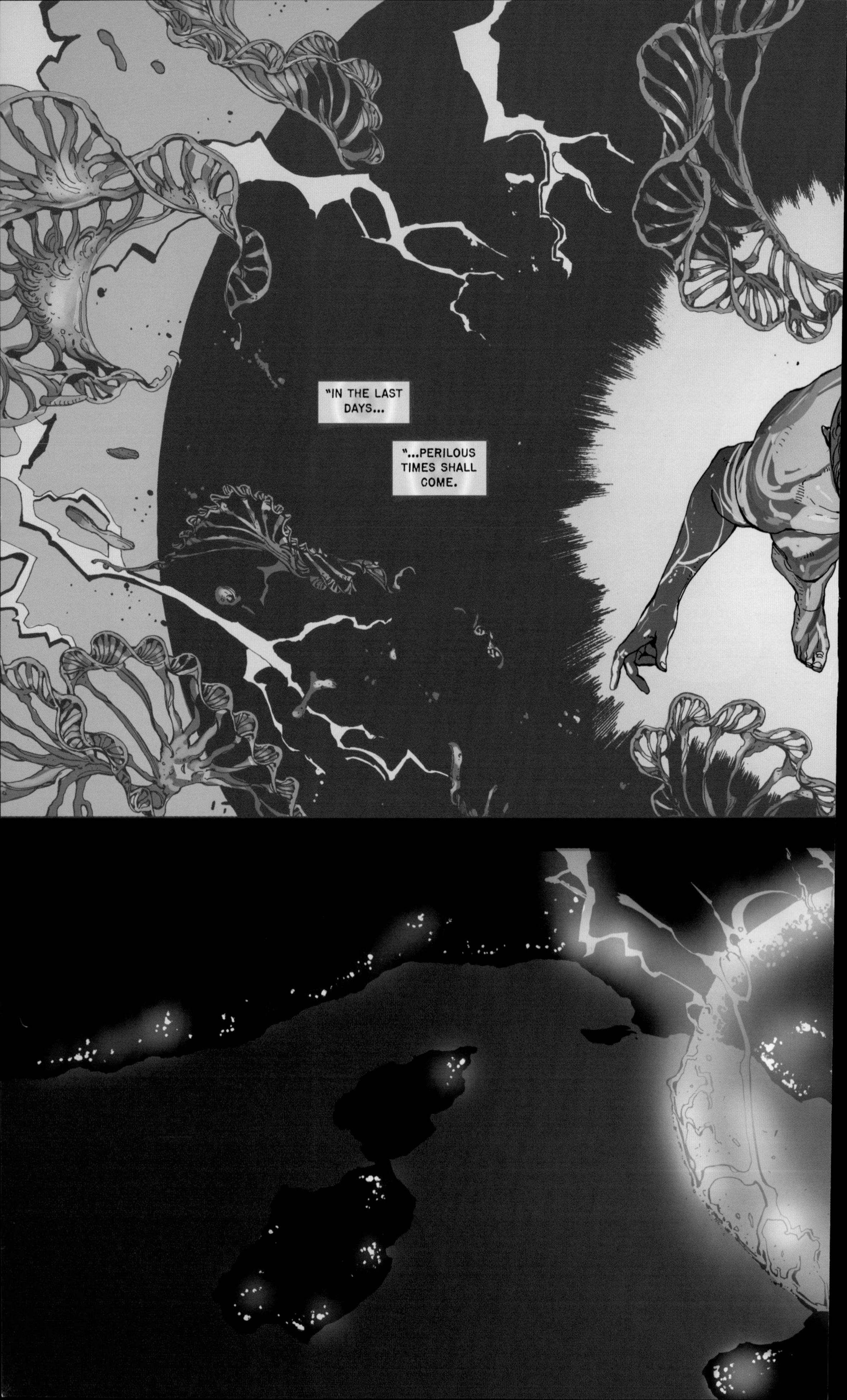
"IN THE LAST DAYS...
"...PERILOUS TIMES SHALL COME.

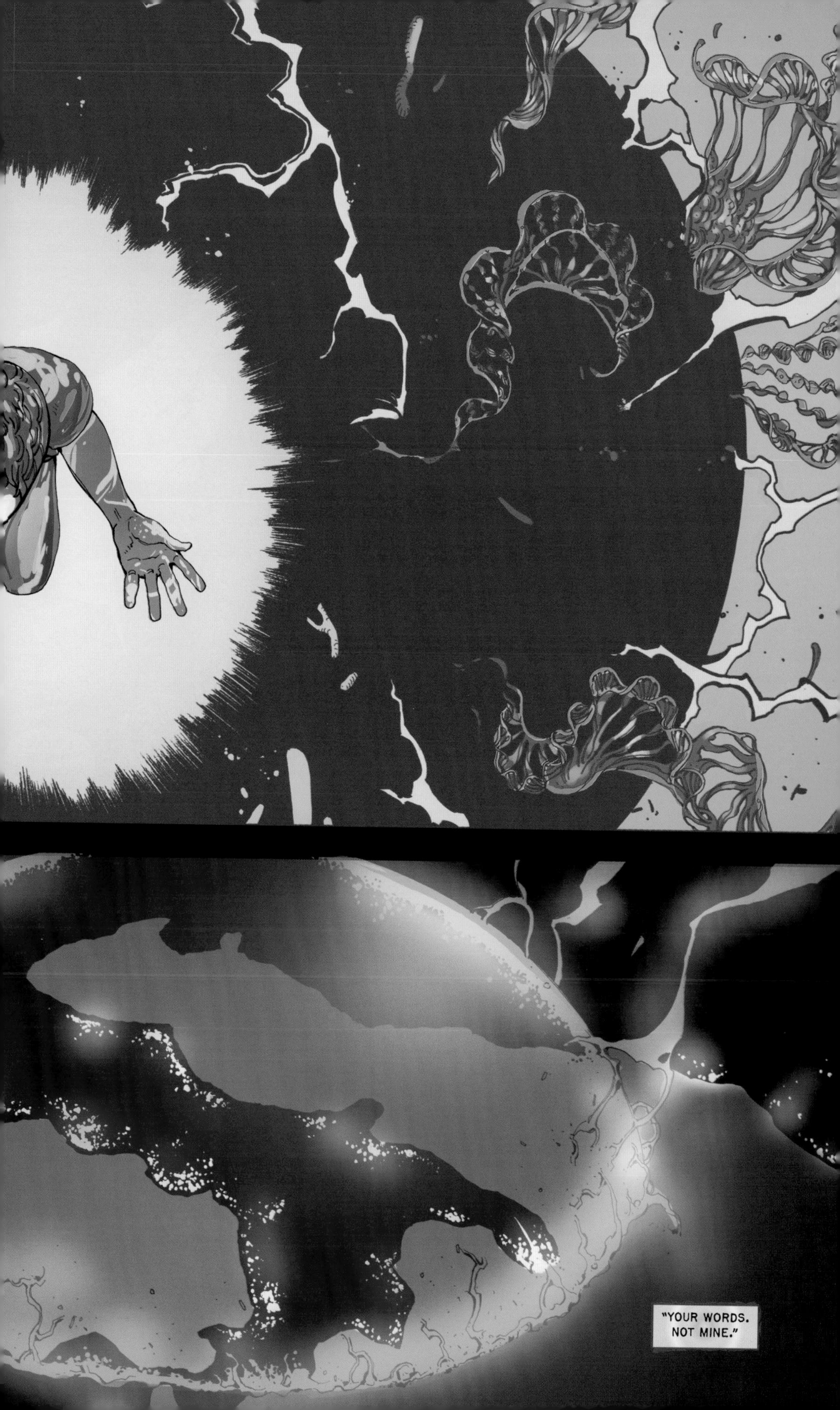
"YOUR WORDS. NOT MINE."

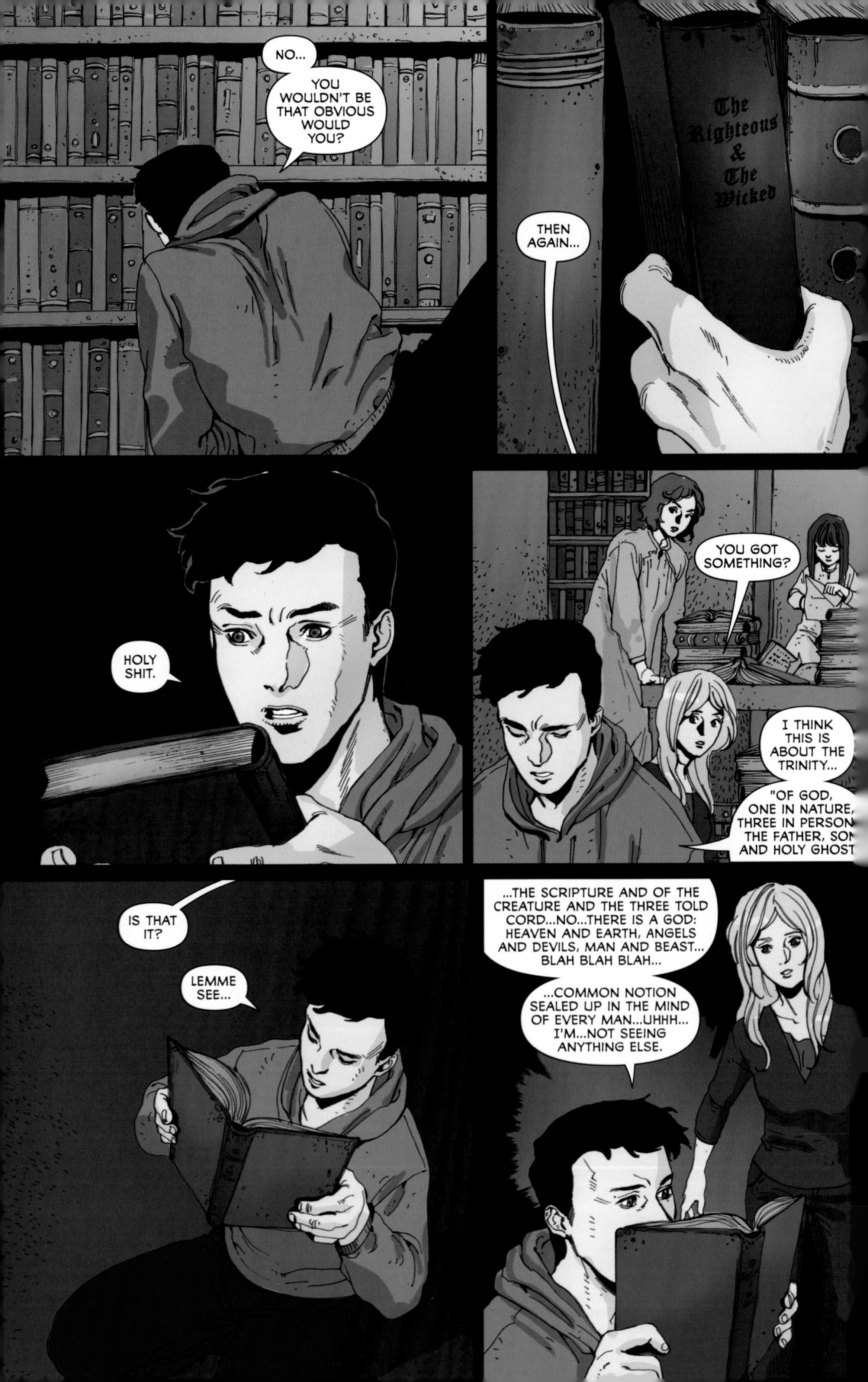

NO...
YOU WOULDN'T BE THAT OBVIOUS WOULD YOU?
The Righteous & The Wicked
THEN AGAIN...
HOLY SHIT.
YOU GOT SOMETHING?
I THINK THIS IS ABOUT THE TRINITY...
"OF GOD, ONE IN NATURE, THREE IN PERSON THE FATHER, SON AND HOLY GHOST
IS THAT IT?
LEMME SEE...
...THE SCRIPTURE AND OF THE CREATURE AND THE THREE TOLD CORD...NO...THERE IS A GOD: HEAVEN AND EARTH, ANGELS AND DEVILS, MAN AND BEAST... BLAH BLAH BLAH...
...COMMON NOTION SEALED UP IN THE MIND OF EVERY MAN...UHHH... I'M...NOT SEEING ANYTHING ELSE.

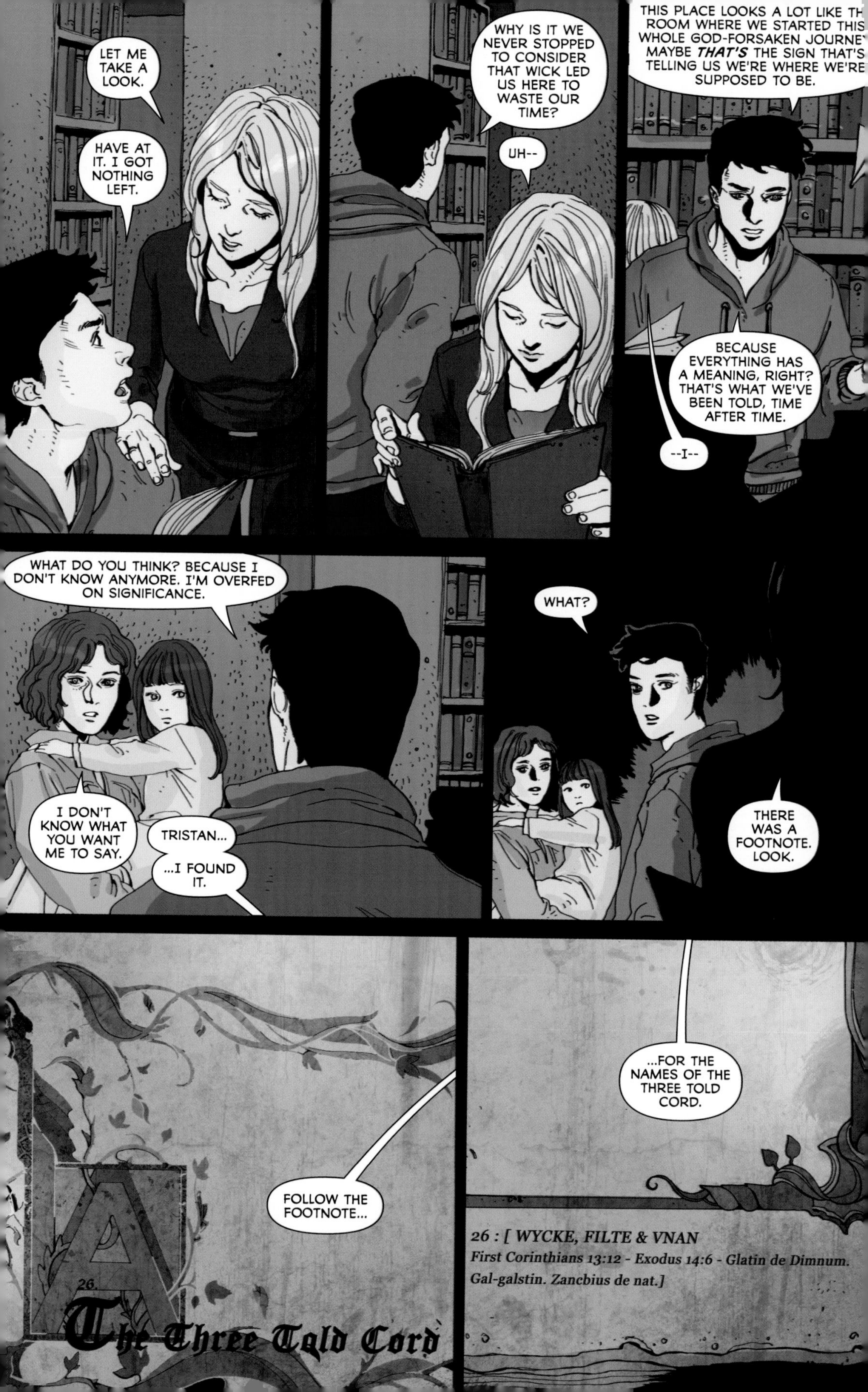
LET ME TAKE A LOOK.
HAVE AT IT. I GOT NOTHING LEFT.
WHY IS IT WE NEVER STOPPED TO CONSIDER THAT WICK LED US HERE TO WASTE OUR TIME?
UH--
THIS PLACE LOOKS A LOT LIKE TH ROOM WHERE WE STARTED THIS WHOLE GOD-FORSAKEN JOURNE MAYBE *THAT'S* THE SIGN THAT'S TELLING US WE'RE WHERE WE'RE SUPPOSED TO BE.
BECAUSE EVERYTHING HAS A MEANING, RIGHT? THAT'S WHAT WE'VE BEEN TOLD, TIME AFTER TIME.
--I--
WHAT DO YOU THINK? BECAUSE I DON'T KNOW ANYMORE. I'M OVERFED ON SIGNIFICANCE.
I DON'T KNOW WHAT YOU WANT ME TO SAY.
TRISTAN...
...I FOUND IT.
WHAT?
THERE WAS A FOOTNOTE. LOOK.
FOLLOW THE FOOTNOTE...
26.
The Three Told Cord
...FOR THE NAMES OF THE THREE TOLD CORD.
26 : [WYCKE, FILTE & VNAN
First Corinthians 13:12 - Exodus 14:6 - Glatin de Dimnum. Gal-galstin. Zancbius de nat.]

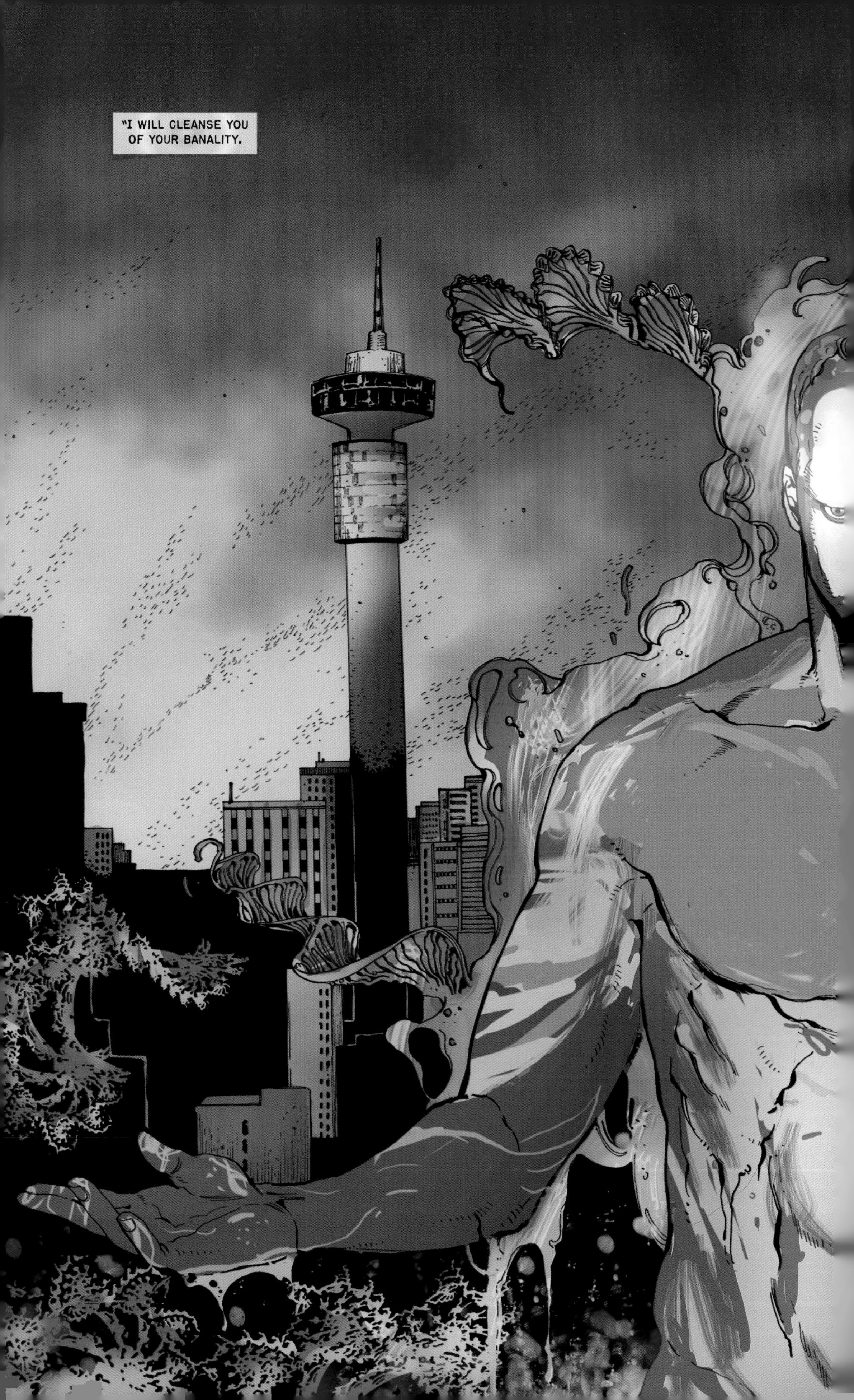
"I WILL CLEANSE YOU OF YOUR BANALITY.

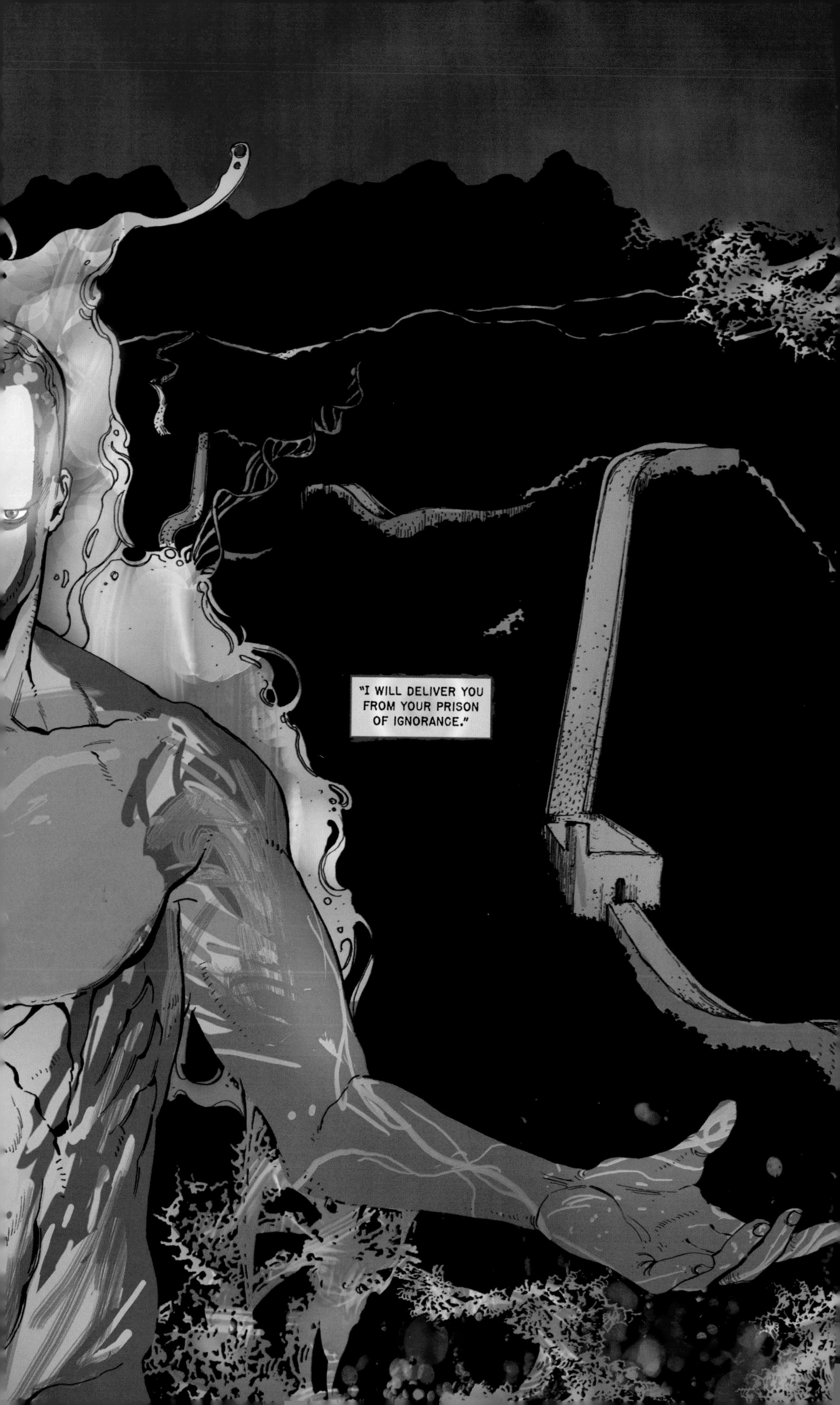
"I WILL DELIVER YOU FROM YOUR PRISON OF IGNORANCE."

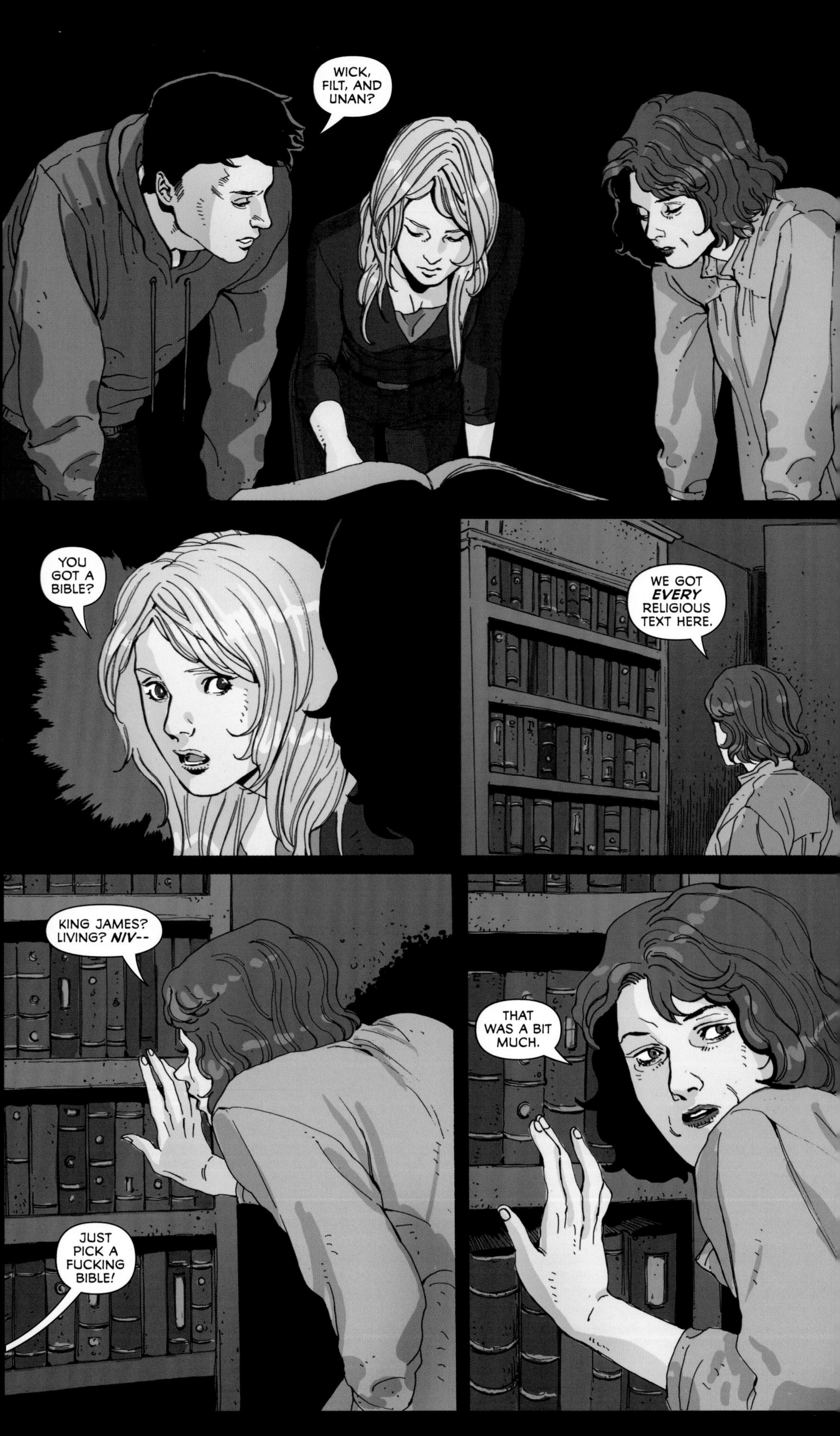
WICK, FILT, AND UNAN?
YOU GOT A BIBLE?
WE GOT *EVERY* RELIGIOUS TEXT HERE.
KING JAMES? LIVING? *NIV*--
JUST PICK A FUCKING BIBLE!
THAT WAS A BIT MUCH.

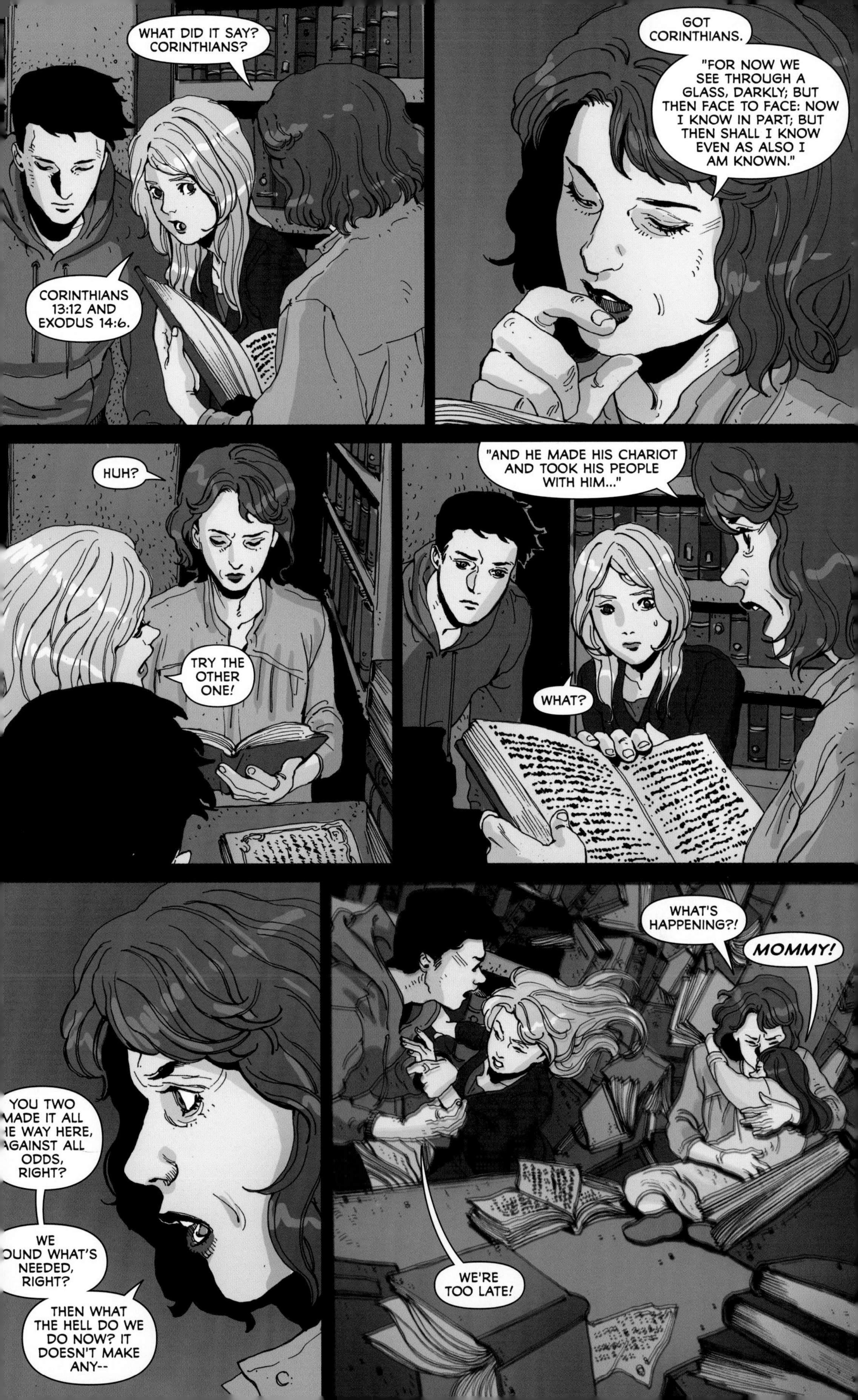
WHAT DID IT SAY? CORINTHIANS?
CORINTHIANS 13:12 AND EXODUS 14:6.
GOT CORINTHIANS.
"FOR NOW WE SEE THROUGH A GLASS, DARKLY; BUT THEN FACE TO FACE: NOW I KNOW IN PART; BUT THEN SHALL I KNOW EVEN AS ALSO I AM KNOWN."
HUH?
TRY THE OTHER ONE!
"AND HE MADE HIS CHARIOT AND TOOK HIS PEOPLE WITH HIM..."
WHAT?
YOU TWO MADE IT ALL THE WAY HERE, AGAINST ALL ODDS, RIGHT?
WE FOUND WHAT'S NEEDED, RIGHT?
THEN WHAT THE HELL DO WE DO NOW? IT DOESN'T MAKE ANY--
WHAT'S HAPPENING?!
MOMMY!
WE'RE TOO LATE!

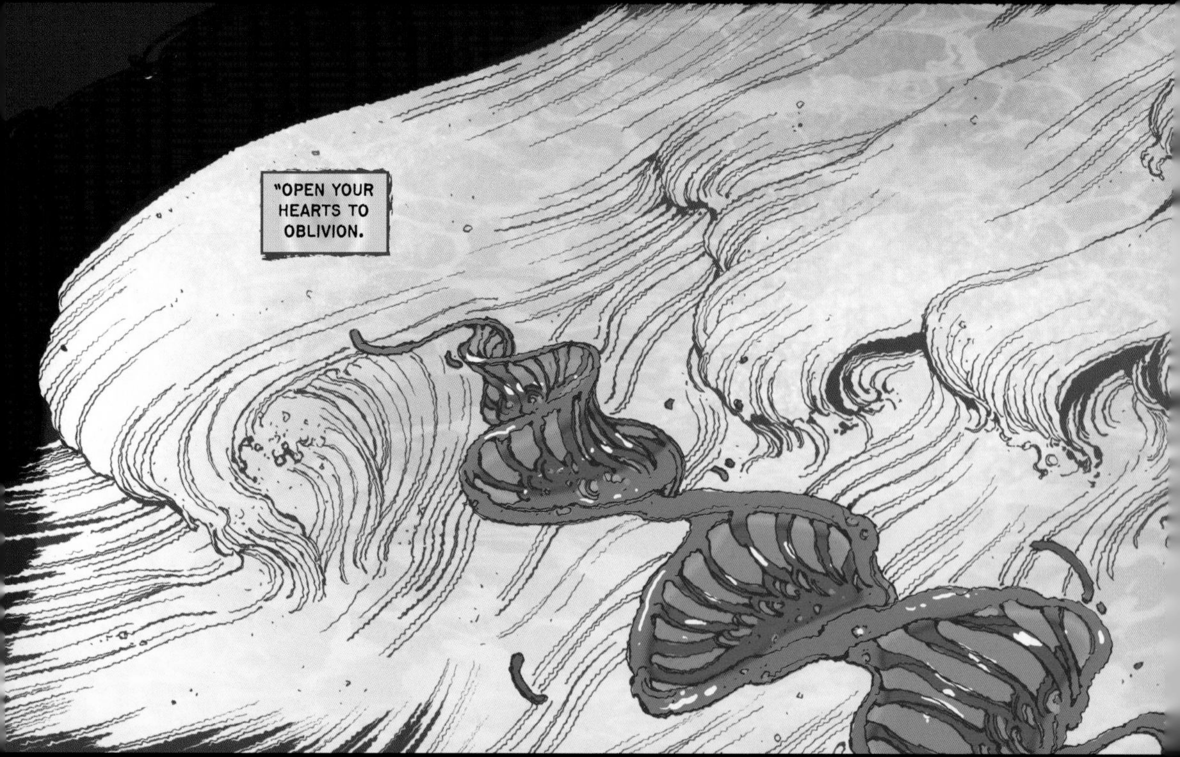
"OPEN YOUR HEARTS TO OBLIVION.

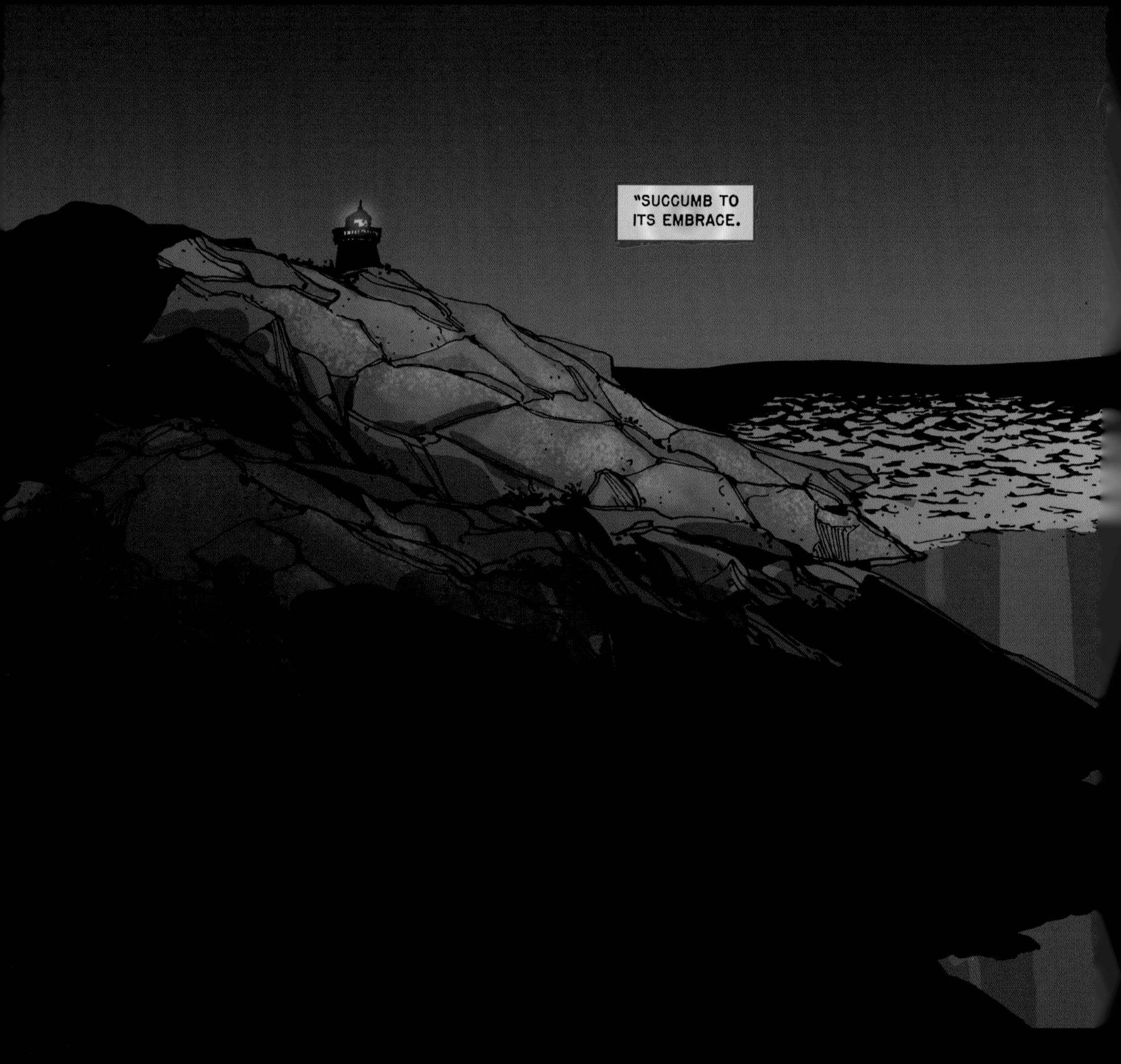
"SUCCUMB TO ITS EMBRACE.

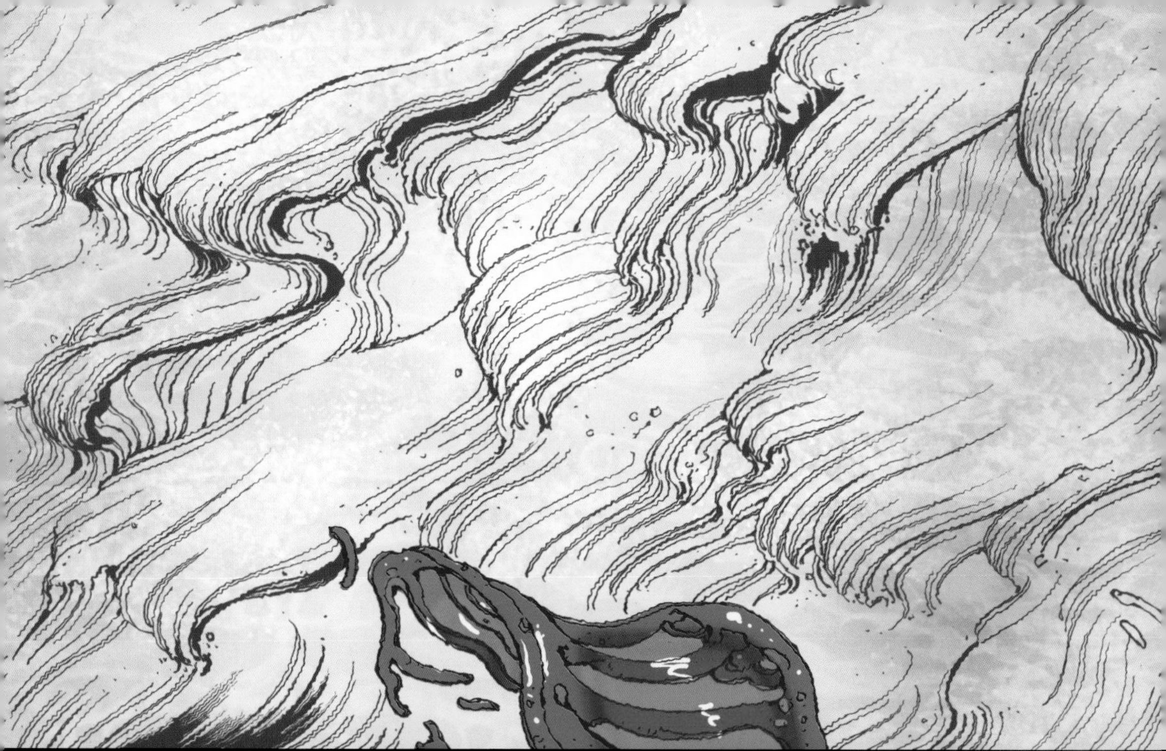

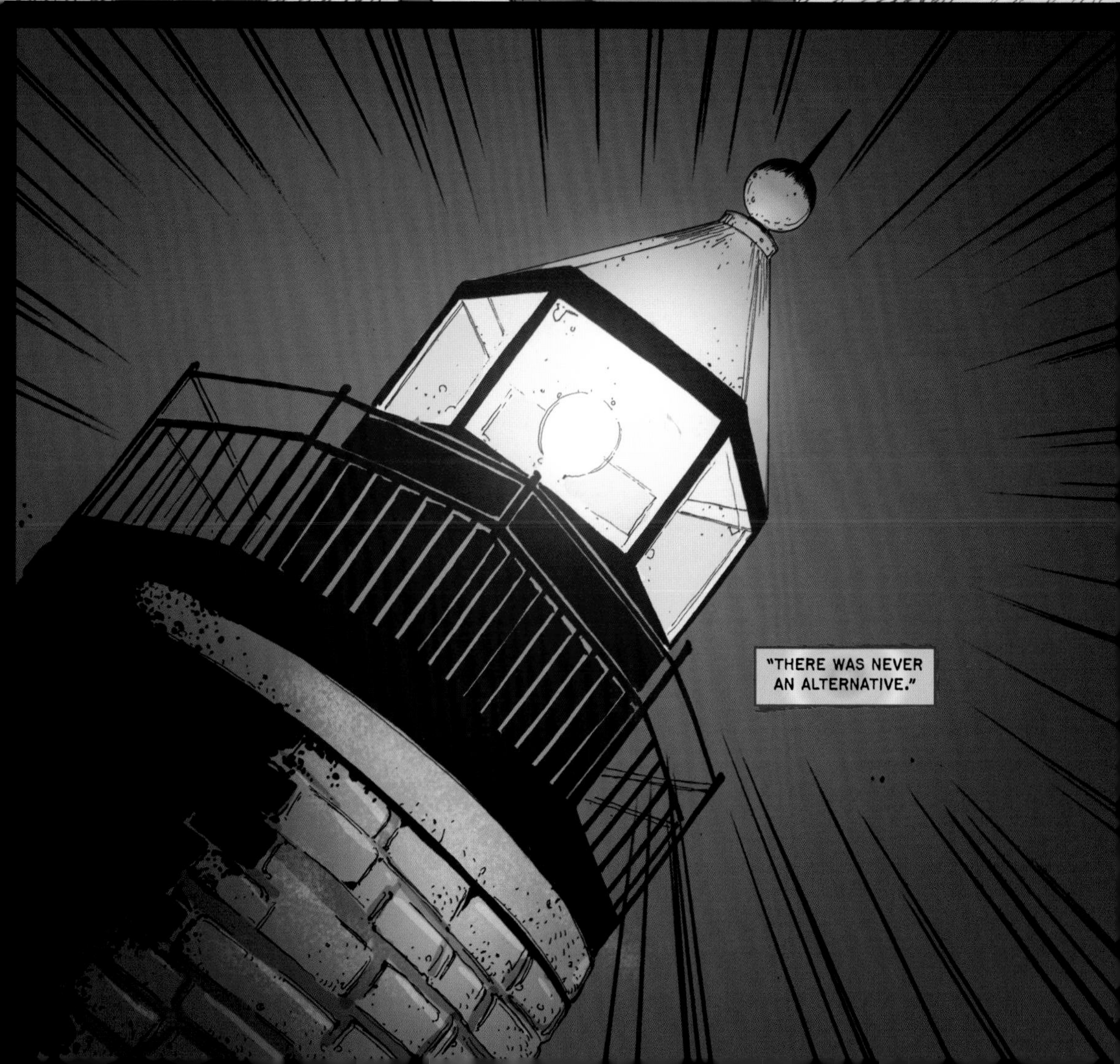
"THERE WAS NEVER AN ALTERNATIVE."

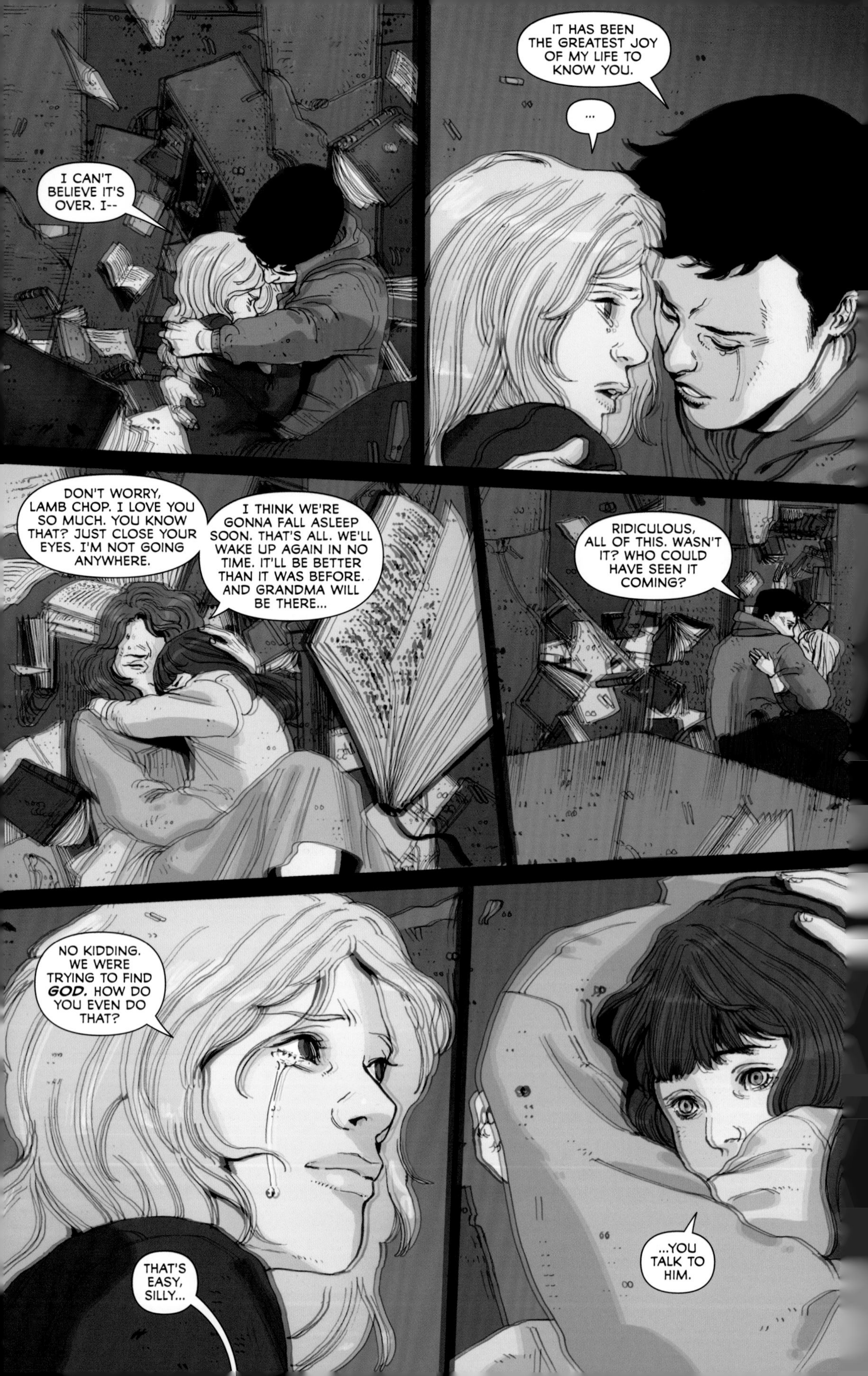
I CAN'T BELIEVE IT'S OVER. I--
IT HAS BEEN THE GREATEST JOY OF MY LIFE TO KNOW YOU.
...
DON'T WORRY, LAMB CHOP. I LOVE YOU SO MUCH. YOU KNOW THAT? JUST CLOSE YOUR EYES. I'M NOT GOING ANYWHERE.
I THINK WE'RE GONNA FALL ASLEEP SOON. THAT'S ALL. WE'LL WAKE UP AGAIN IN NO TIME. IT'LL BE BETTER THAN IT WAS BEFORE. AND GRANDMA WILL BE THERE...
RIDICULOUS, ALL OF THIS. WASN'T IT? WHO COULD HAVE SEEN IT COMING?
NO KIDDING. WE WERE TRYING TO FIND ***GOD.*** HOW DO YOU EVEN DO THAT?
THAT'S EASY, SILLY...
...YOU TALK TO HIM.

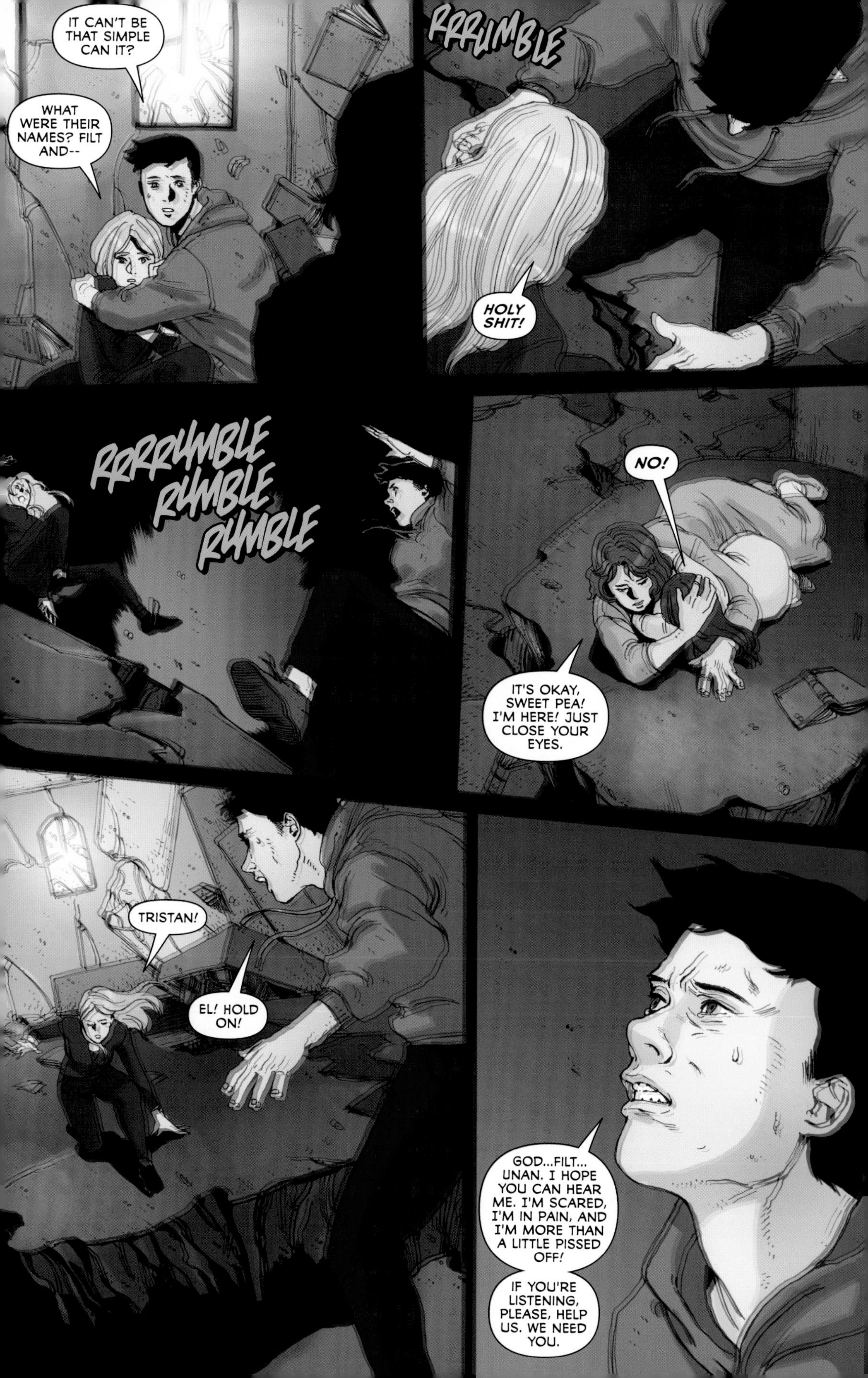
IT CAN'T BE THAT SIMPLE CAN IT?
WHAT WERE THEIR NAMES? FILT AND--
RRRUMBLE
HOLY SHIT!
RRRRUMBLE RUMBLE RUMBLE
NO!
IT'S OKAY, SWEET PEA! I'M HERE! JUST CLOSE YOUR EYES.
TRISTAN!
EL! HOLD ON!
GOD...FILT... UNAN. I HOPE YOU CAN HEAR ME. I'M SCARED, I'M IN PAIN, AND I'M MORE THAN A LITTLE PISSED OFF!
IF YOU'RE LISTENING, PLEASE, HELP US. WE NEED YOU.

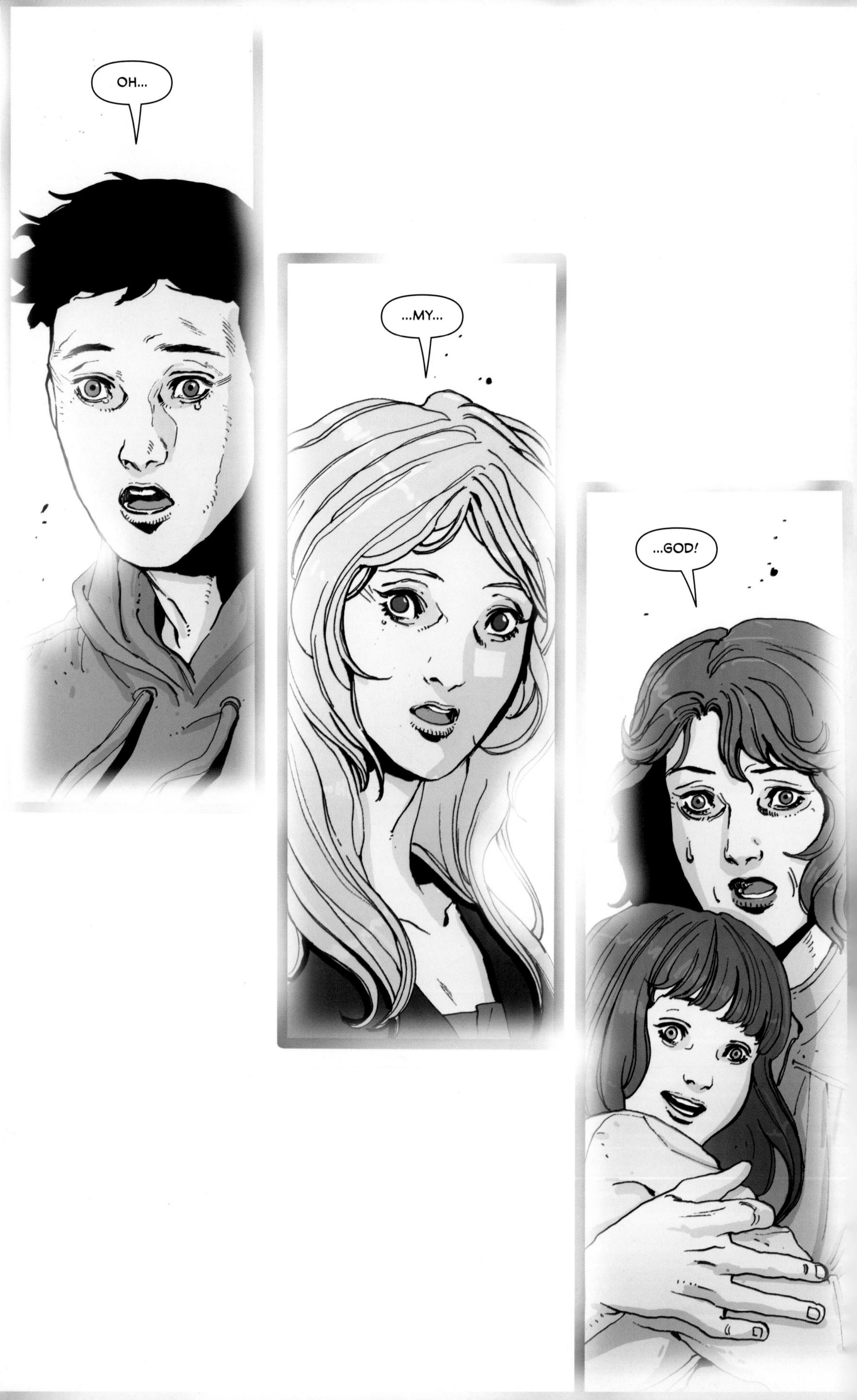
OH...
...MY...
...GOD!

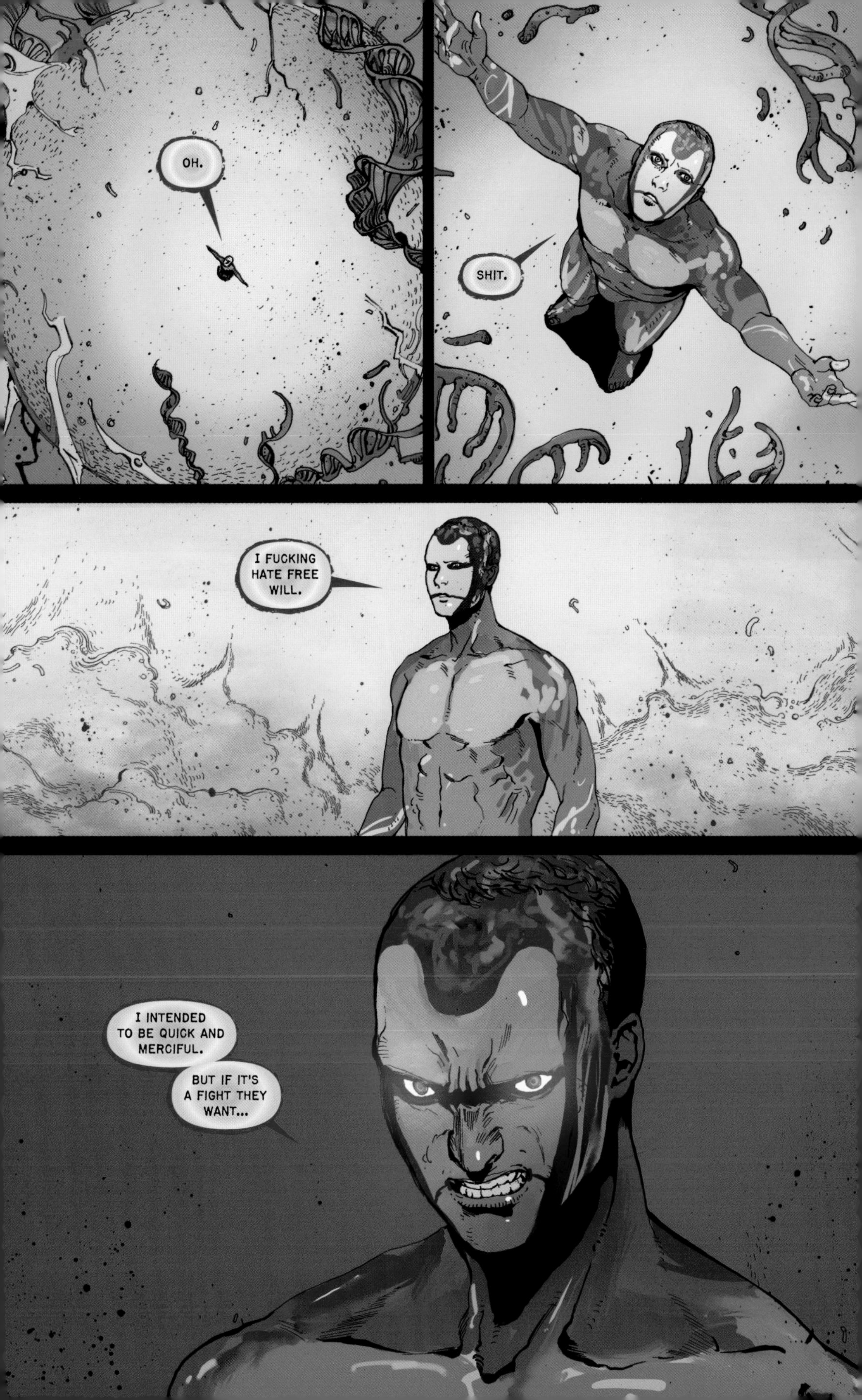
OH.
SHIT.
I FUCKING HATE FREE WILL.
I INTENDED TO BE QUICK AND MERCIFUL.
BUT IF IT'S A FIGHT THEY WANT...

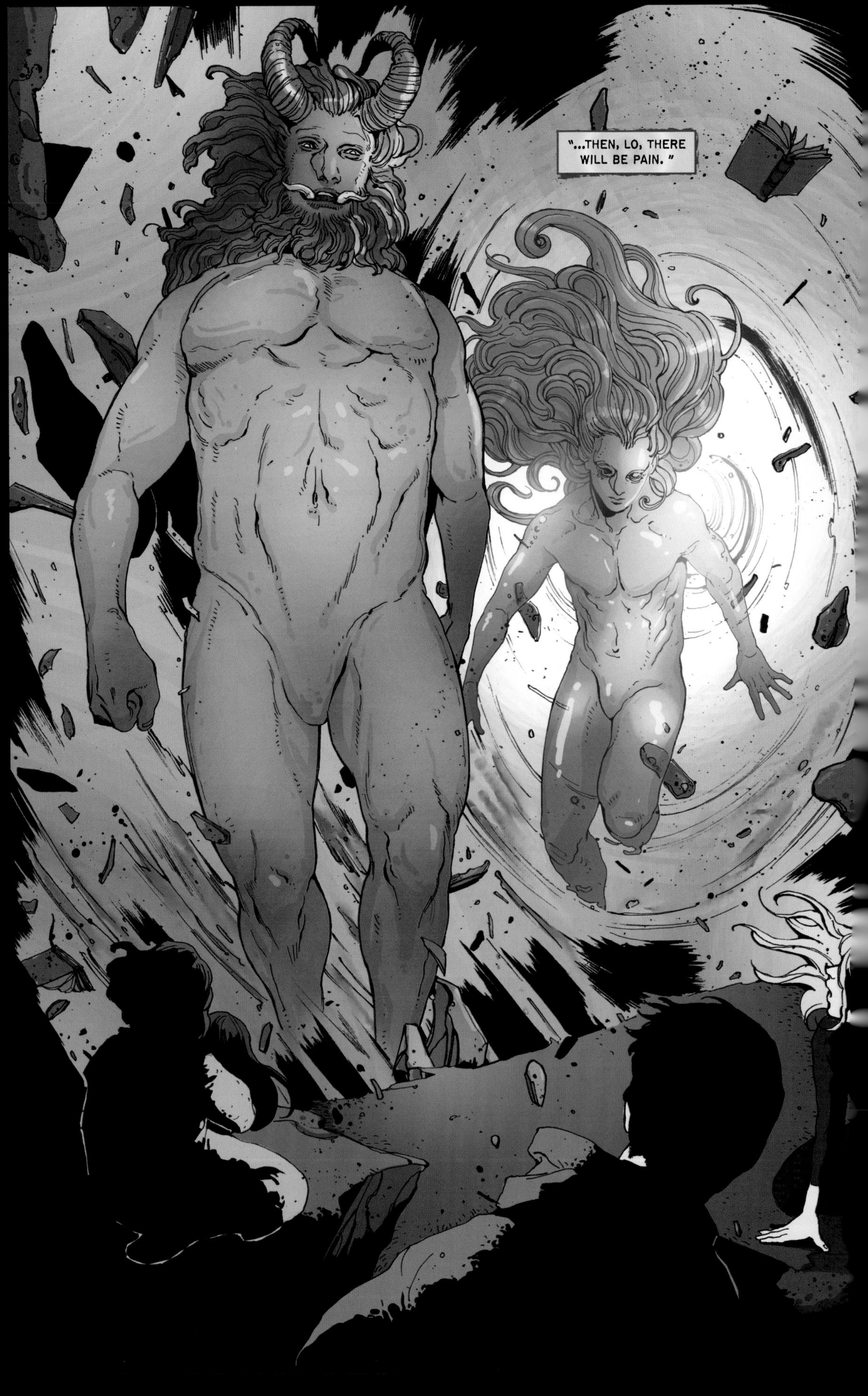
"...THEN, LO, THERE WILL BE PAIN."

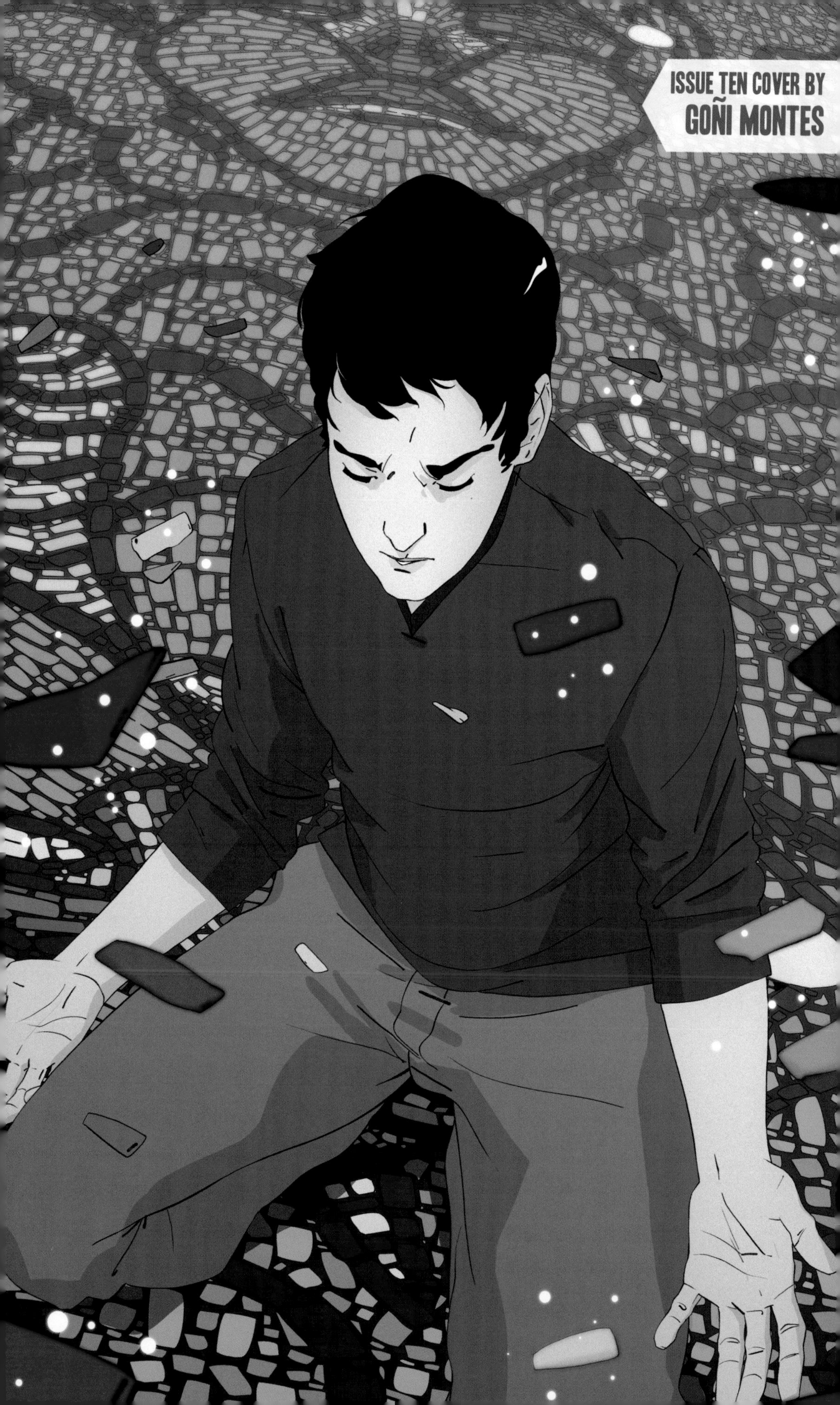

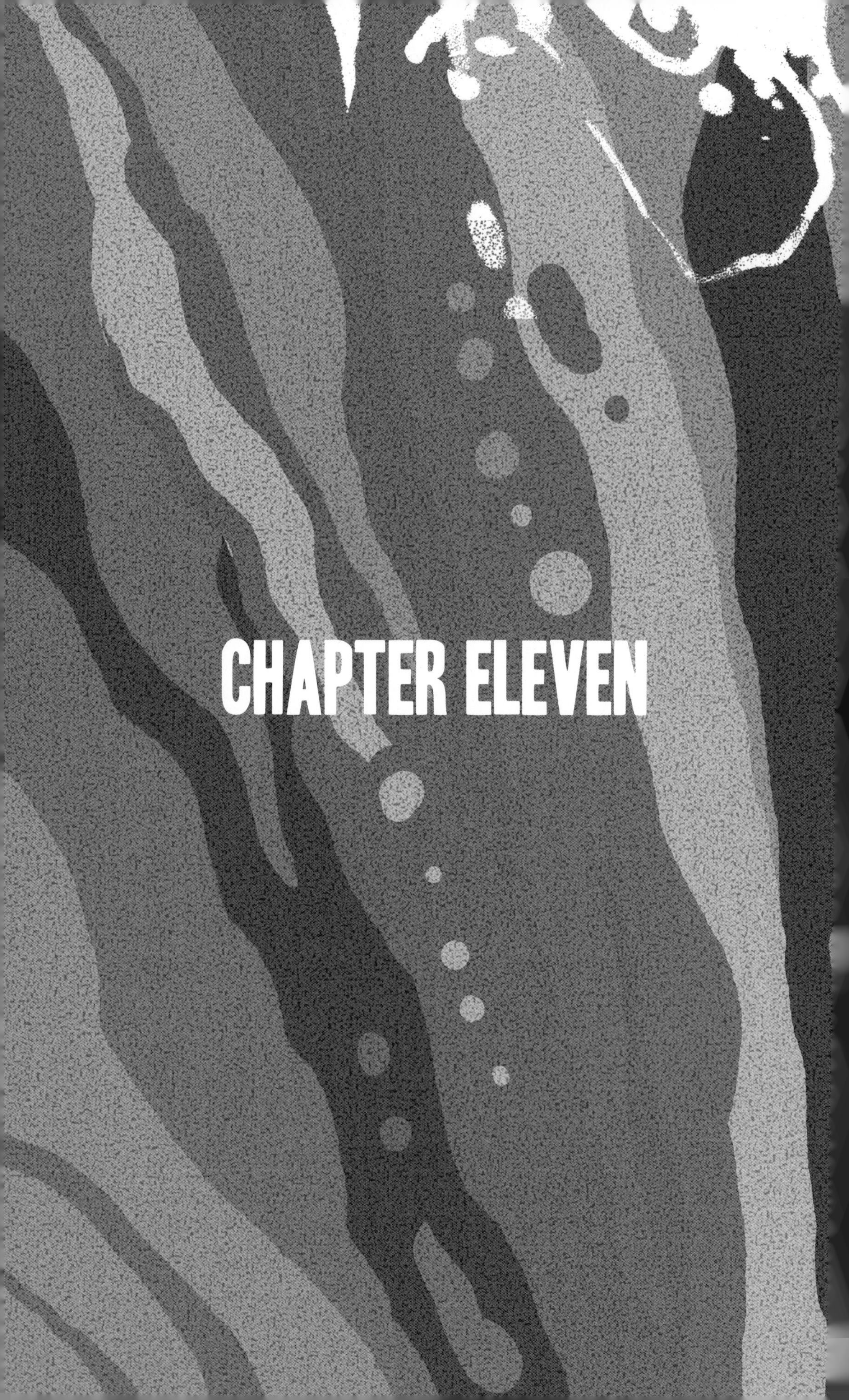

CHAPTER ELEVEN

CHAPTER 11: OUT OF THE MOUTHS OF BABES

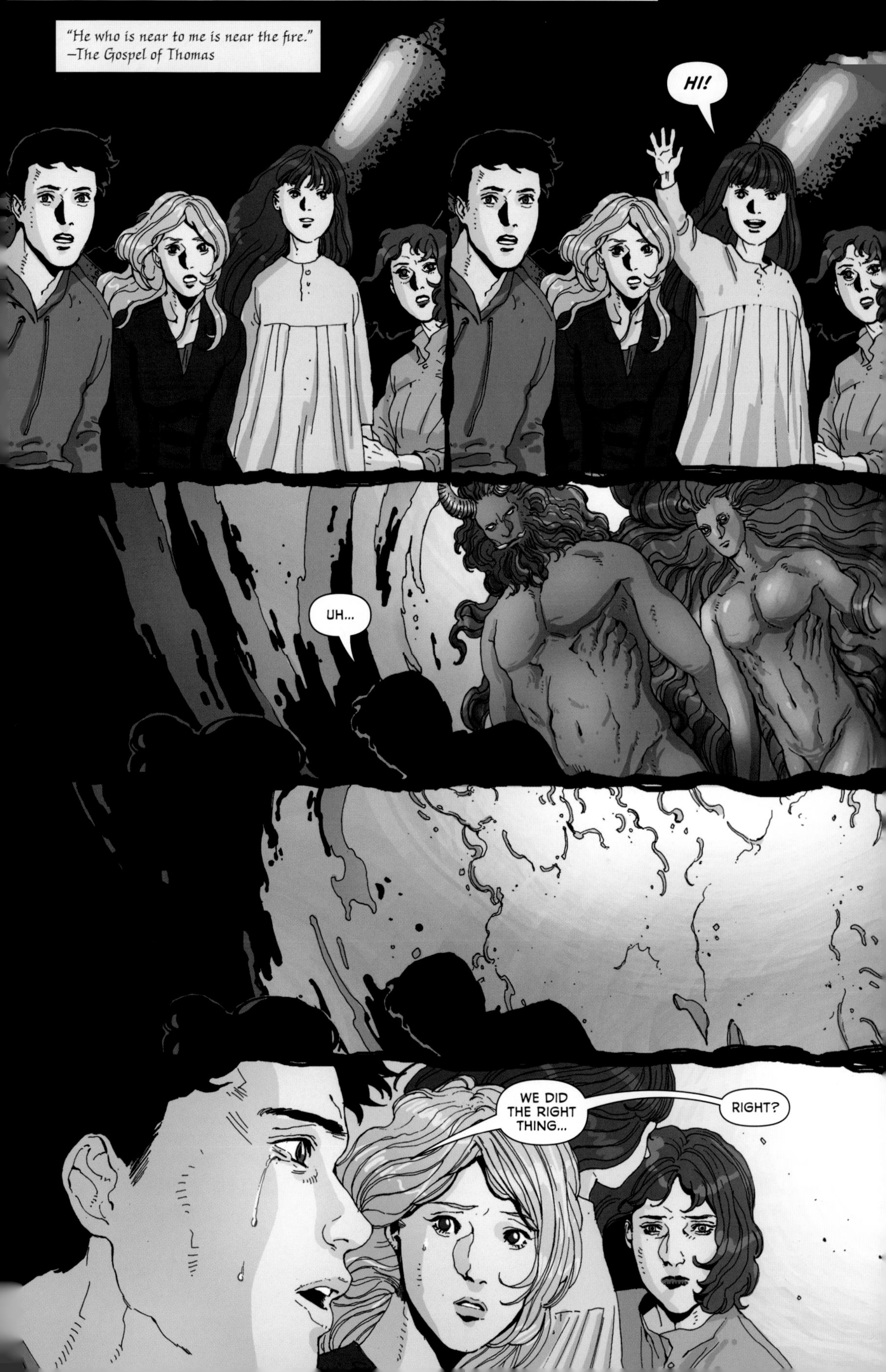
"He who is near to me is near the fire."
—The Gospel of Thomas
HI!
UH...
WE DID THE RIGHT THING...
RIGHT?

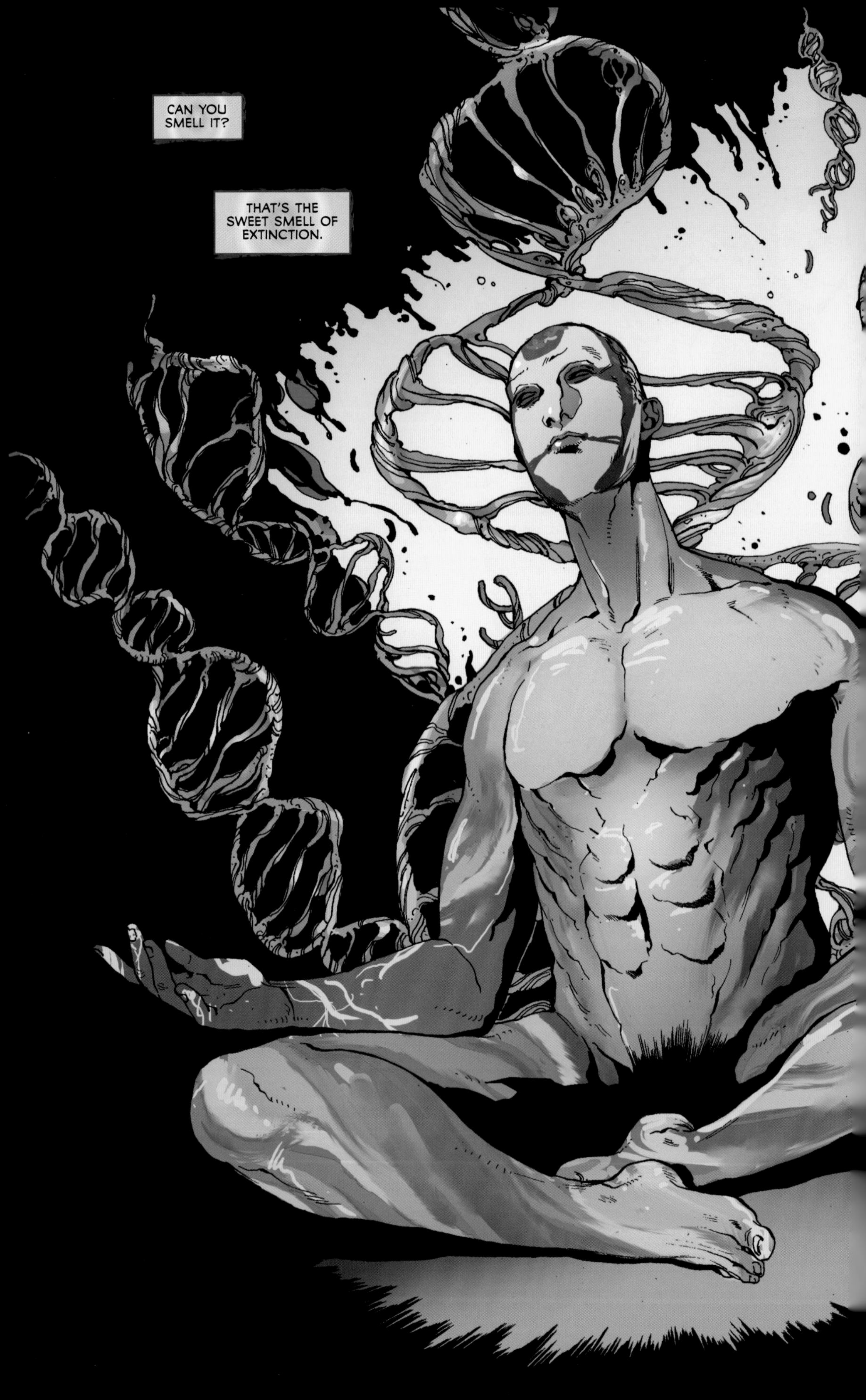
CAN YOU SMELL IT?
THAT'S THE SWEET SMELL OF EXTINCTION.

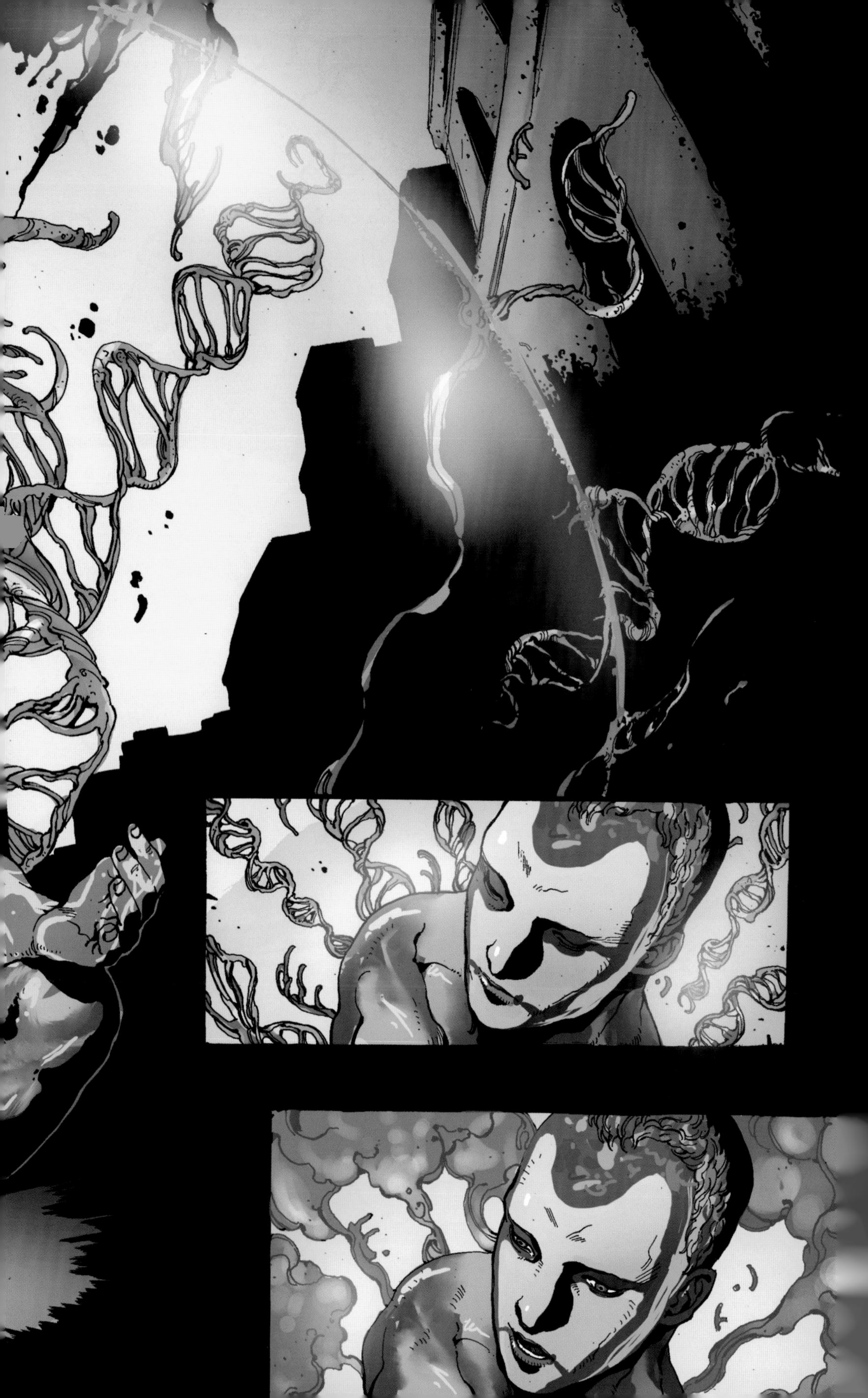

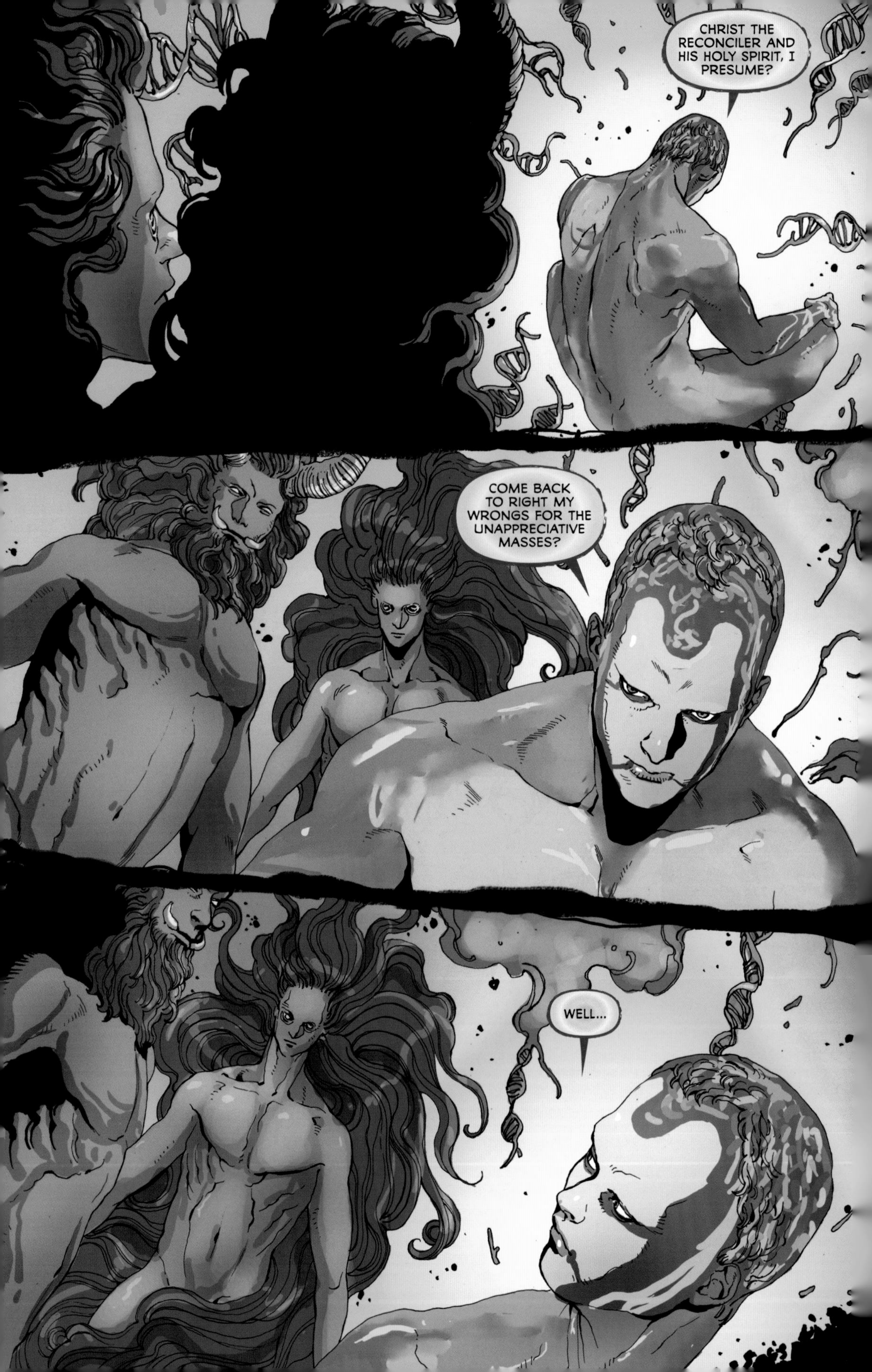
CHRIST THE RECONCILER AND HIS HOLY SPIRIT, I PRESUME?
COME BACK TO RIGHT MY WRONGS FOR THE UNAPPRECIATIVE MASSES?
WELL...

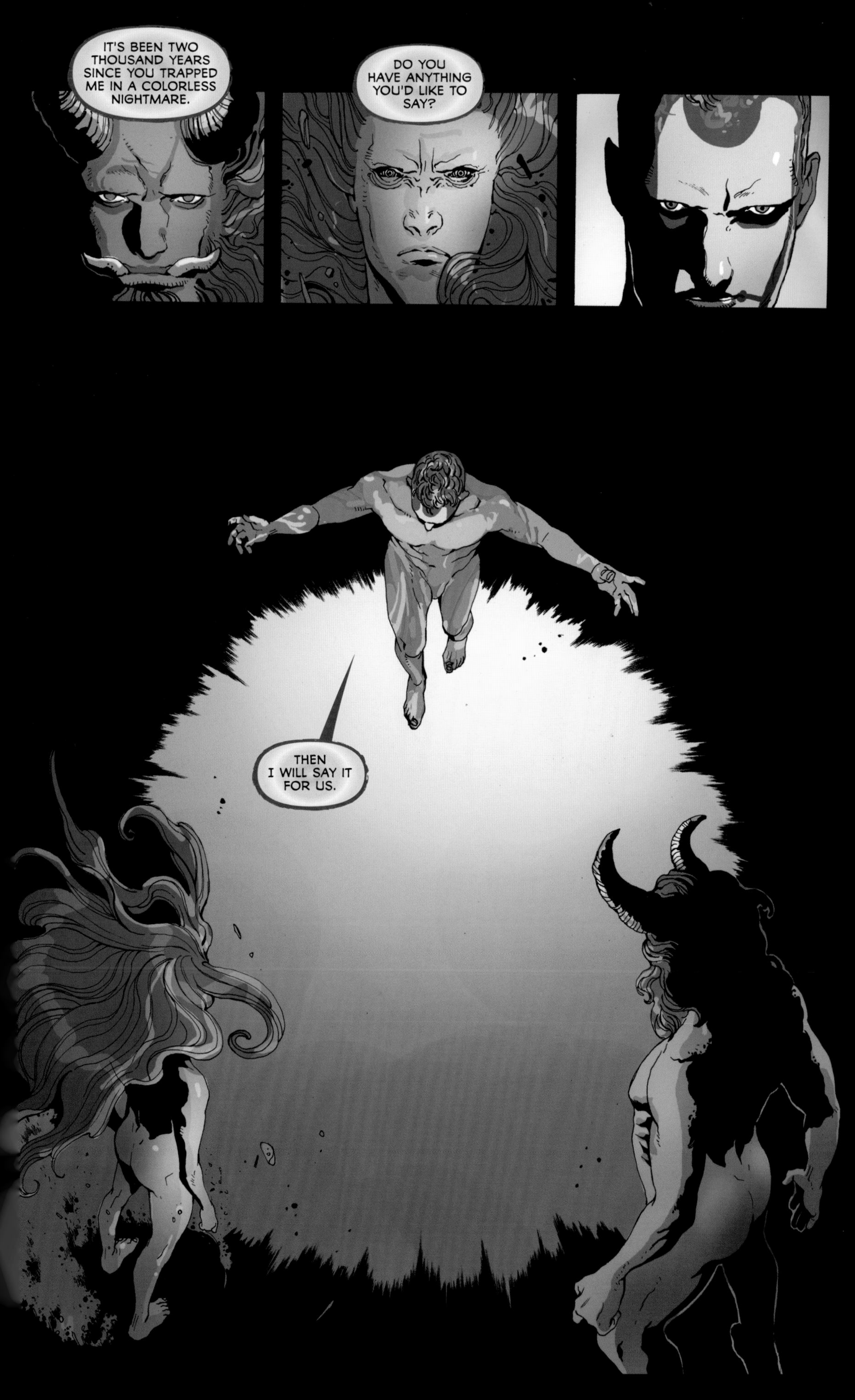
IT'S BEEN TWO THOUSAND YEARS SINCE YOU TRAPPED ME IN A COLORLESS NIGHTMARE.
DO YOU HAVE ANYTHING YOU'D LIKE TO SAY?
THEN I WILL SAY IT FOR US.

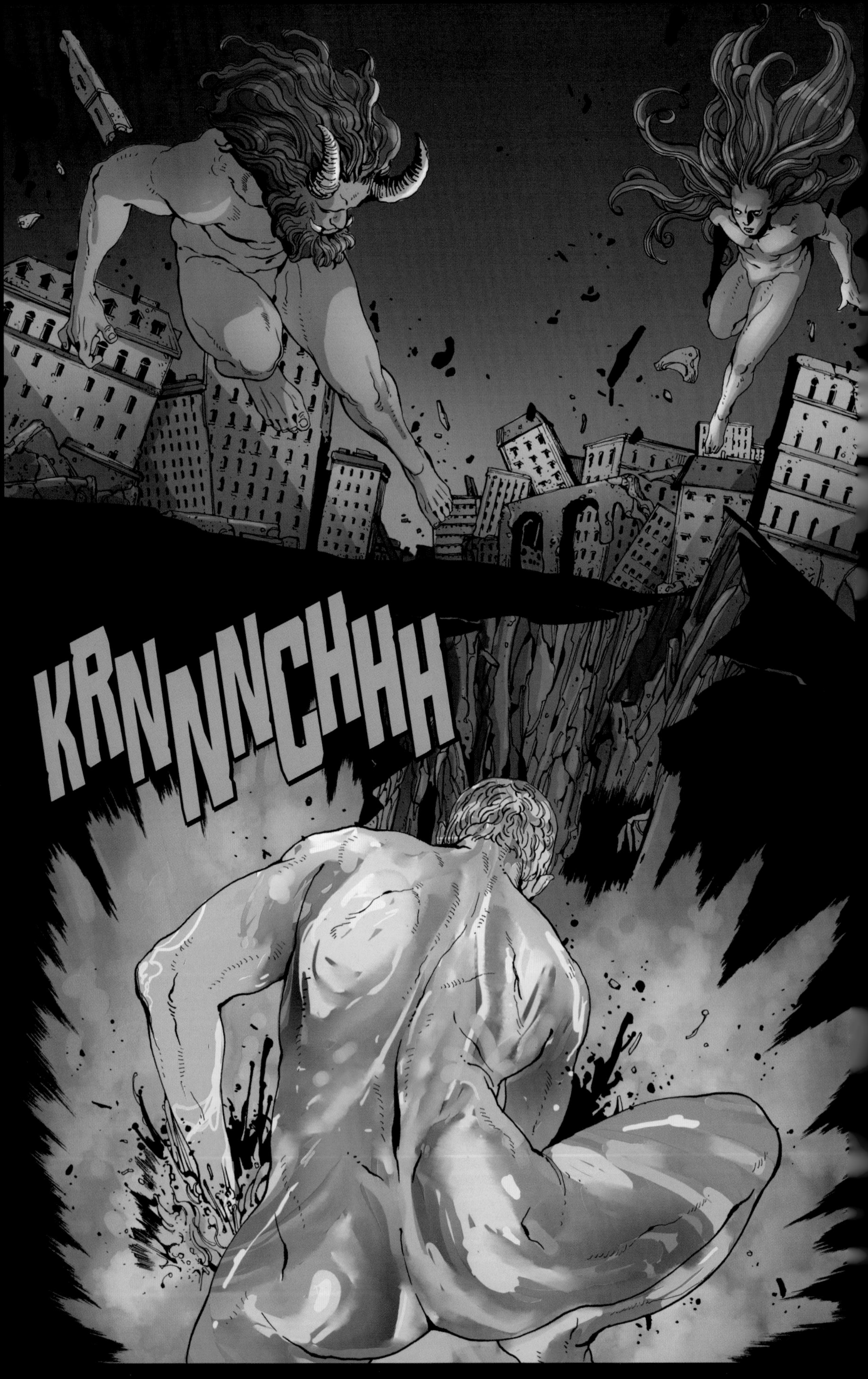
KRNNNCHHH

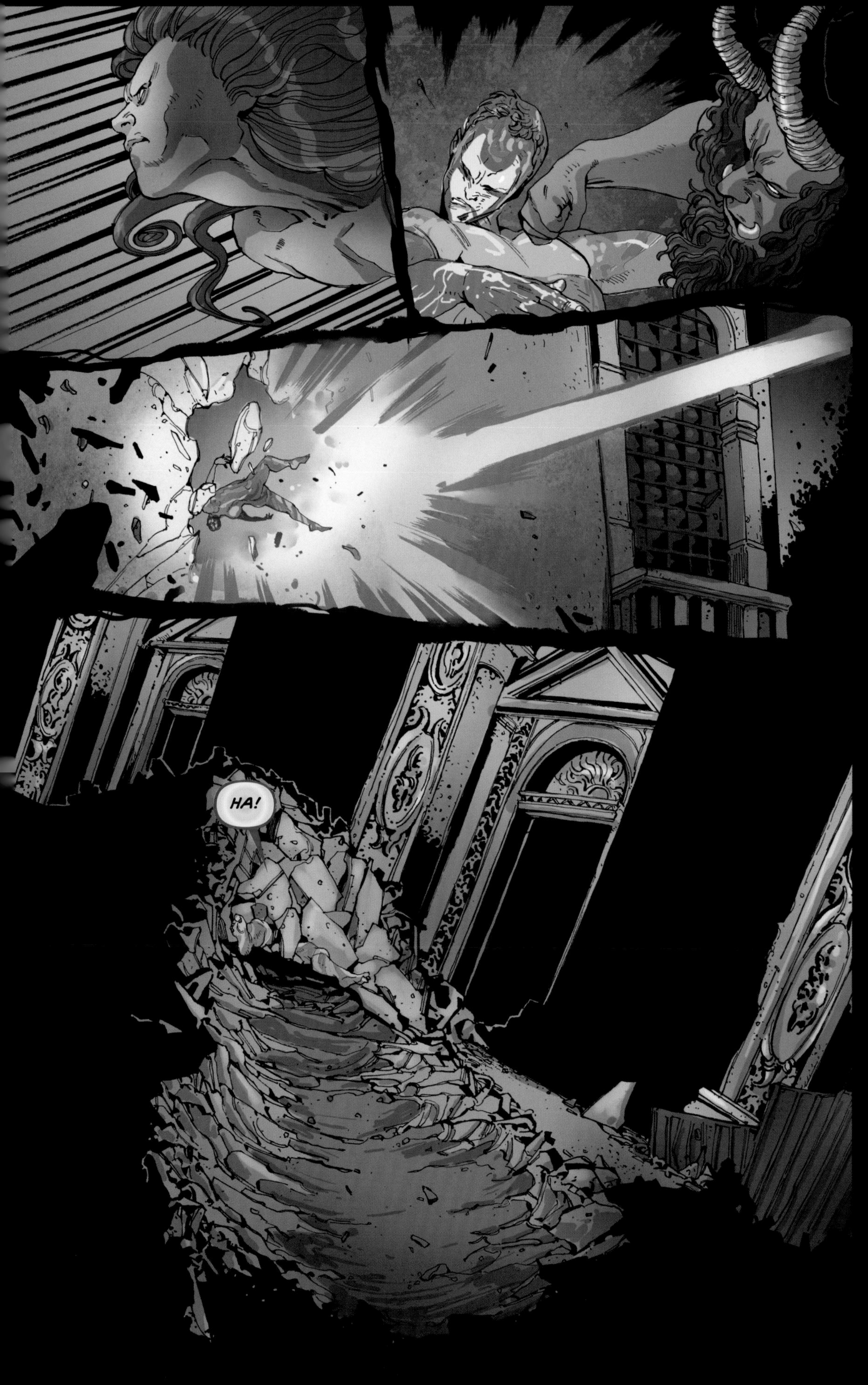
HA!

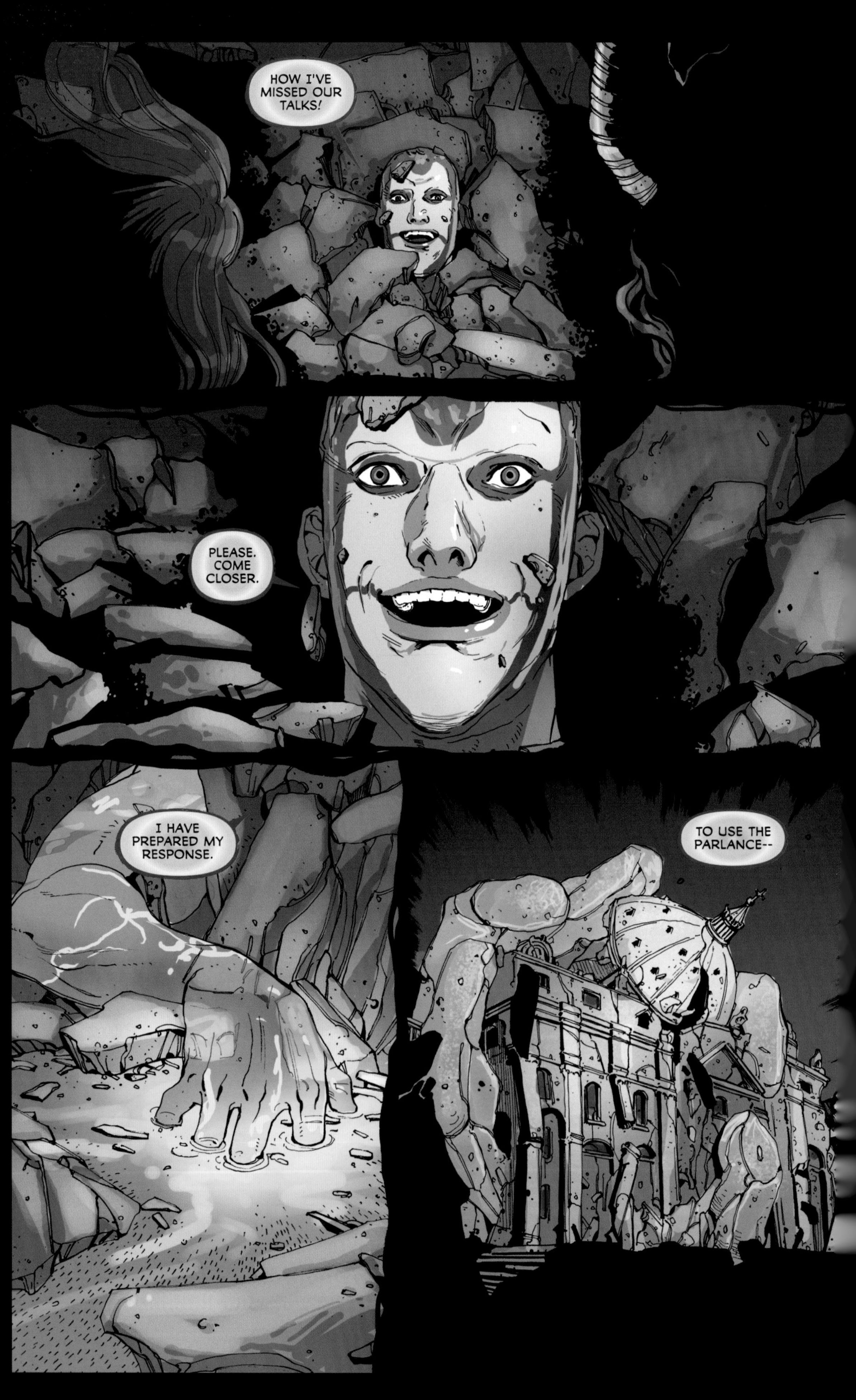
HOW I'VE MISSED OUR TALKS!
PLEASE. COME CLOSER.
I HAVE PREPARED MY RESPONSE.
TO USE THE PARLANCE--

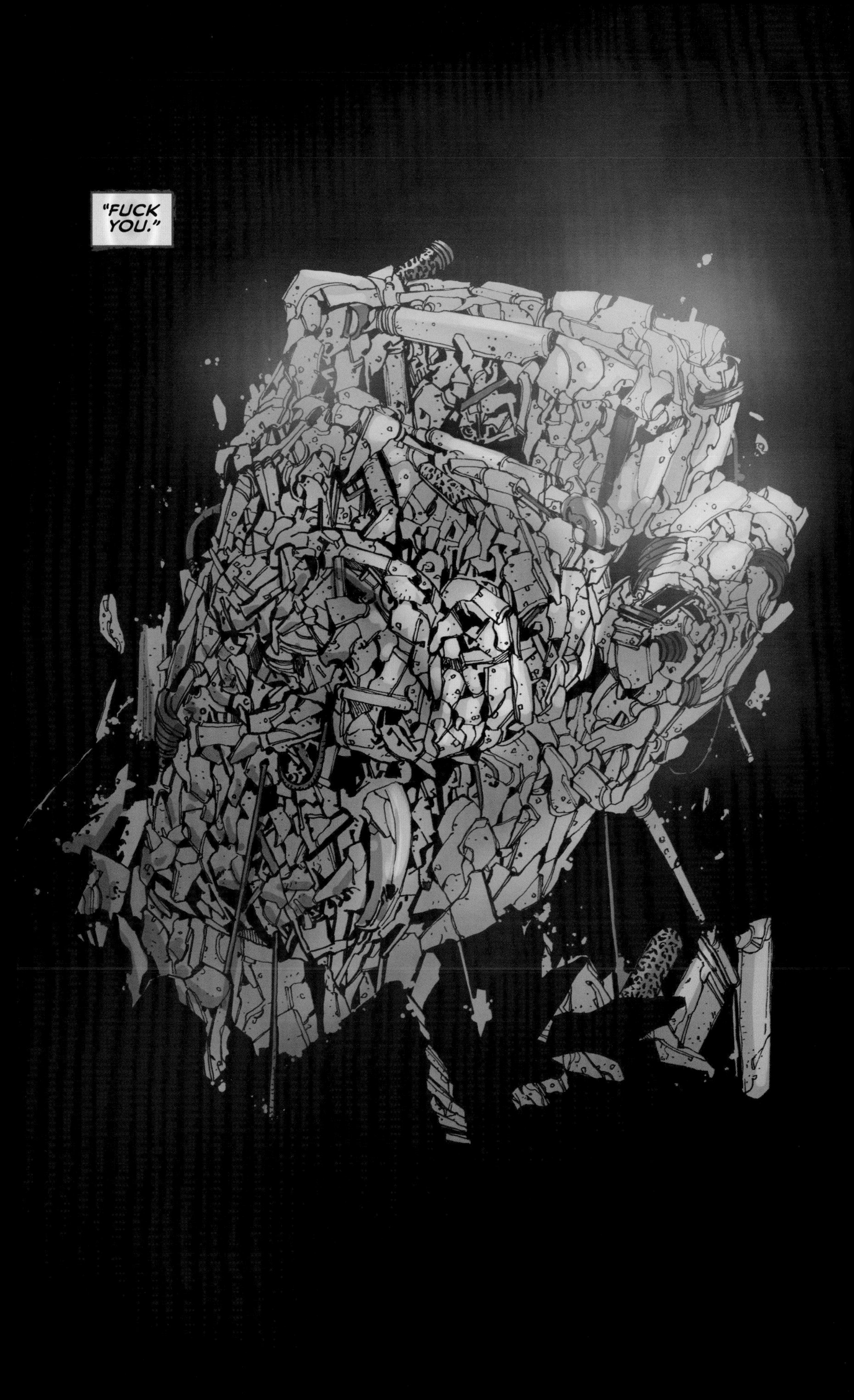
"FUCK YOU."

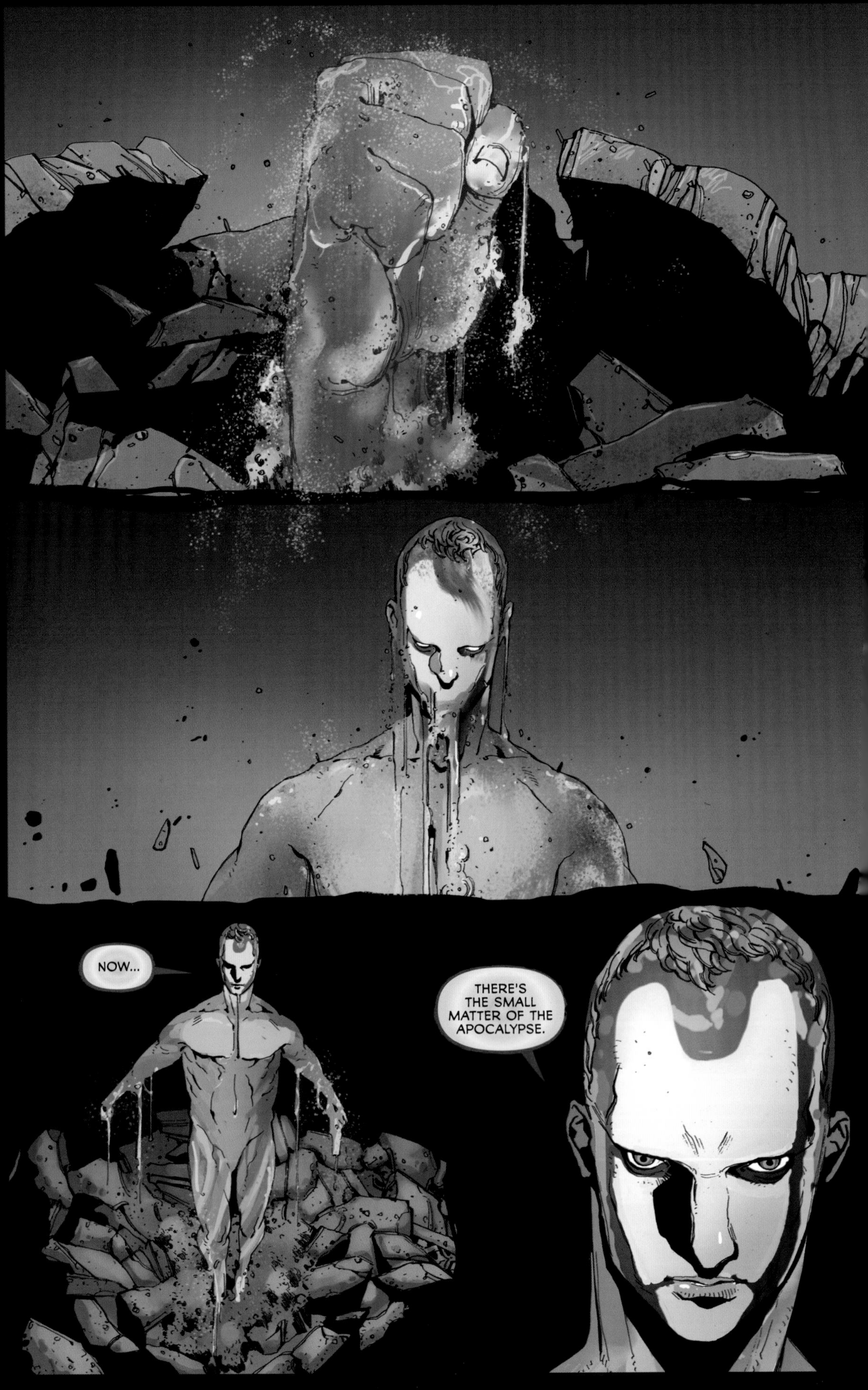
NOW...
THERE'S THE SMALL MATTER OF THE APOCALYPSE.

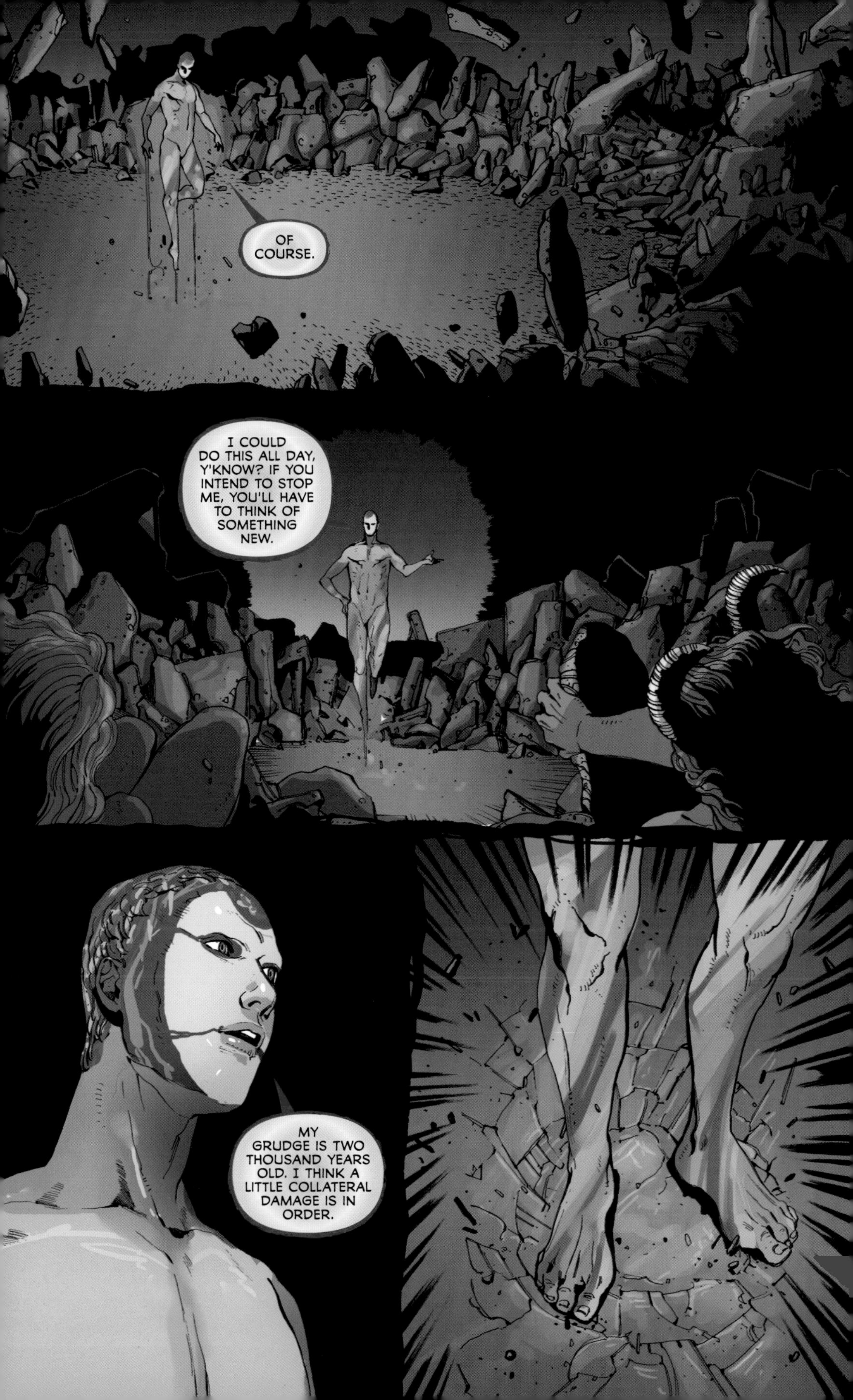
OF COURSE.
I COULD DO THIS ALL DAY, Y'KNOW? IF YOU INTEND TO STOP ME, YOU'LL HAVE TO THINK OF SOMETHING NEW.
MY GRUDGE IS TWO THOUSAND YEARS OLD. I THINK A LITTLE COLLATERAL DAMAGE IS IN ORDER.

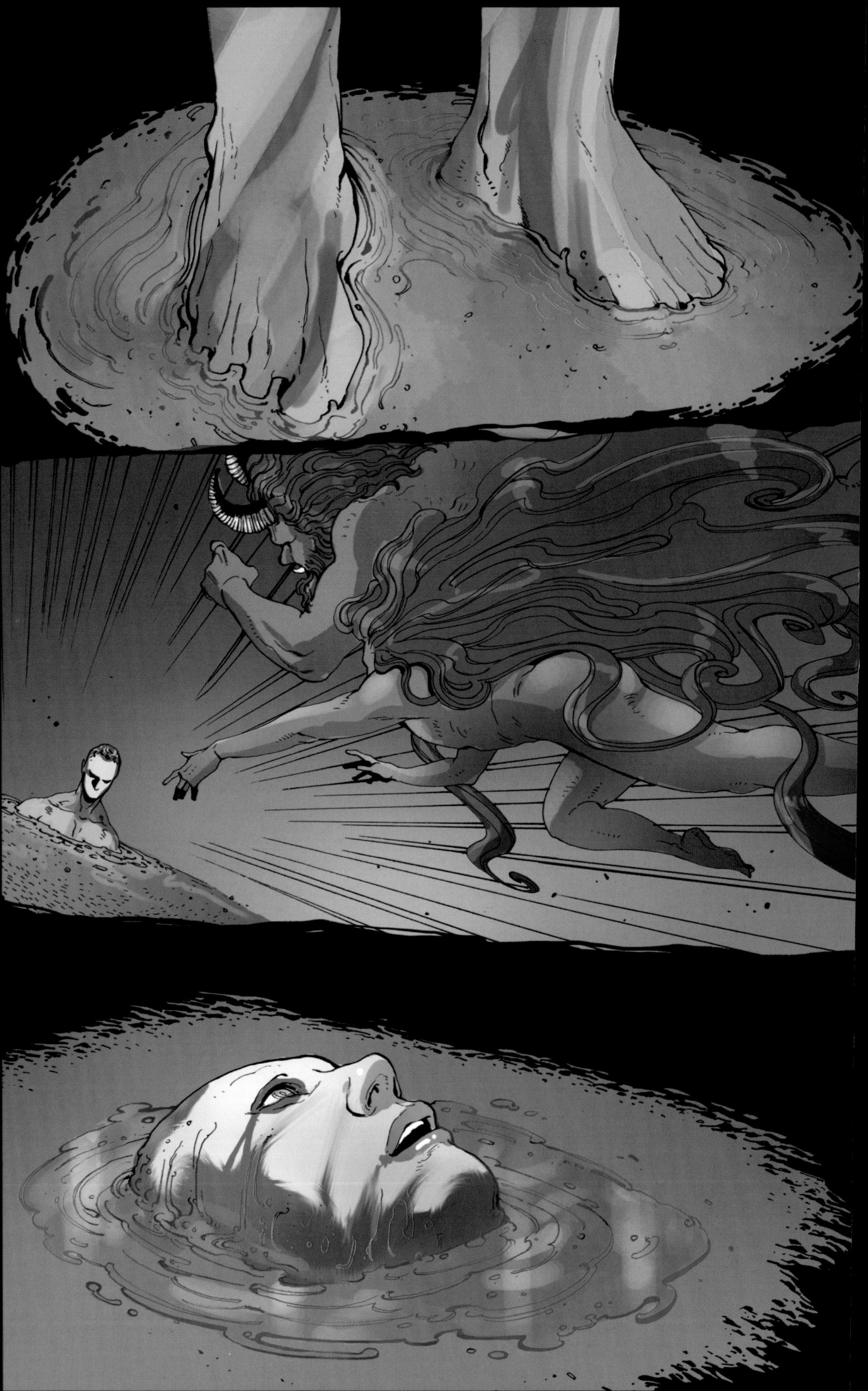

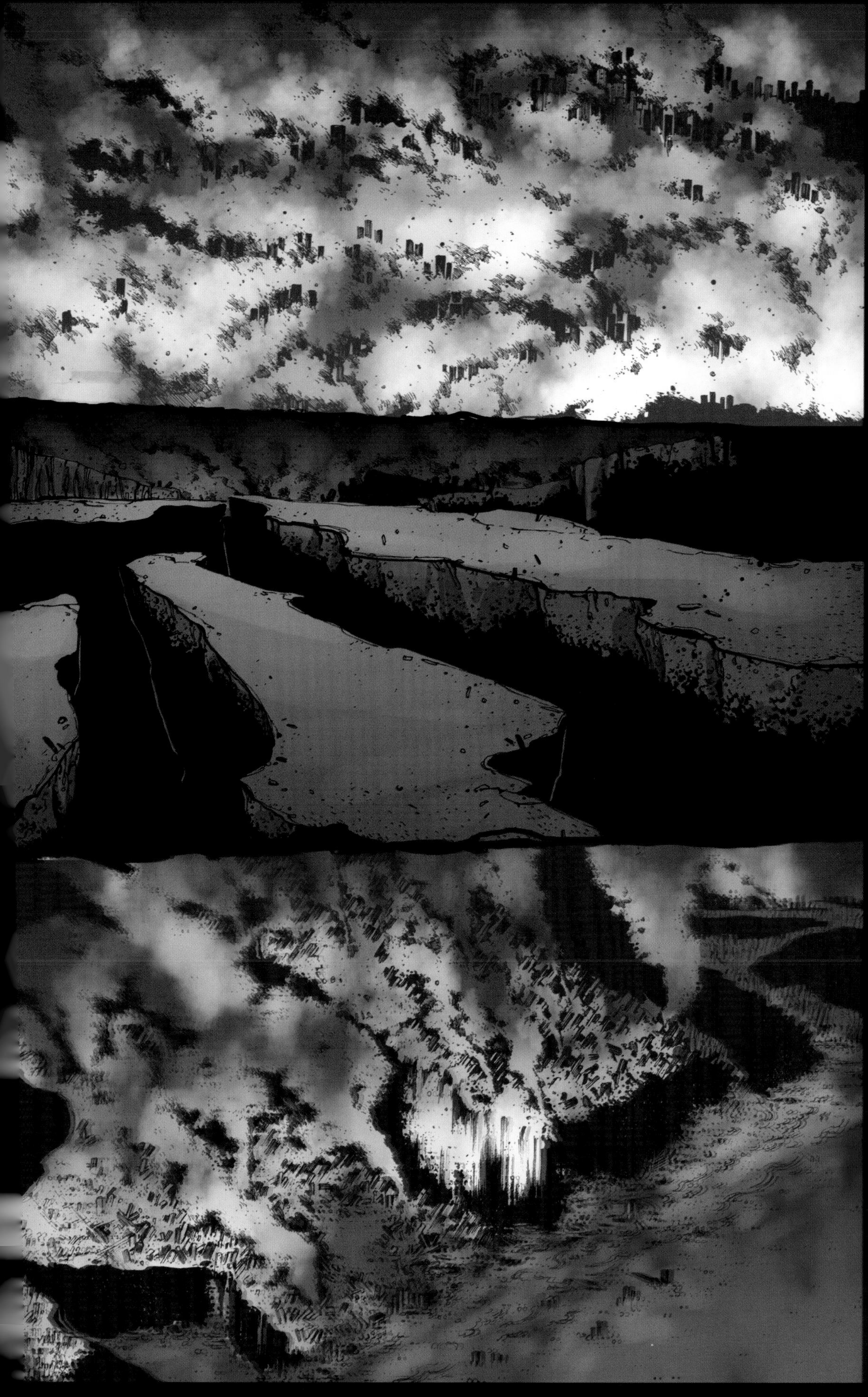

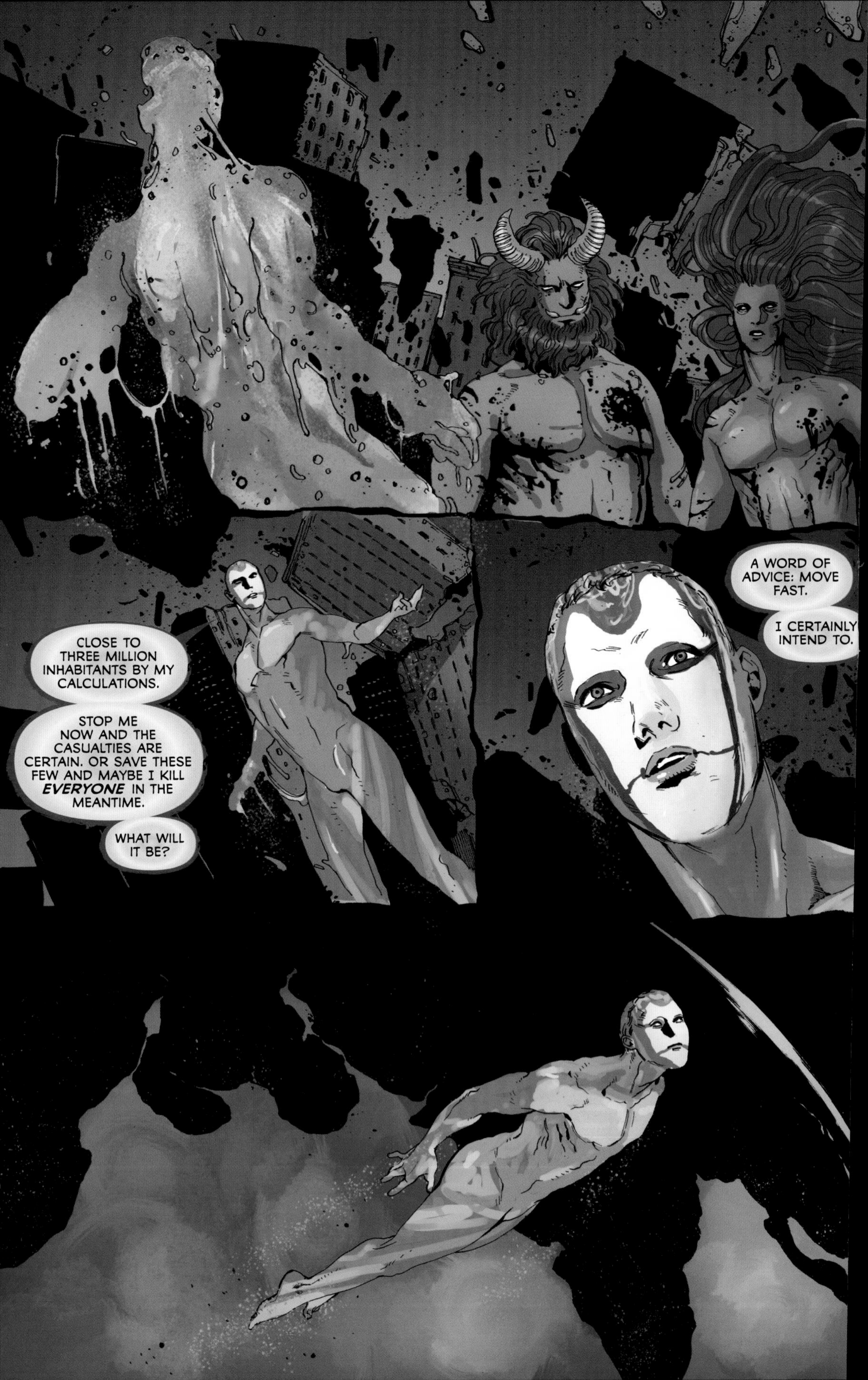
CLOSE TO THREE MILLION INHABITANTS BY MY CALCULATIONS.
STOP ME NOW AND THE CASUALTIES ARE CERTAIN. OR SAVE THESE FEW AND MAYBE I KILL *EVERYONE* IN THE MEANTIME.
WHAT WILL IT BE?
A WORD OF ADVICE: MOVE FAST.
I CERTAINLY INTEND TO.

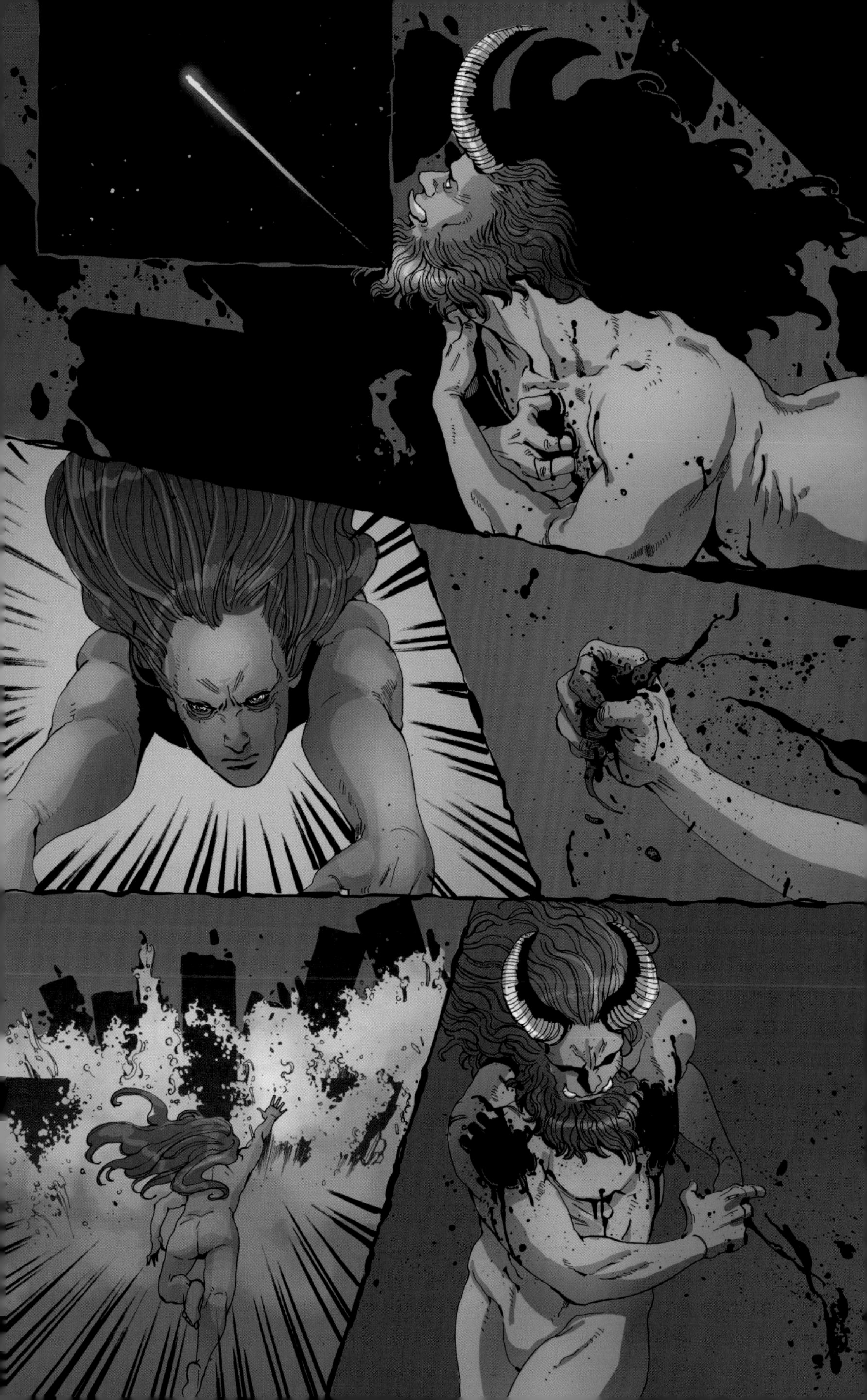

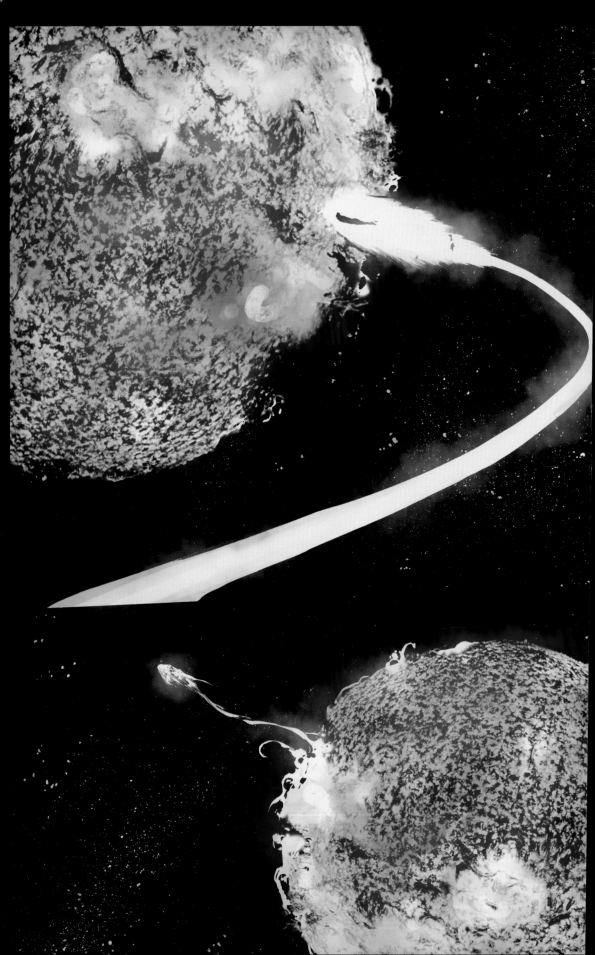

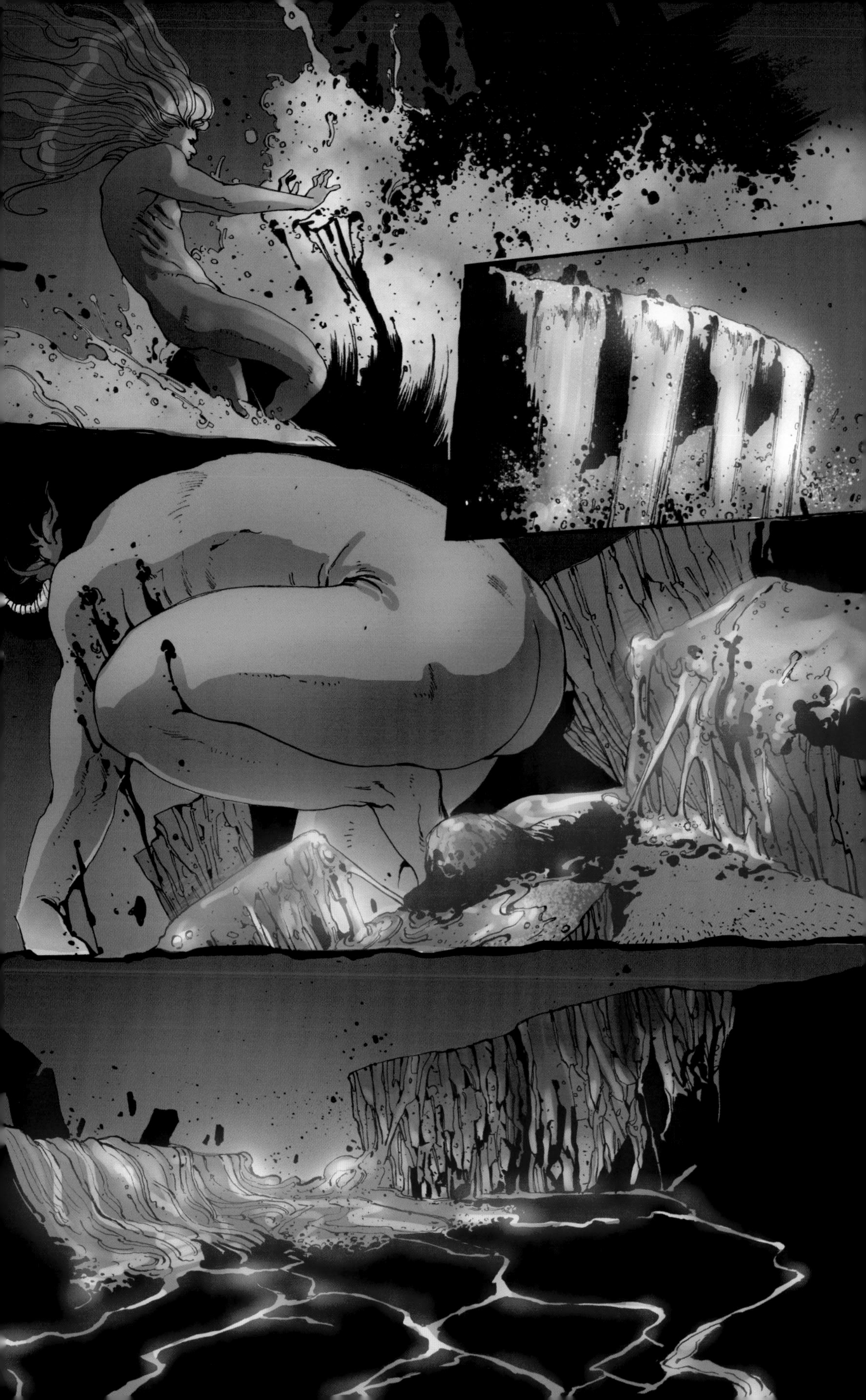

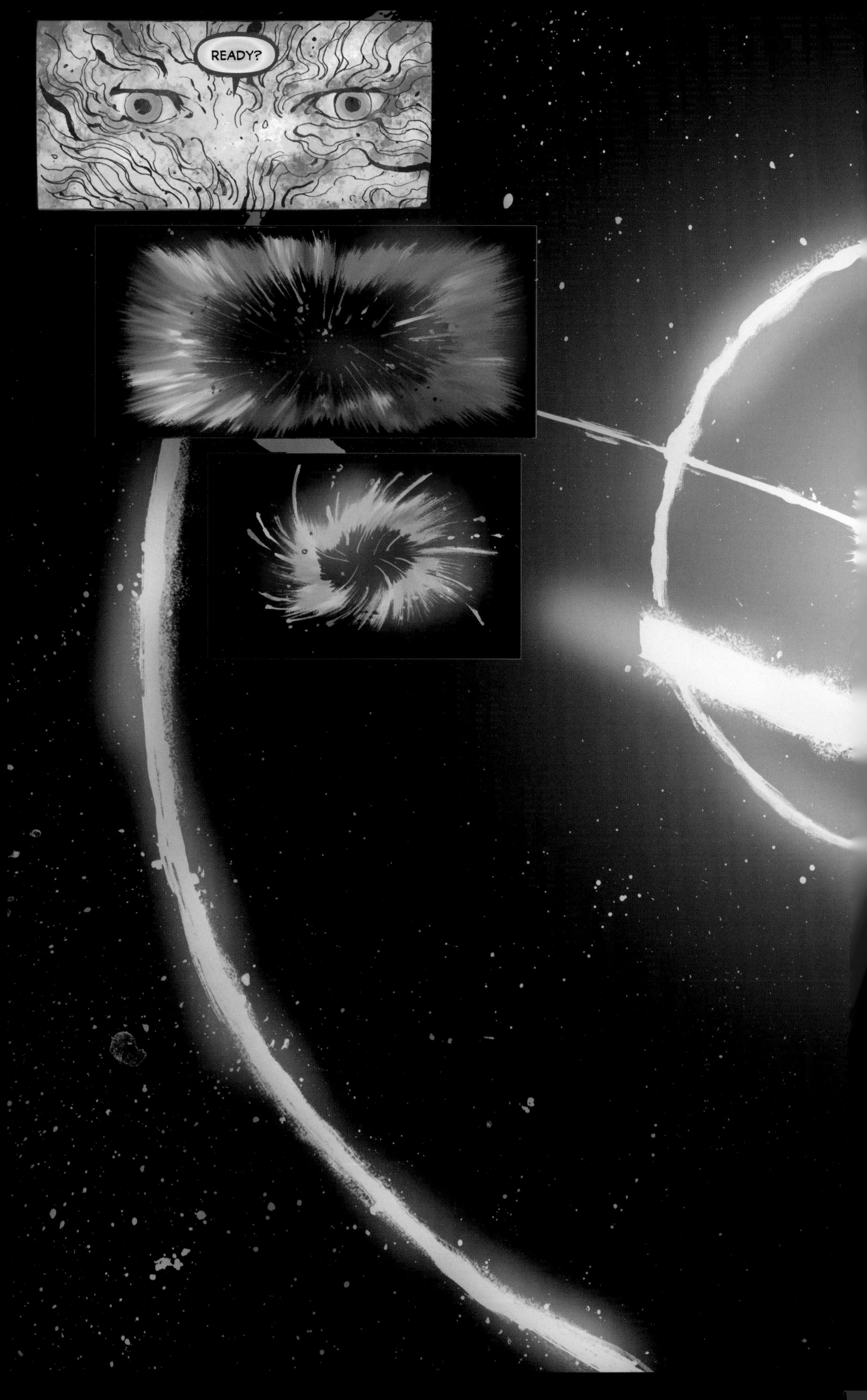
READY?

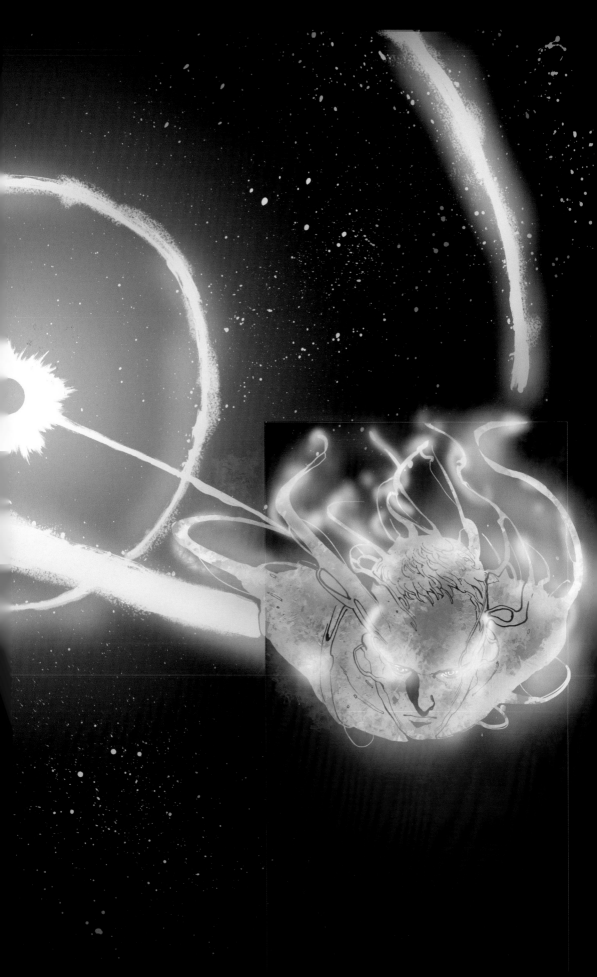

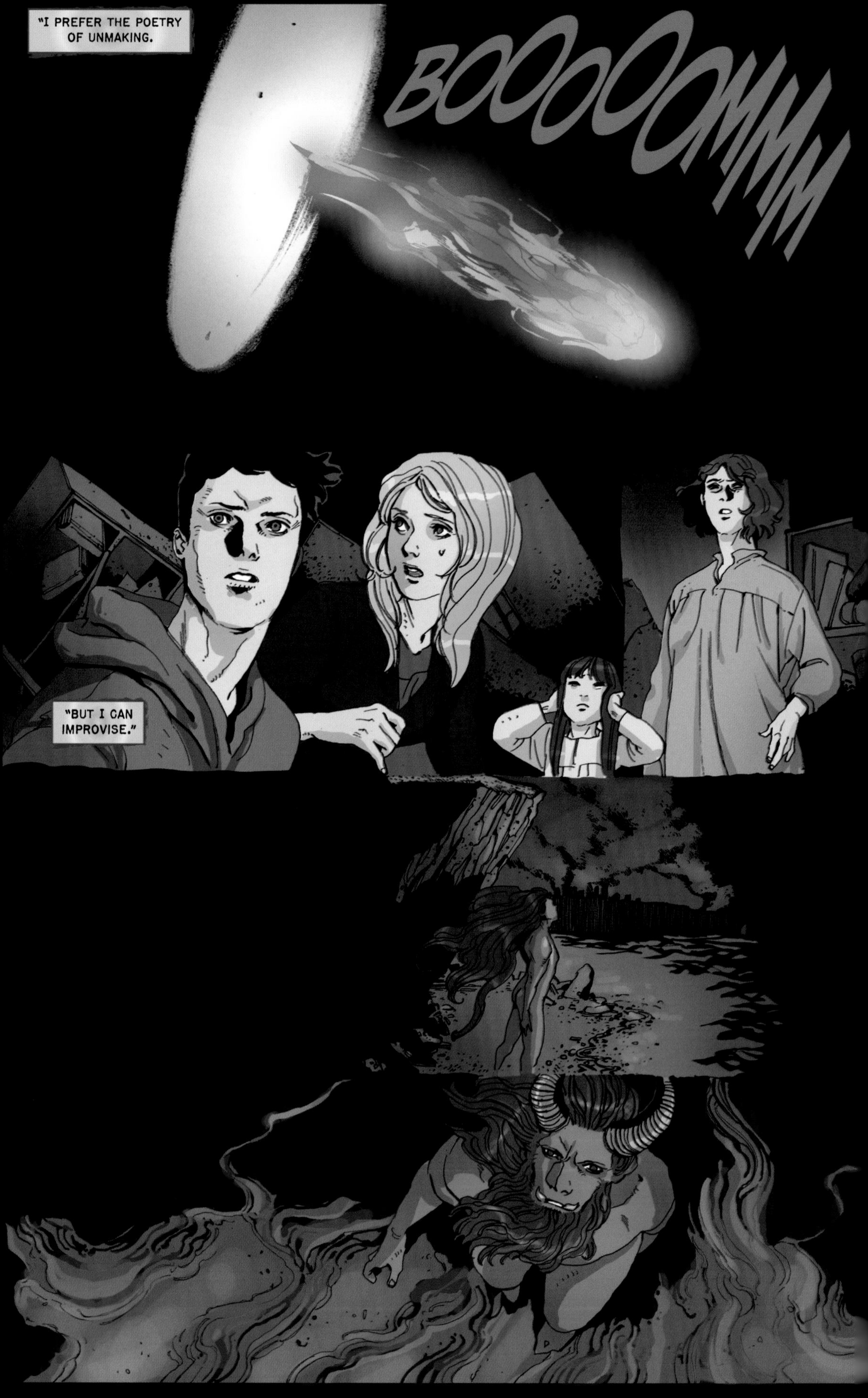
"I PREFER THE POETRY OF UNMAKING.
BOOOOOMMM
"BUT I CAN IMPROVISE."

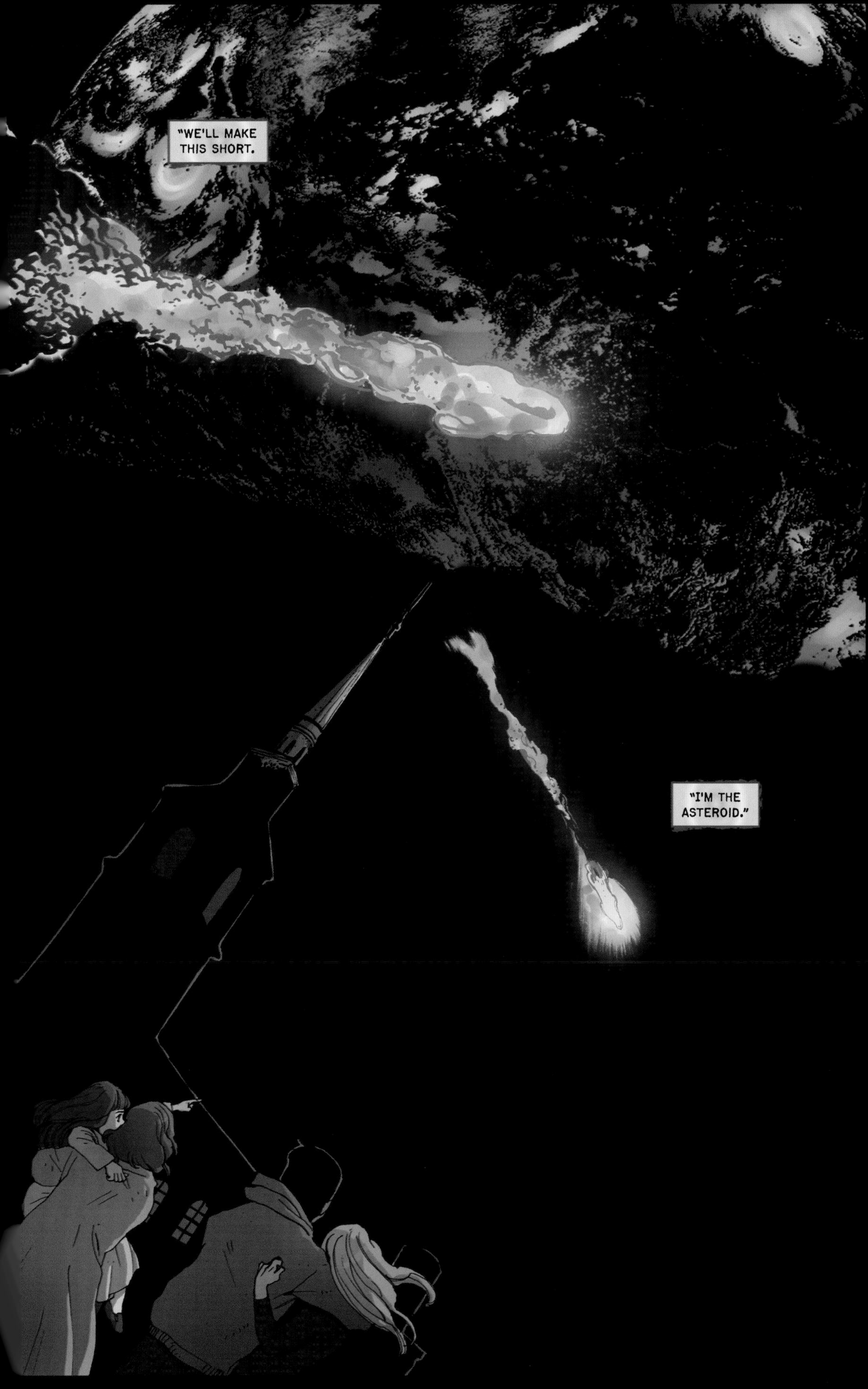
"WE'LL MAKE THIS SHORT.
"I'M THE ASTEROID."

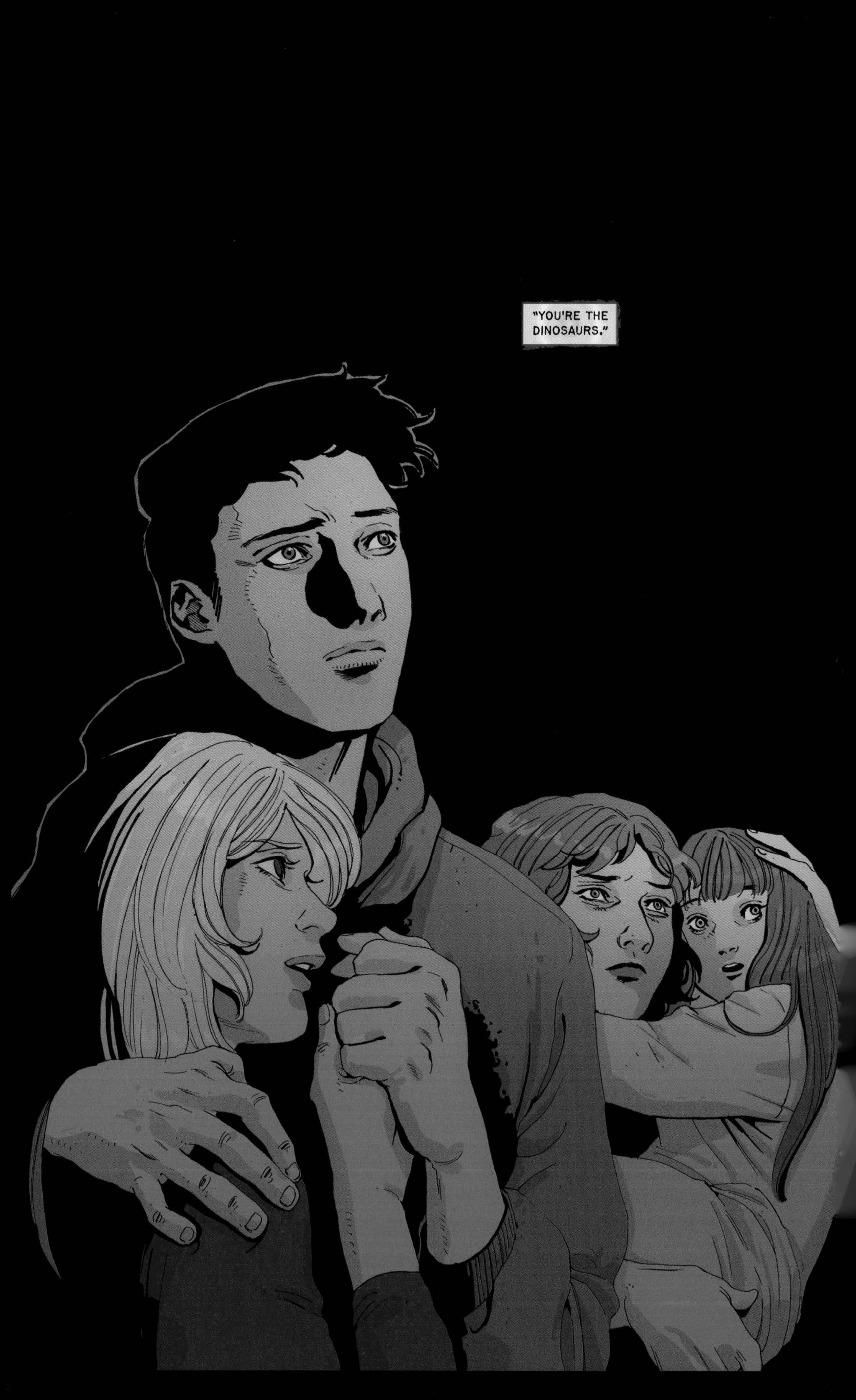
"YOU'RE THE DINOSAURS."

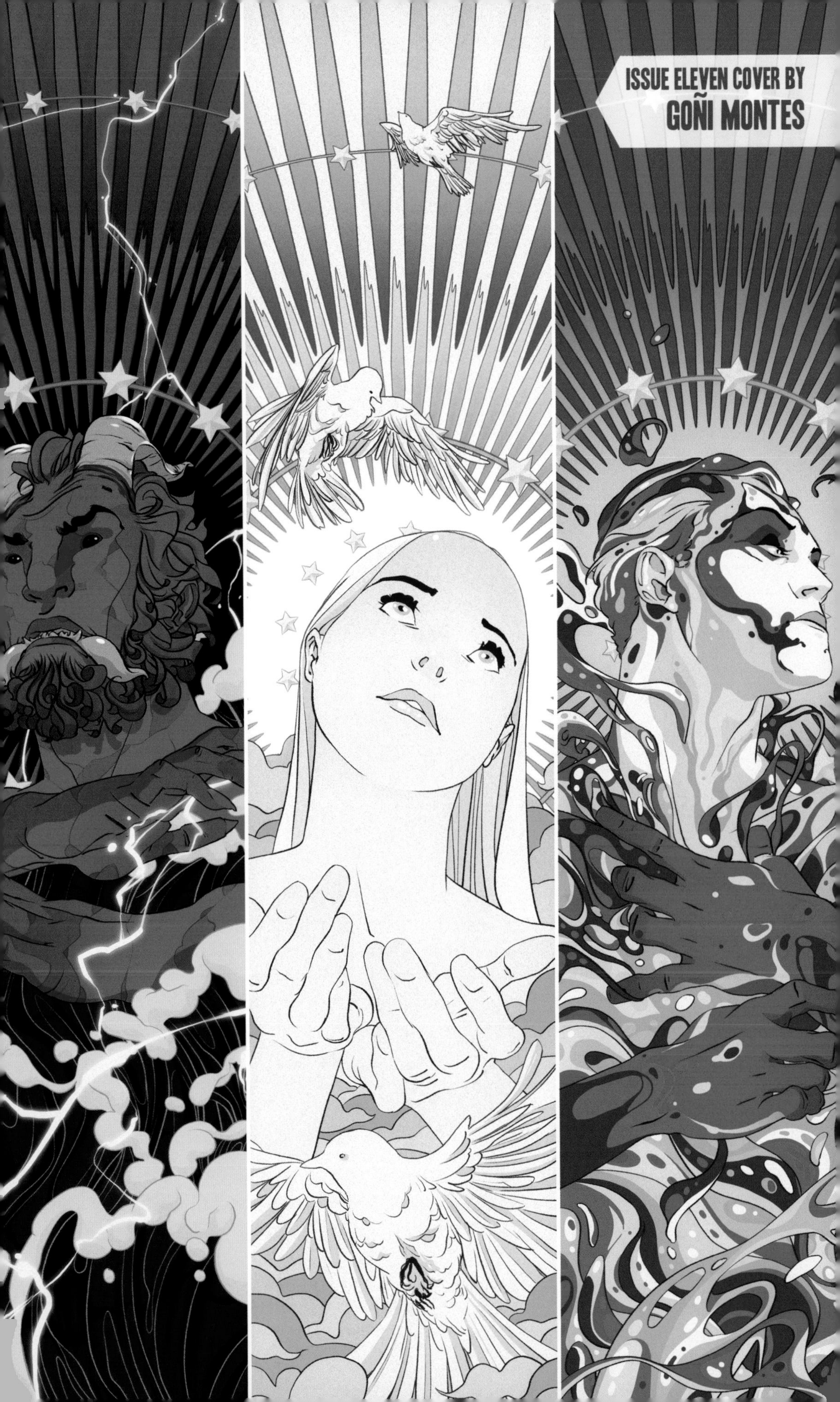
ISSUE ELEVEN COVER BY
GOÑI MONTES

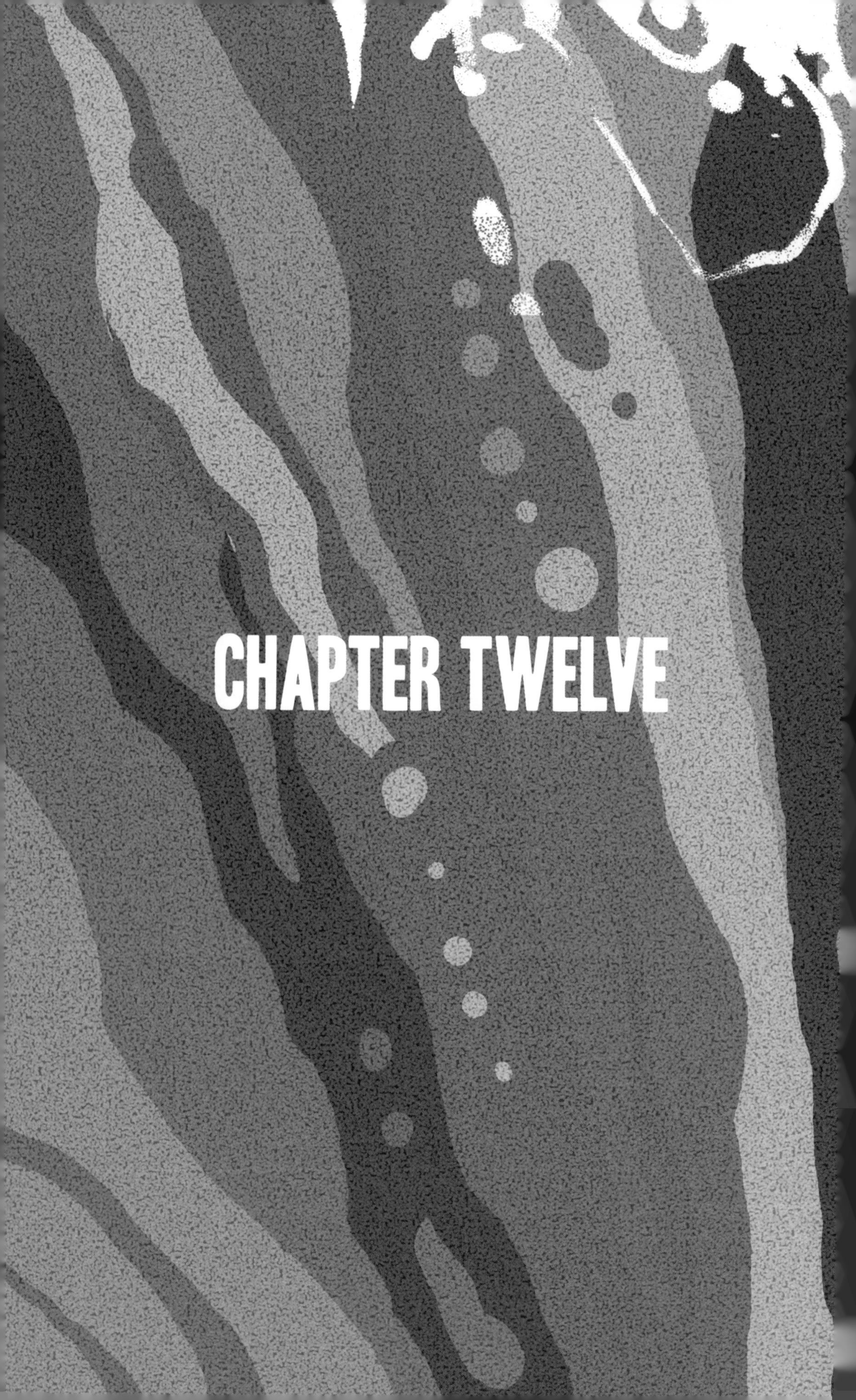

CHAPTER TWELVE

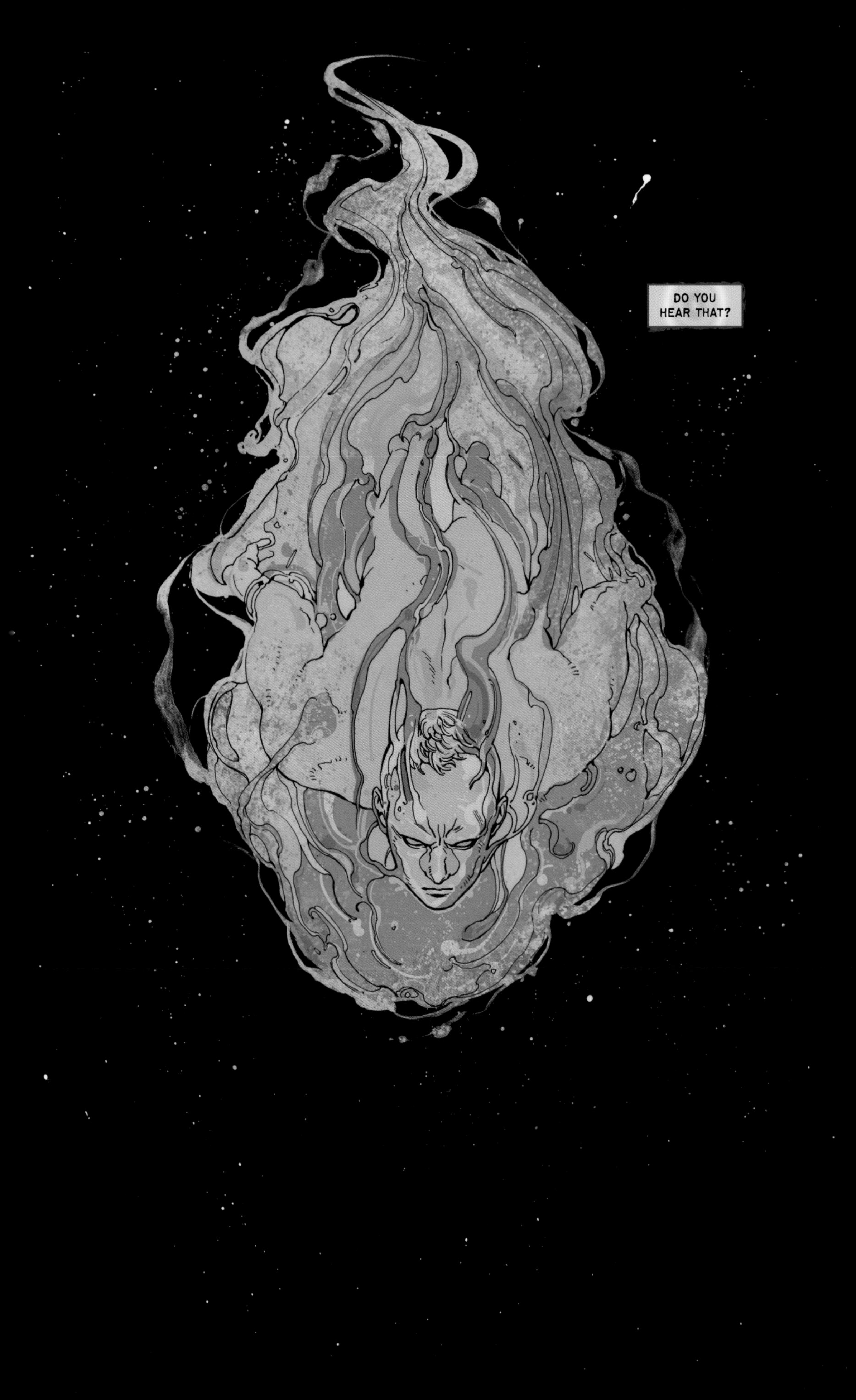
DO YOU
HEAR THAT?

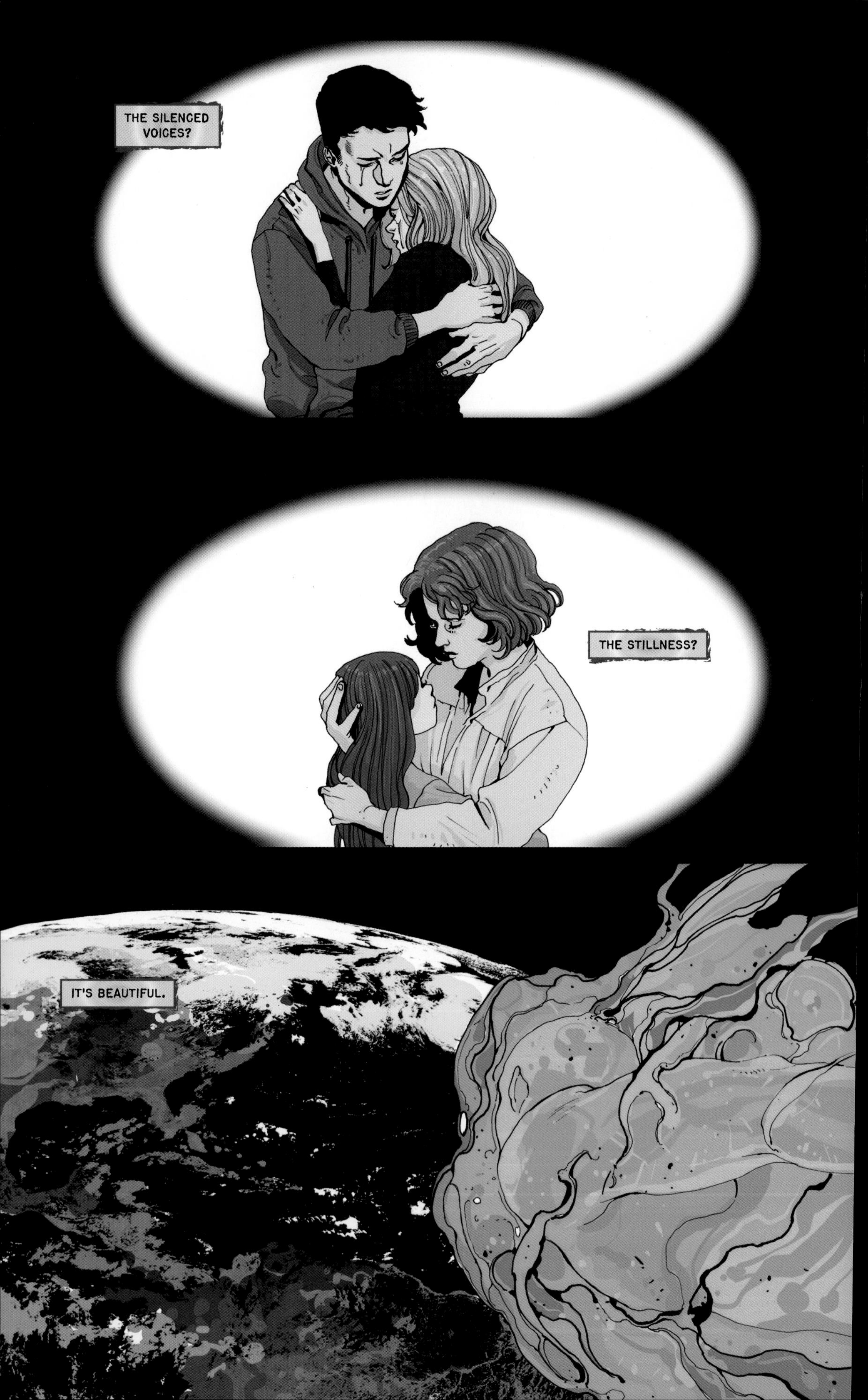
THE SILENCED VOICES?
THE STILLNESS?
IT'S BEAUTIFUL.

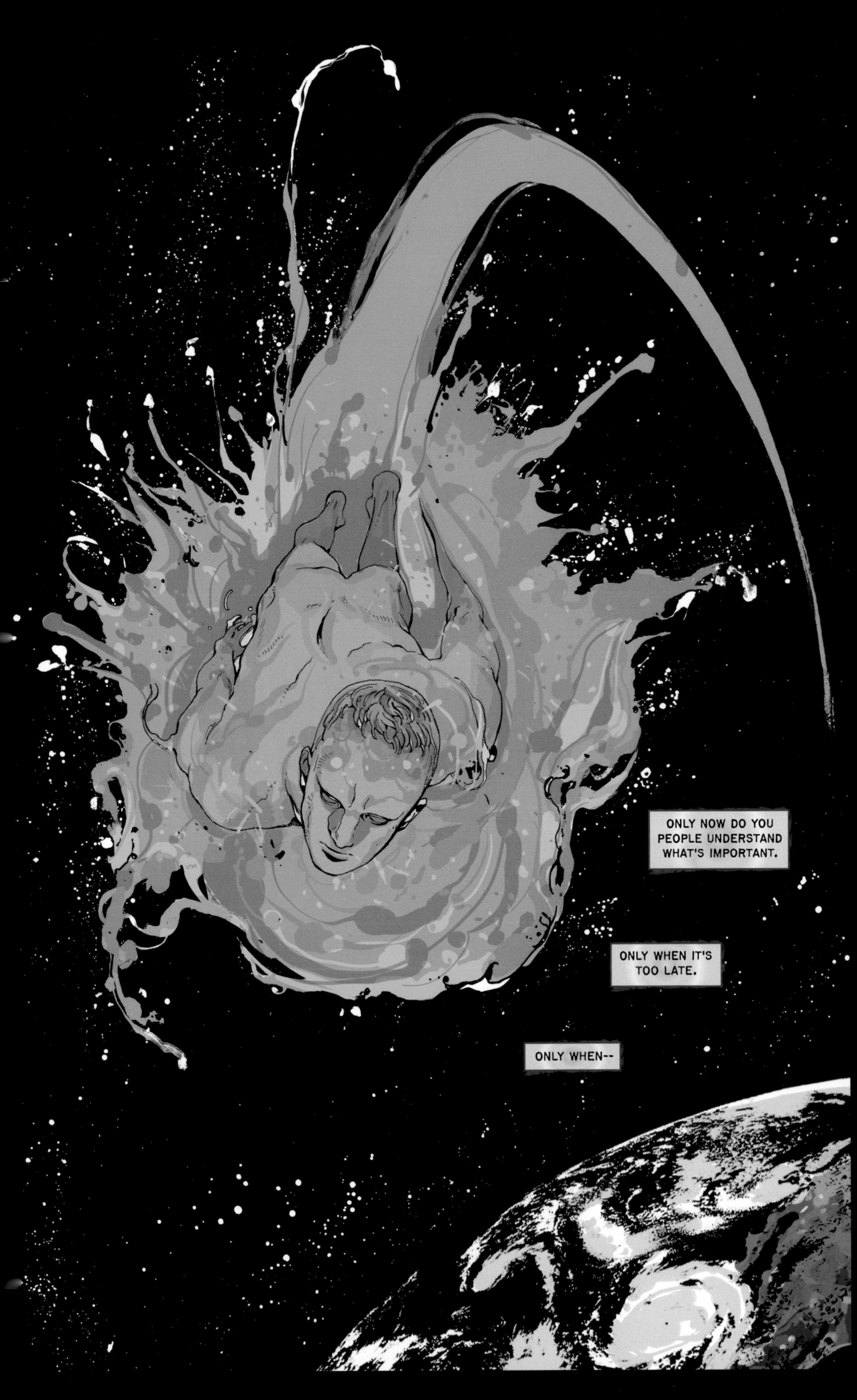
ONLY NOW DO YOU PEOPLE UNDERSTAND WHAT'S IMPORTANT.
ONLY WHEN IT'S TOO LATE.
ONLY WHEN--

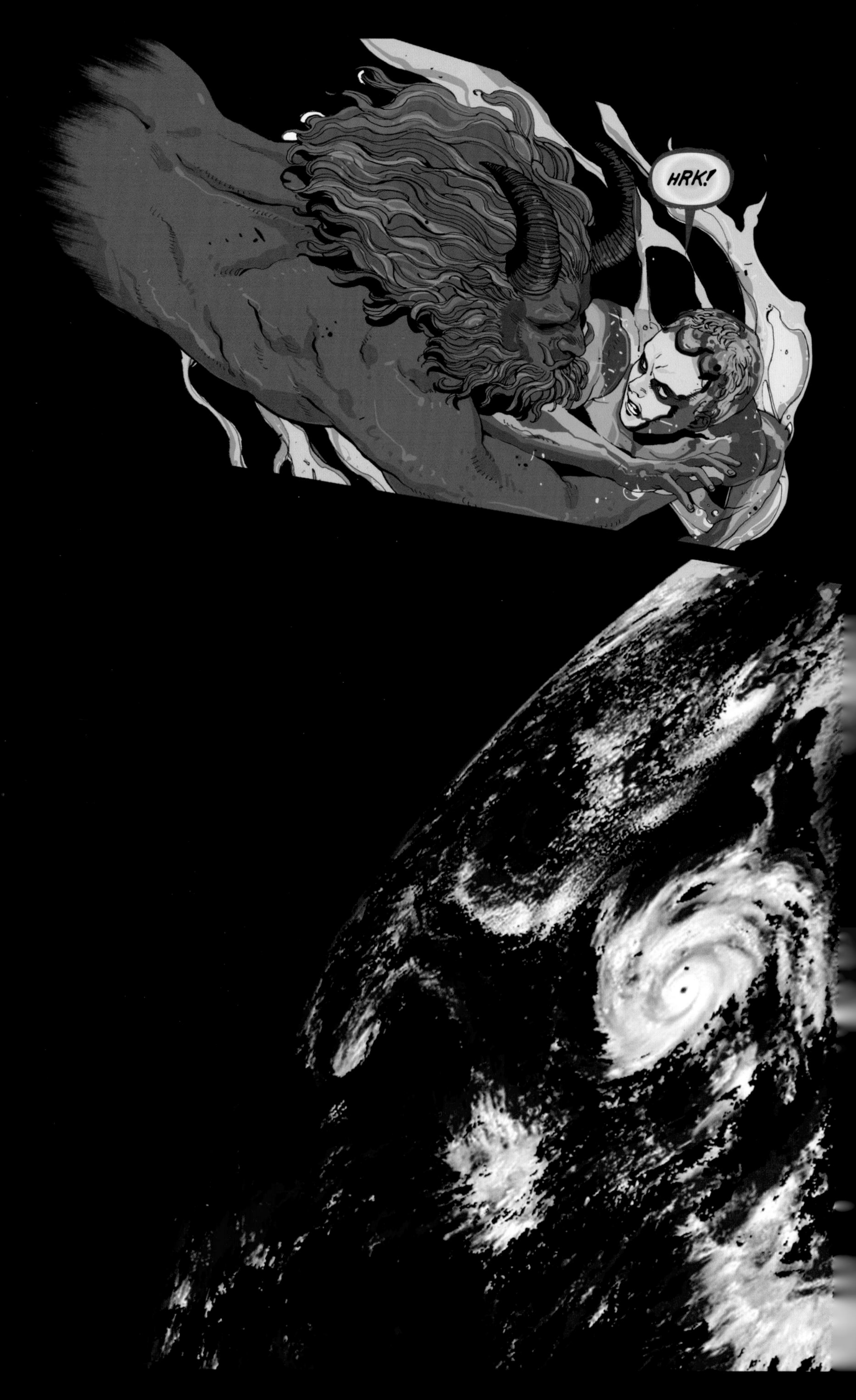
HRK!

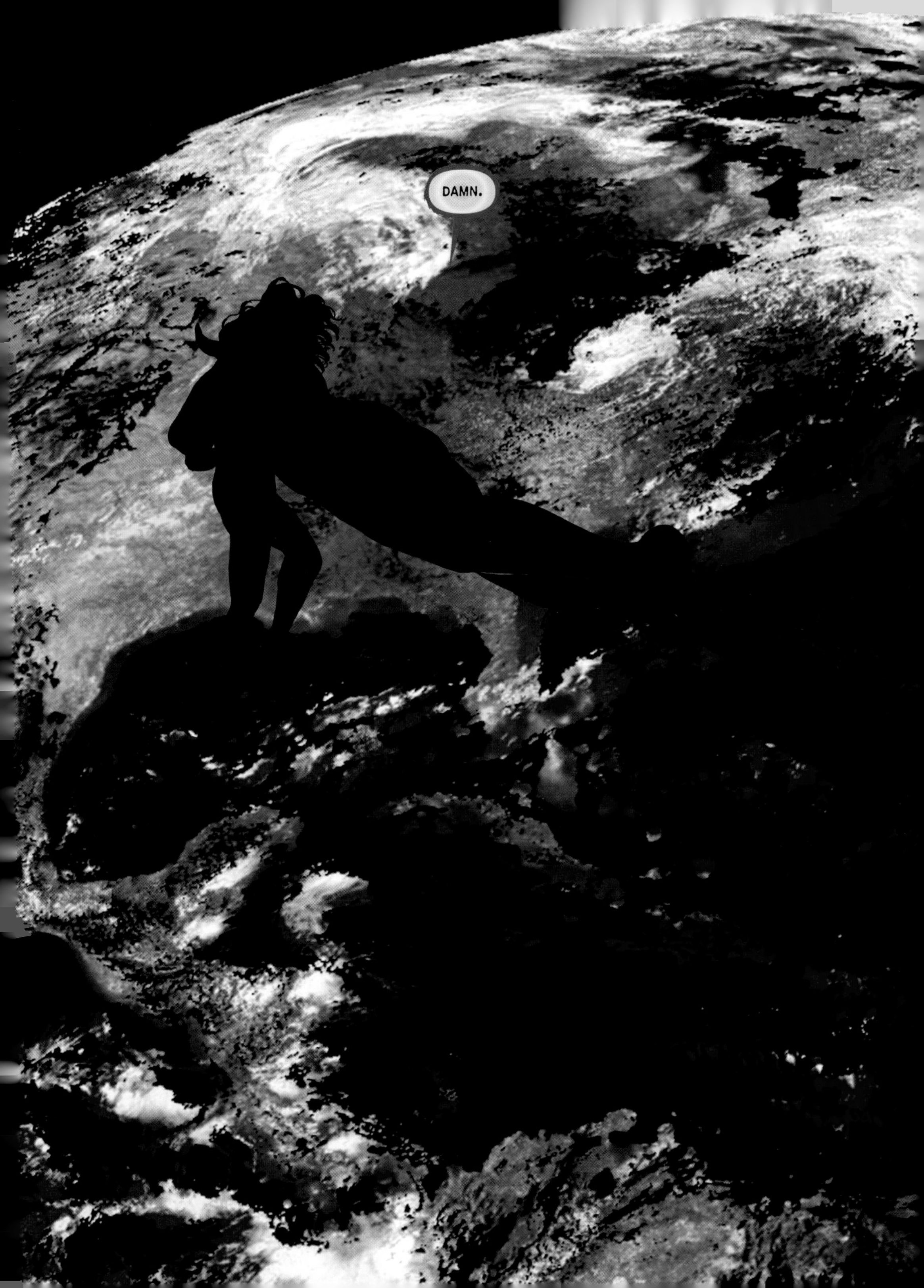
DAMN.

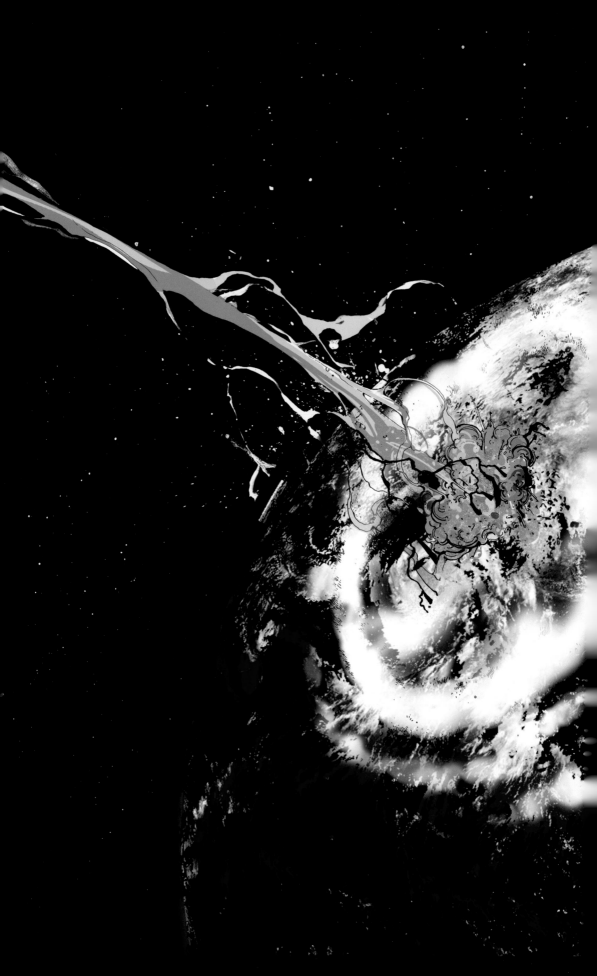

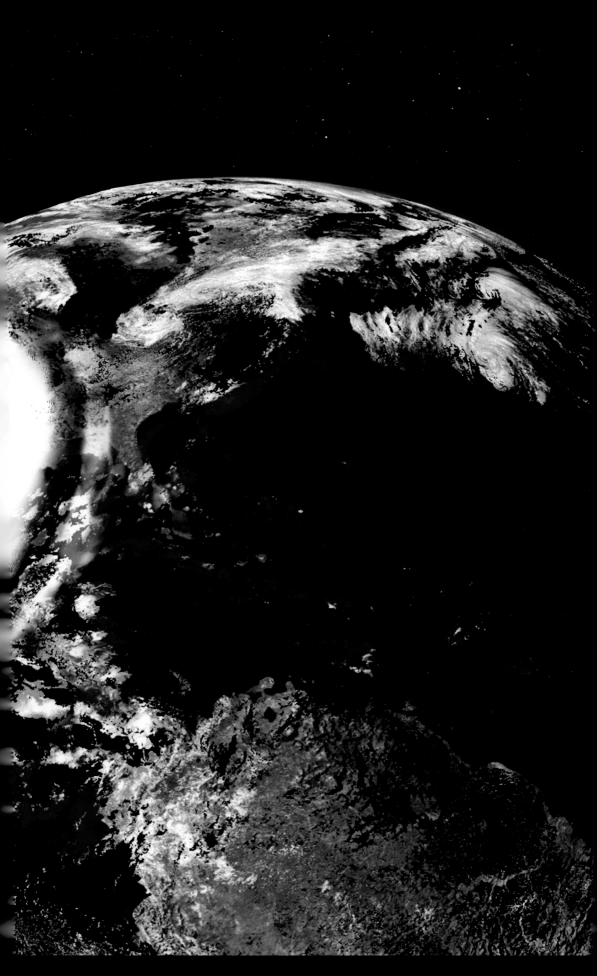

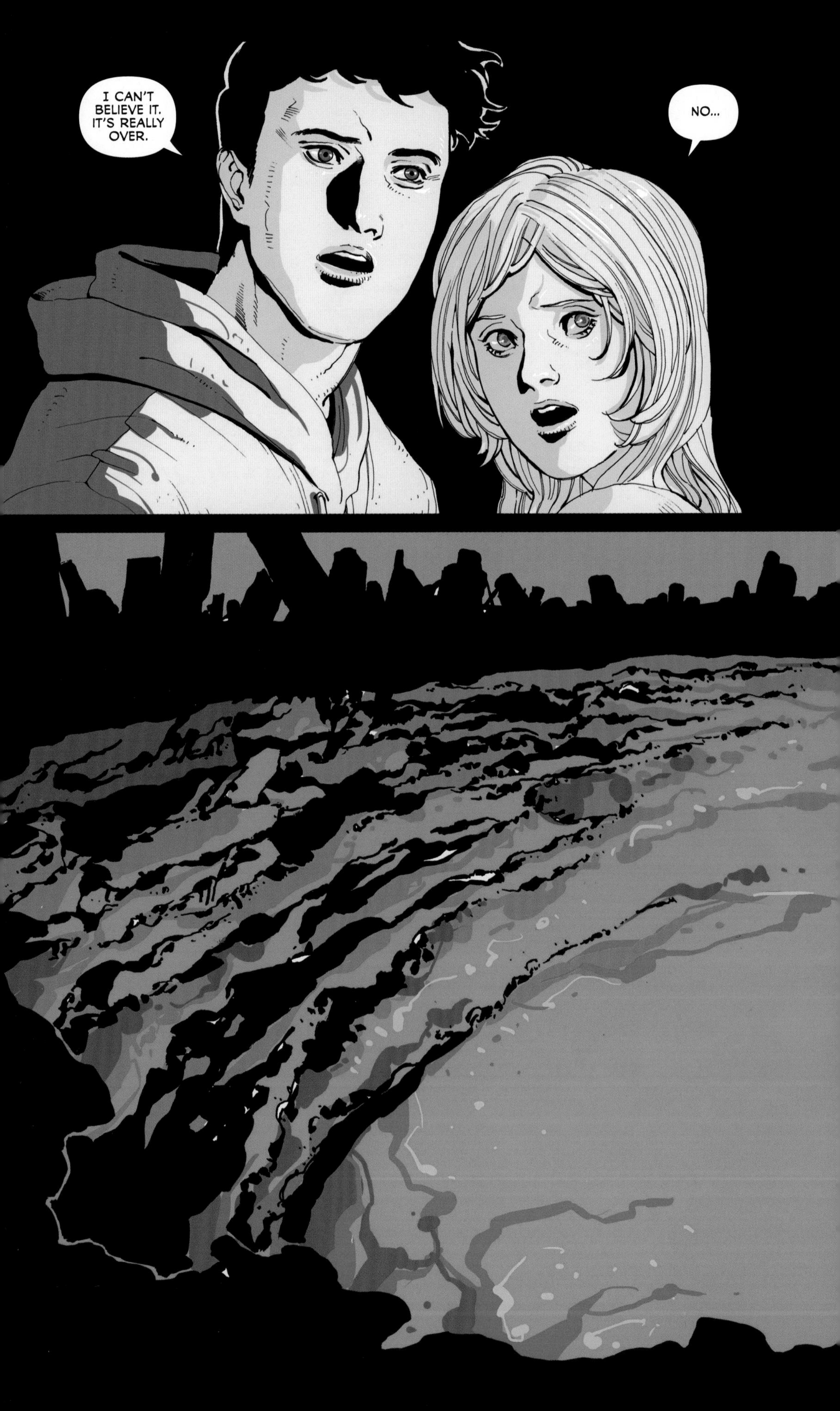
I CAN'T BELIEVE IT. IT'S REALLY OVER.
NO...

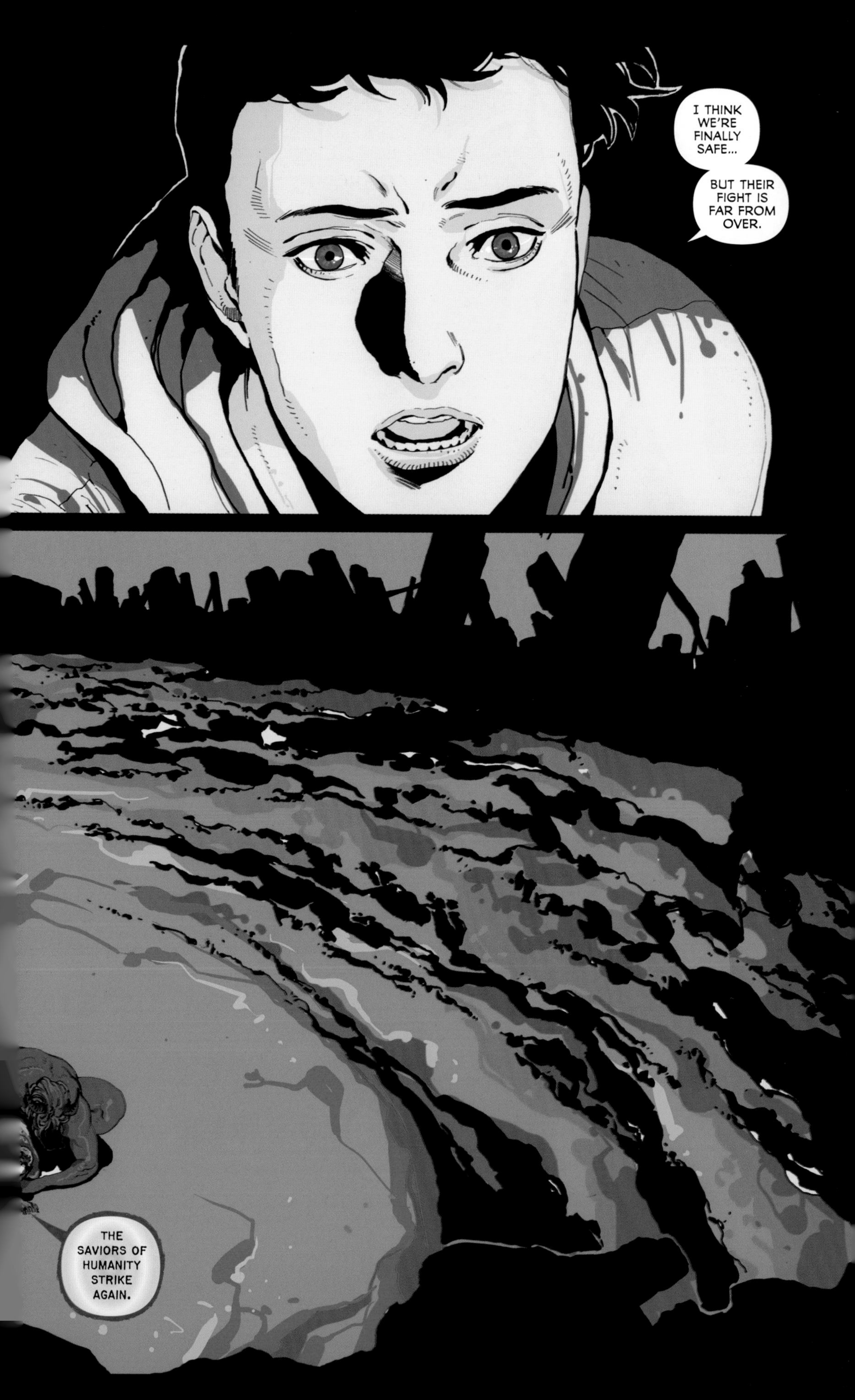
I THINK WE'RE FINALLY SAFE...
BUT THEIR FIGHT IS FAR FROM OVER.
THE SAVIORS OF HUMANITY STRIKE AGAIN.

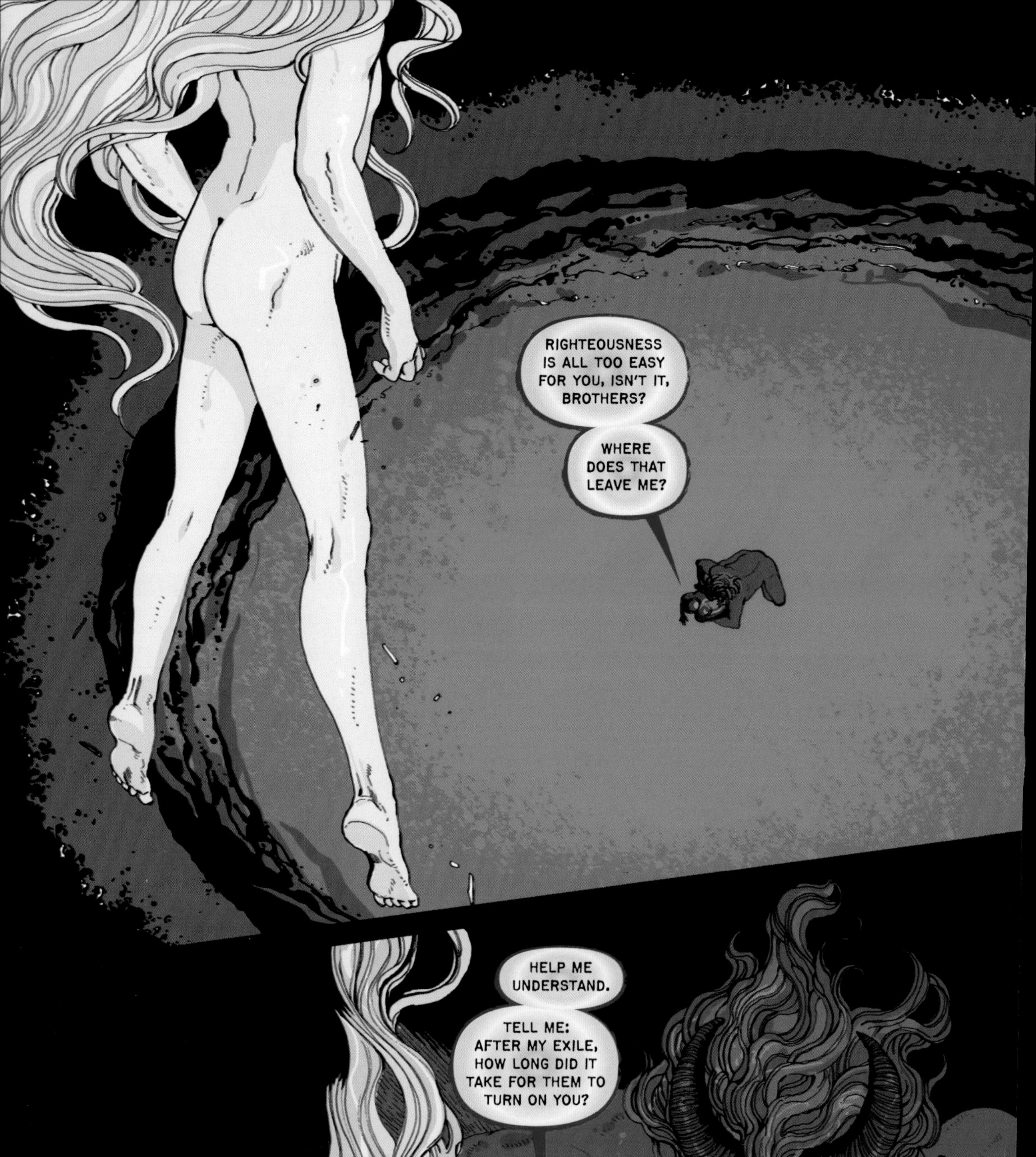
RIGHTEOUSNESS IS ALL TOO EASY FOR YOU, ISN'T IT, BROTHERS?
WHERE DOES THAT LEAVE ME?

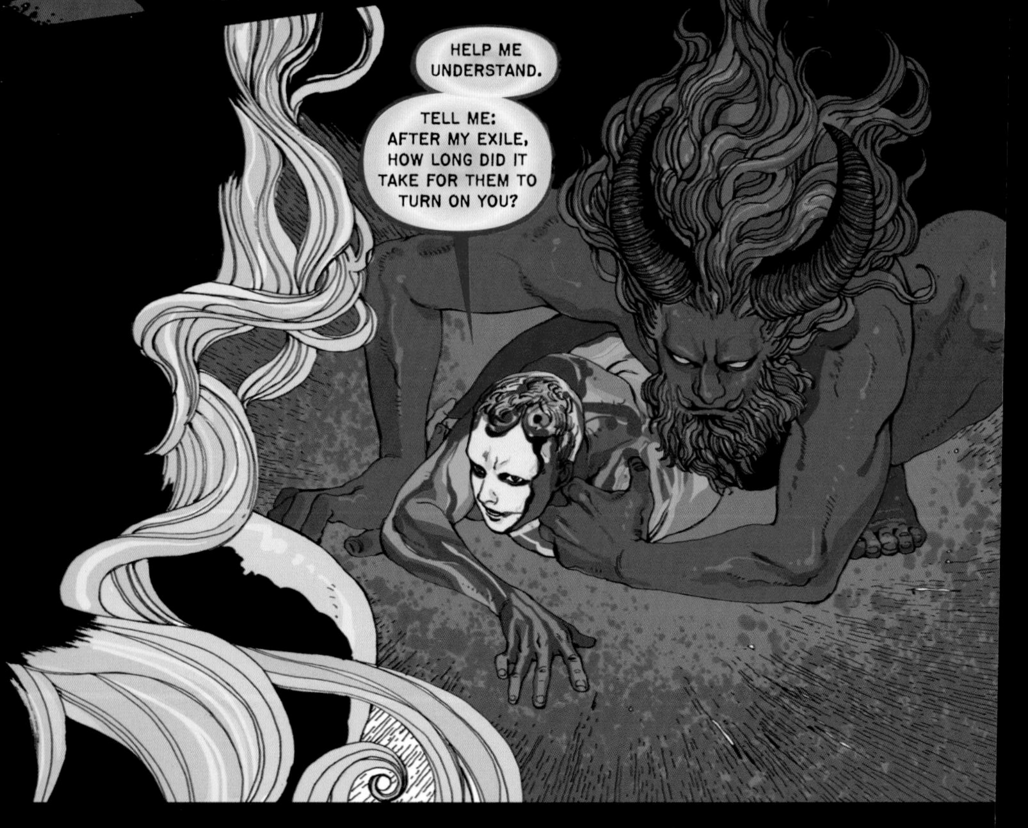
HELP ME UNDERSTAND.
TELL ME: AFTER MY EXILE, HOW LONG DID IT TAKE FOR THEM TO TURN ON YOU?

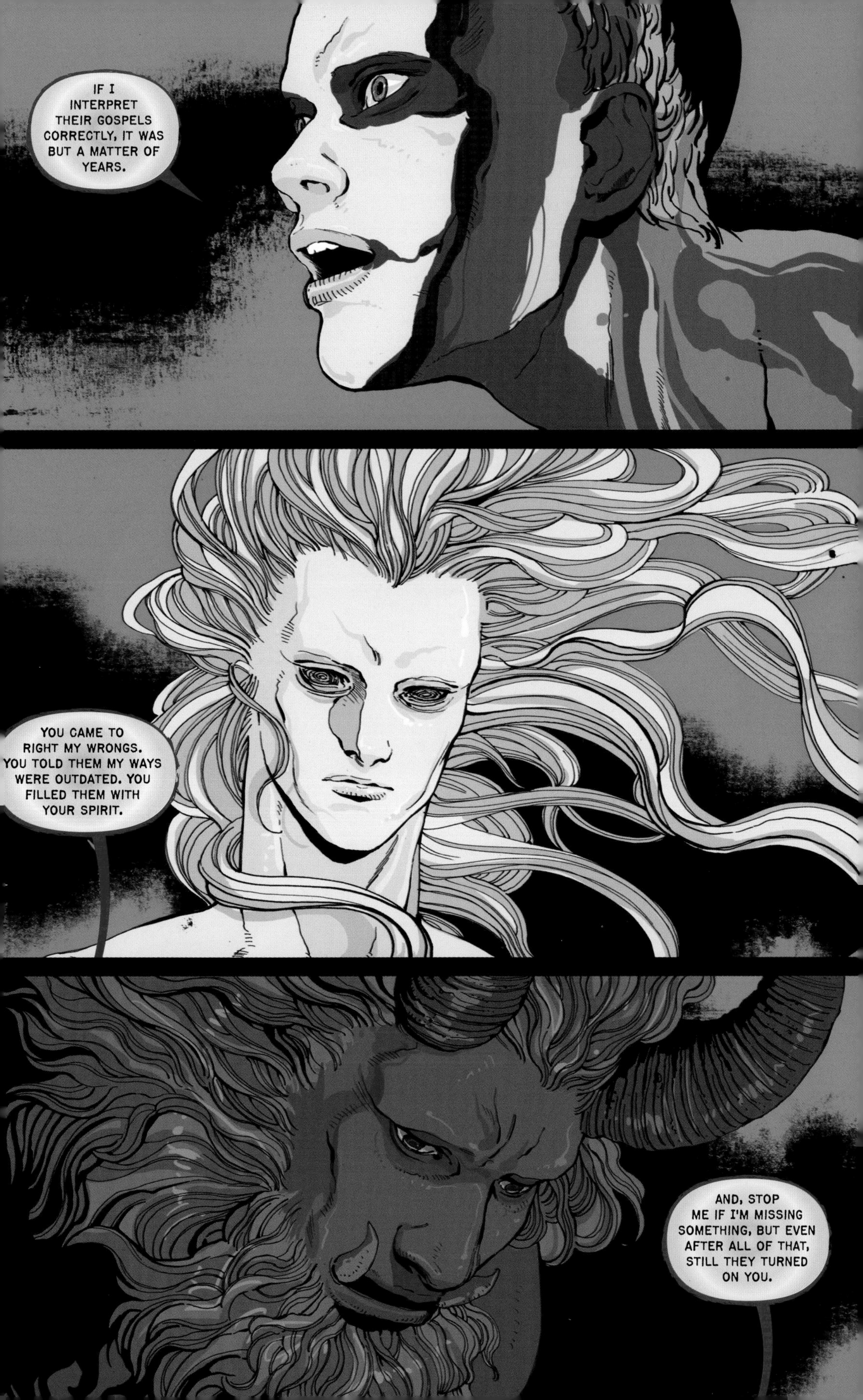
IF I INTERPRET THEIR GOSPELS CORRECTLY, IT WAS BUT A MATTER OF YEARS.
YOU CAME TO RIGHT MY WRONGS. YOU TOLD THEM MY WAYS WERE OUTDATED. YOU FILLED THEM WITH YOUR SPIRIT.
AND, STOP ME IF I'M MISSING SOMETHING, BUT EVEN AFTER ALL OF THAT, STILL THEY TURNED ON YOU.

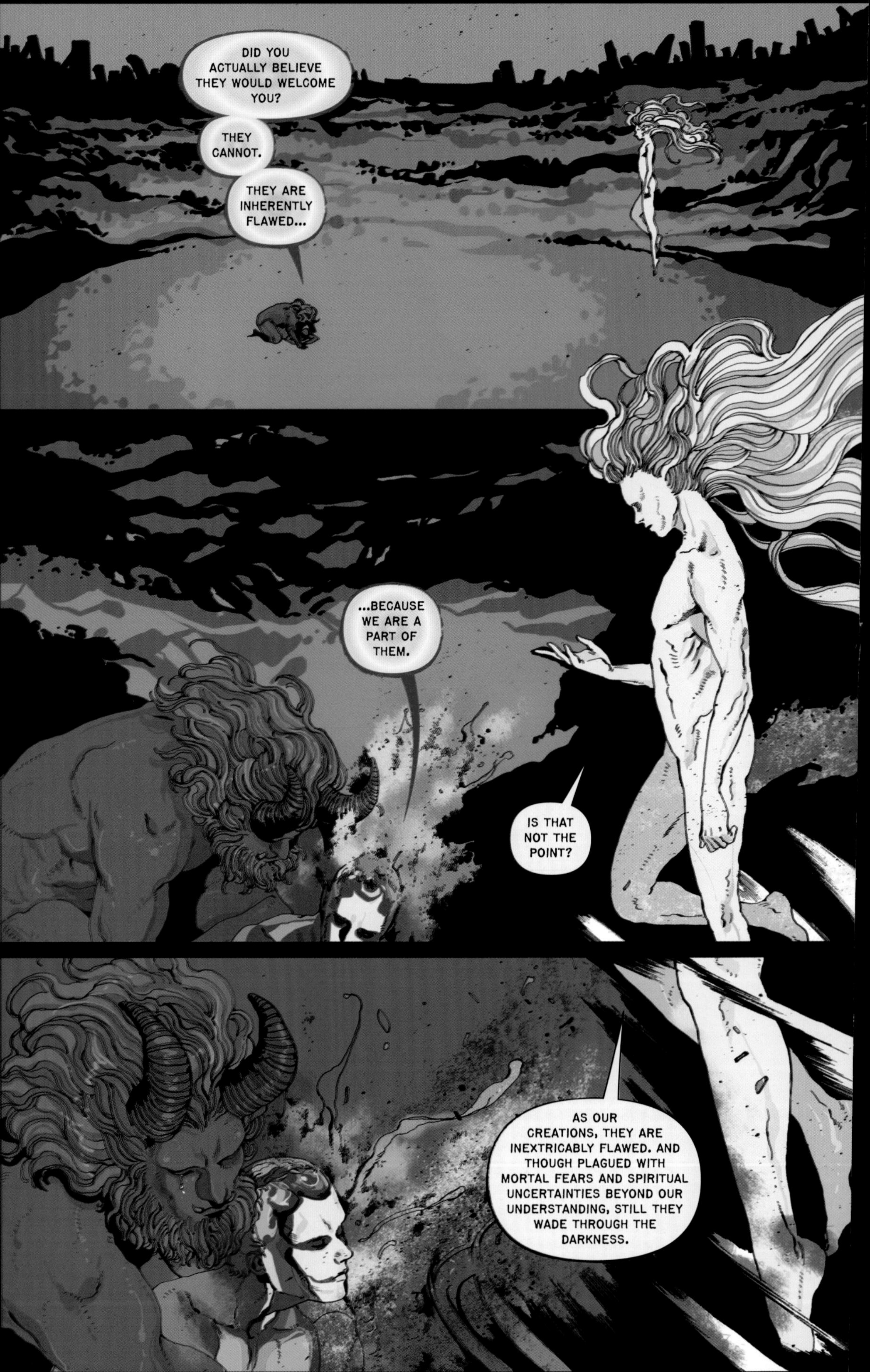
DID YOU ACTUALLY BELIEVE THEY WOULD WELCOME YOU?
THEY CANNOT.
THEY ARE INHERENTLY FLAWED...
...BECAUSE WE ARE A PART OF THEM.
IS THAT NOT THE POINT?
AS OUR CREATIONS, THEY ARE INEXTRICABLY FLAWED. AND THOUGH PLAGUED WITH MORTAL FEARS AND SPIRITUAL UNCERTAINTIES BEYOND OUR UNDERSTANDING, STILL THEY WADE THROUGH THE DARKNESS.

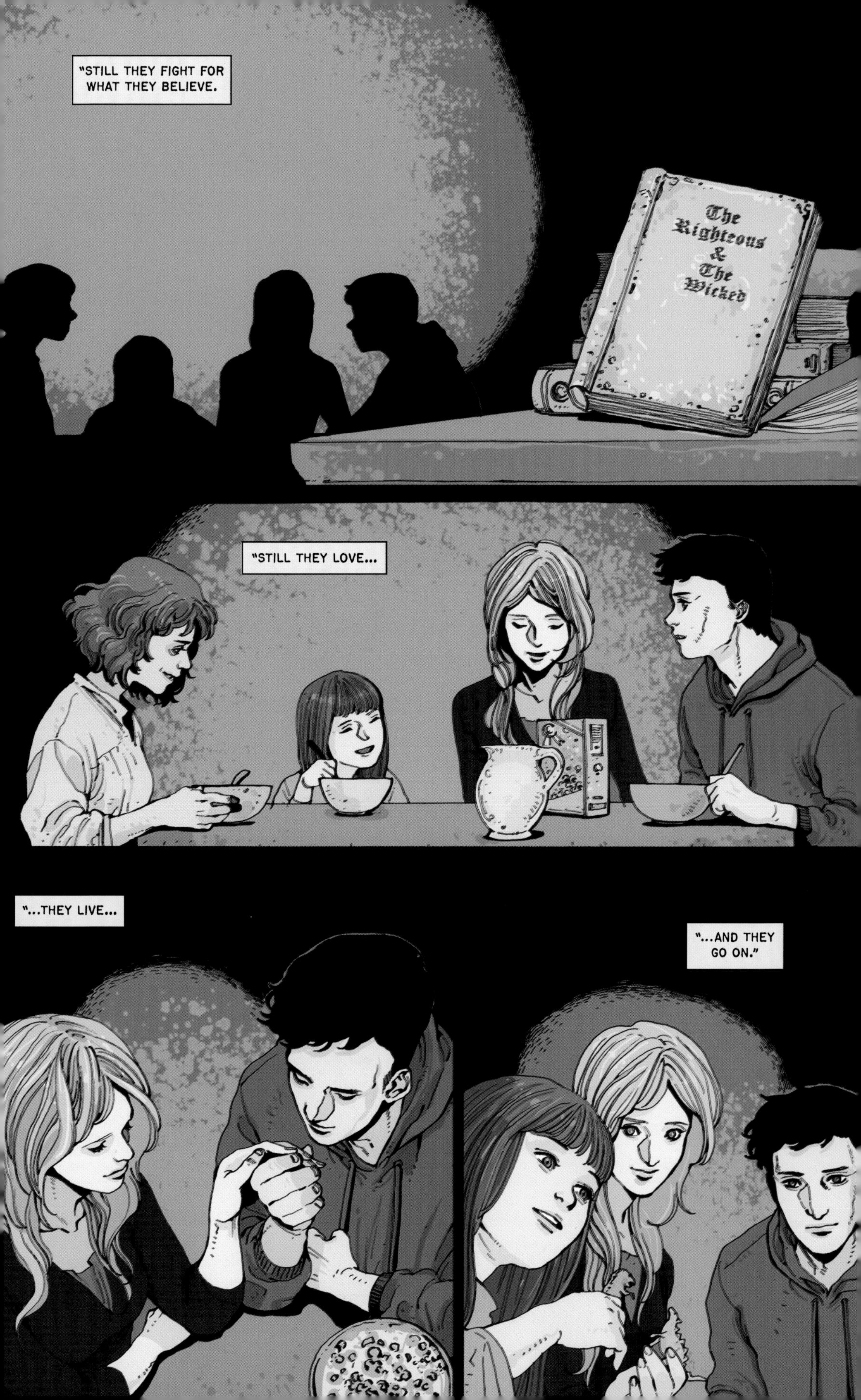
"STILL THEY FIGHT FOR WHAT THEY BELIEVE.
The Righteous & The Wicked
"STILL THEY LOVE...
"...THEY LIVE...
"...AND THEY GO ON."

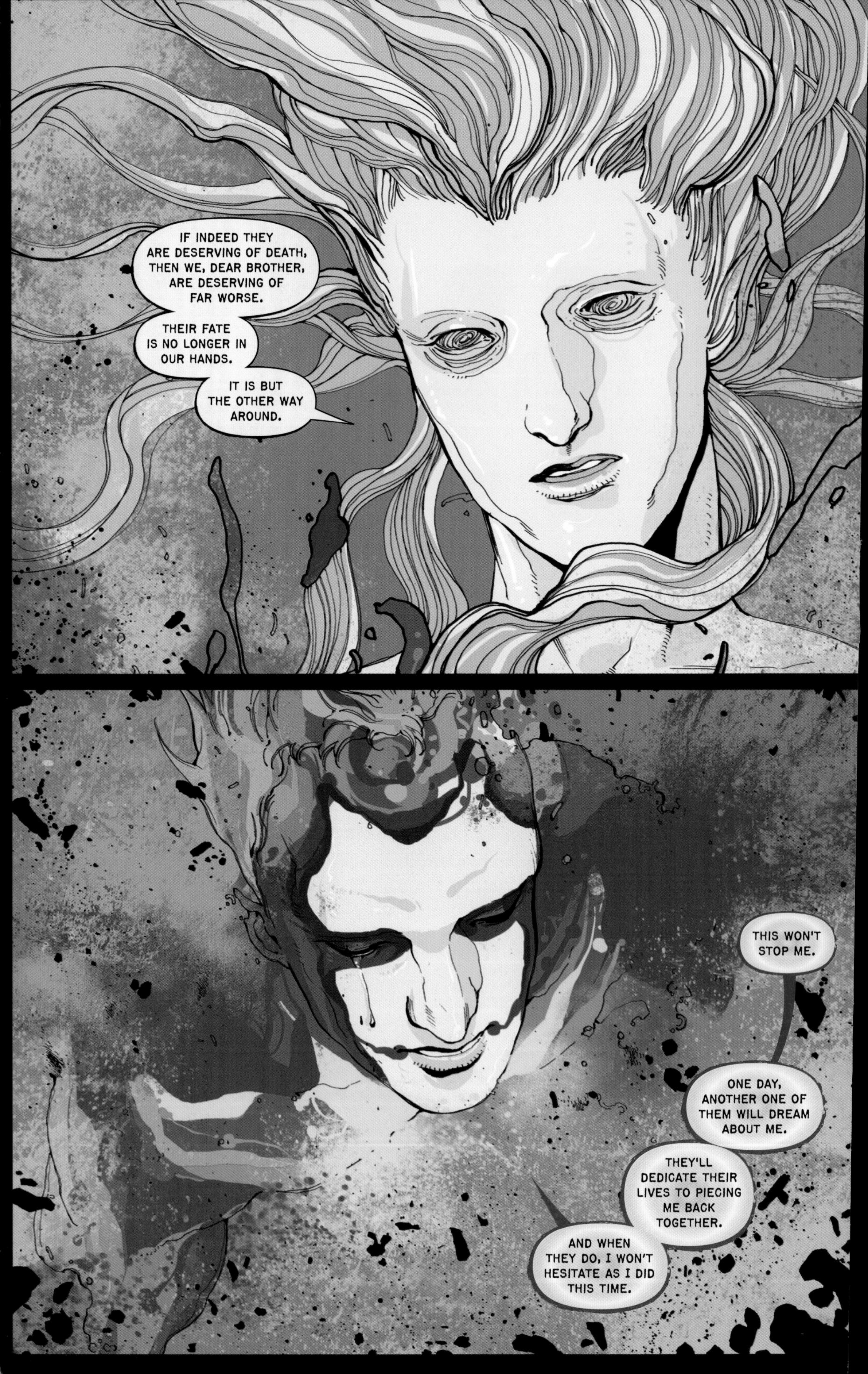
IF INDEED THEY ARE DESERVING OF DEATH, THEN WE, DEAR BROTHER, ARE DESERVING OF FAR WORSE.
THEIR FATE IS NO LONGER IN OUR HANDS.
IT IS BUT THE OTHER WAY AROUND.
THIS WON'T STOP ME.
ONE DAY, ANOTHER ONE OF THEM WILL DREAM ABOUT ME.
THEY'LL DEDICATE THEIR LIVES TO PIECING ME BACK TOGETHER.
AND WHEN THEY DO, I WON'T HESITATE AS I DID THIS TIME.

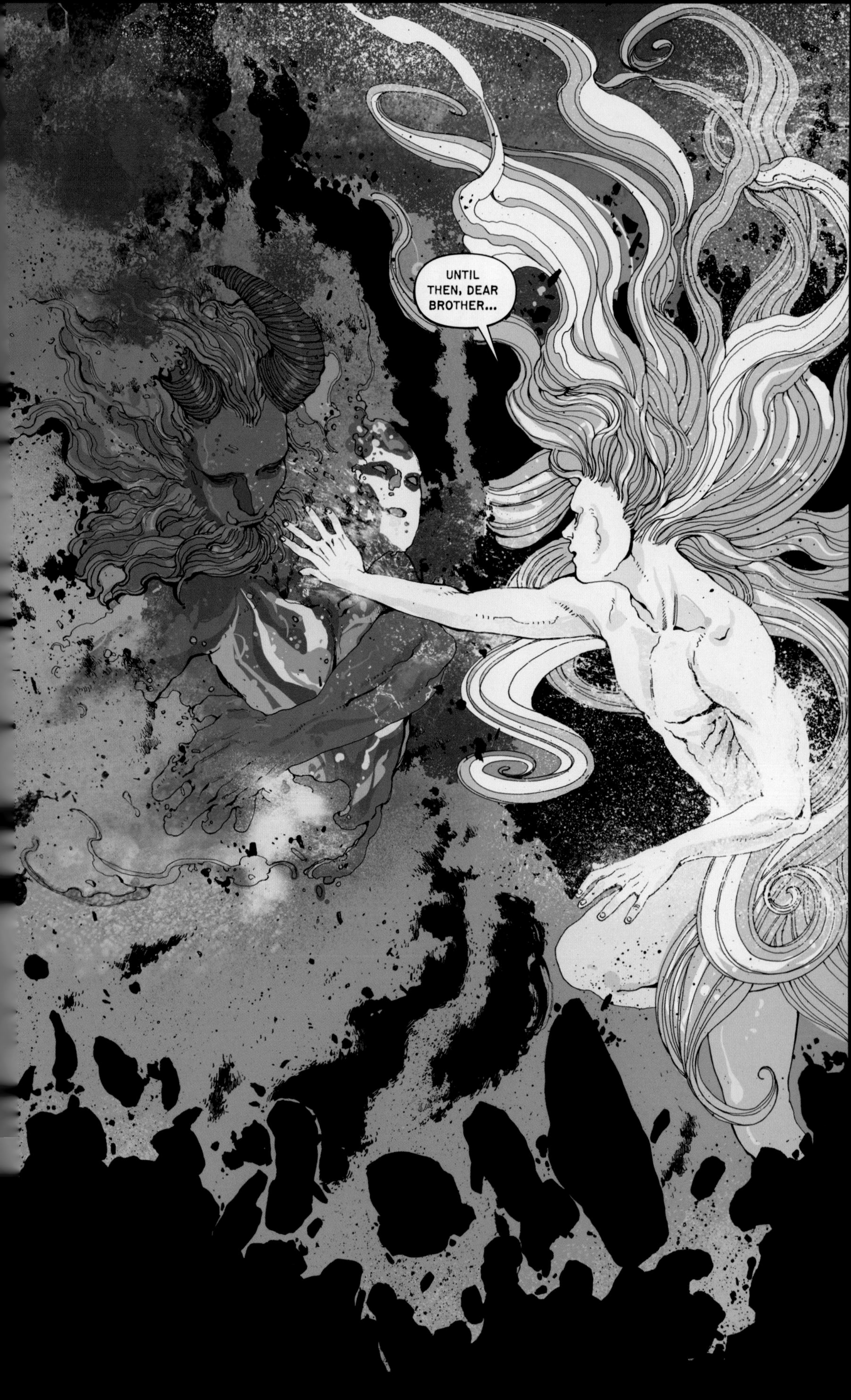
UNTIL THEN, DEAR BROTHER...

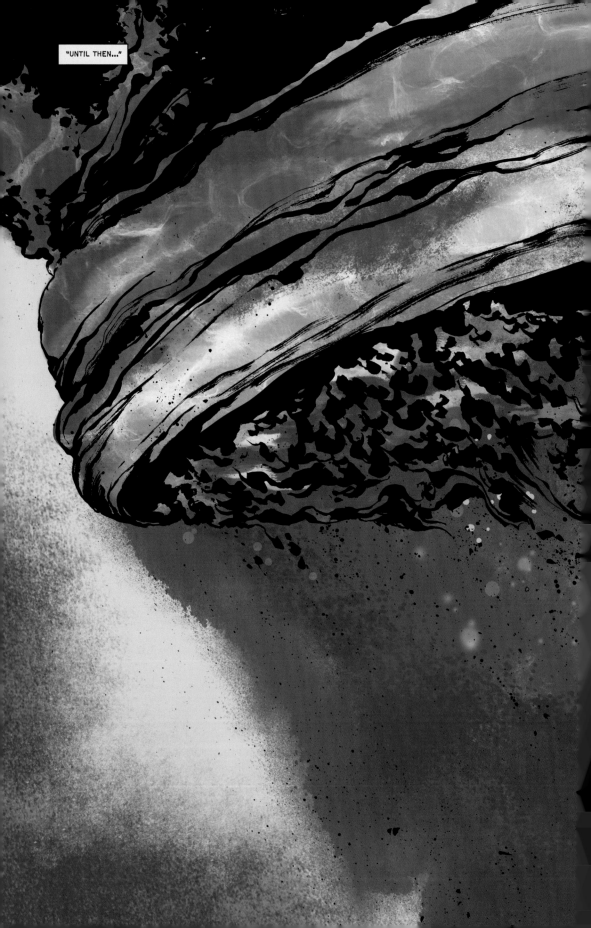

"UNTIL THEN..."

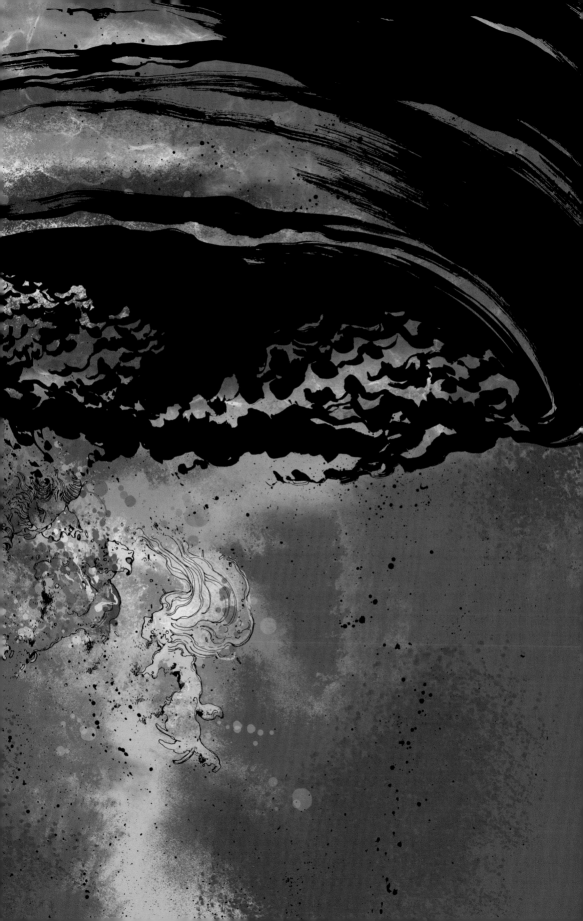

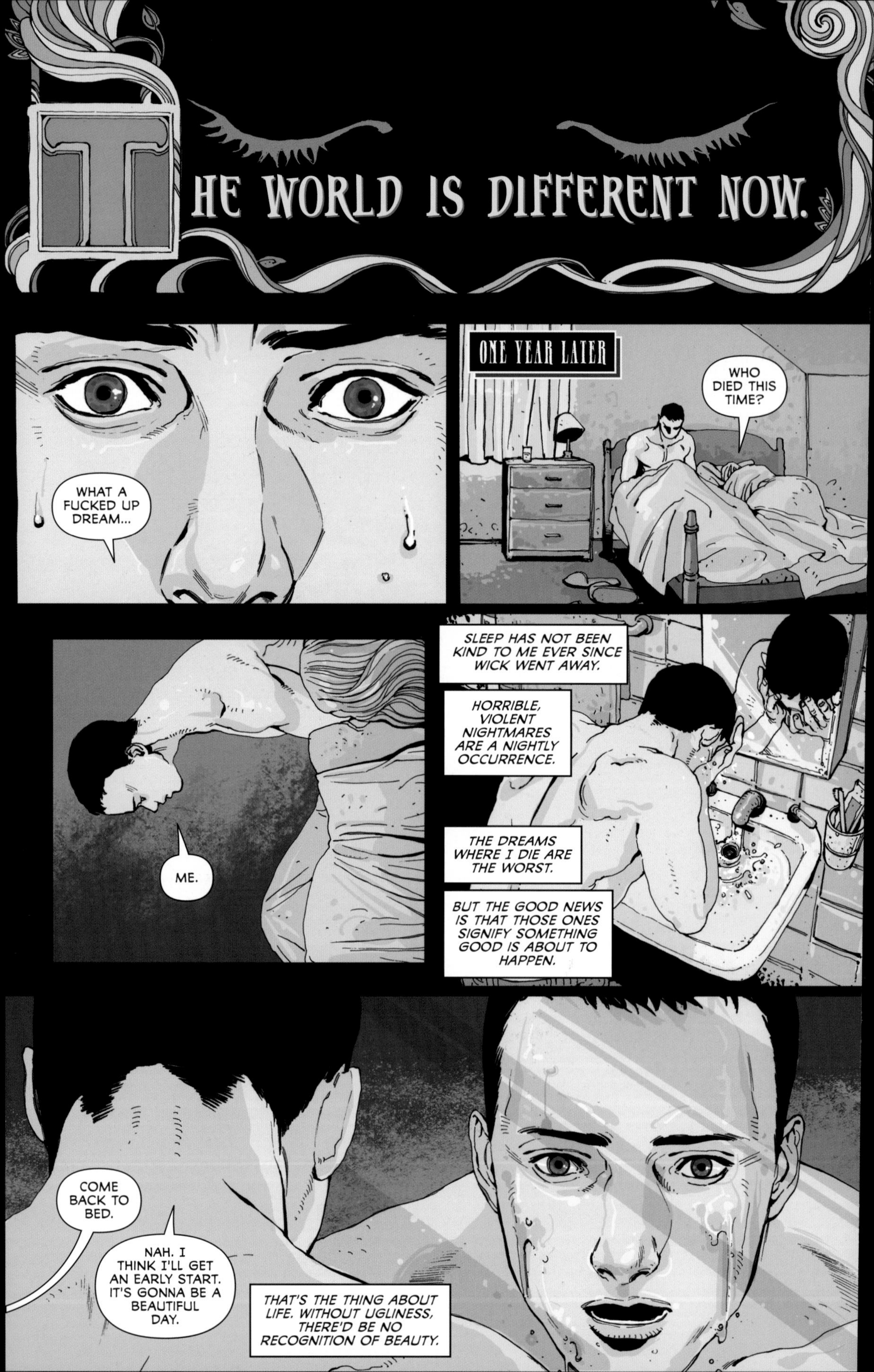
THE WORLD IS DIFFERENT NOW.
WHAT A FUCKED UP DREAM...
ONE YEAR LATER
WHO DIED THIS TIME?
ME.
SLEEP HAS NOT BEEN KIND TO ME EVER SINCE WICK WENT AWAY.
HORRIBLE, VIOLENT NIGHTMARES ARE A NIGHTLY OCCURRENCE.
THE DREAMS WHERE I DIE ARE THE WORST.
BUT THE GOOD NEWS IS THAT THOSE ONES SIGNIFY SOMETHING GOOD IS ABOUT TO HAPPEN.
COME BACK TO BED.
NAH. I THINK I'LL GET AN EARLY START. IT'S GONNA BE A BEAUTIFUL DAY.
THAT'S THE THING ABOUT LIFE. WITHOUT UGLINESS, THERE'D BE NO RECOGNITION OF BEAUTY.

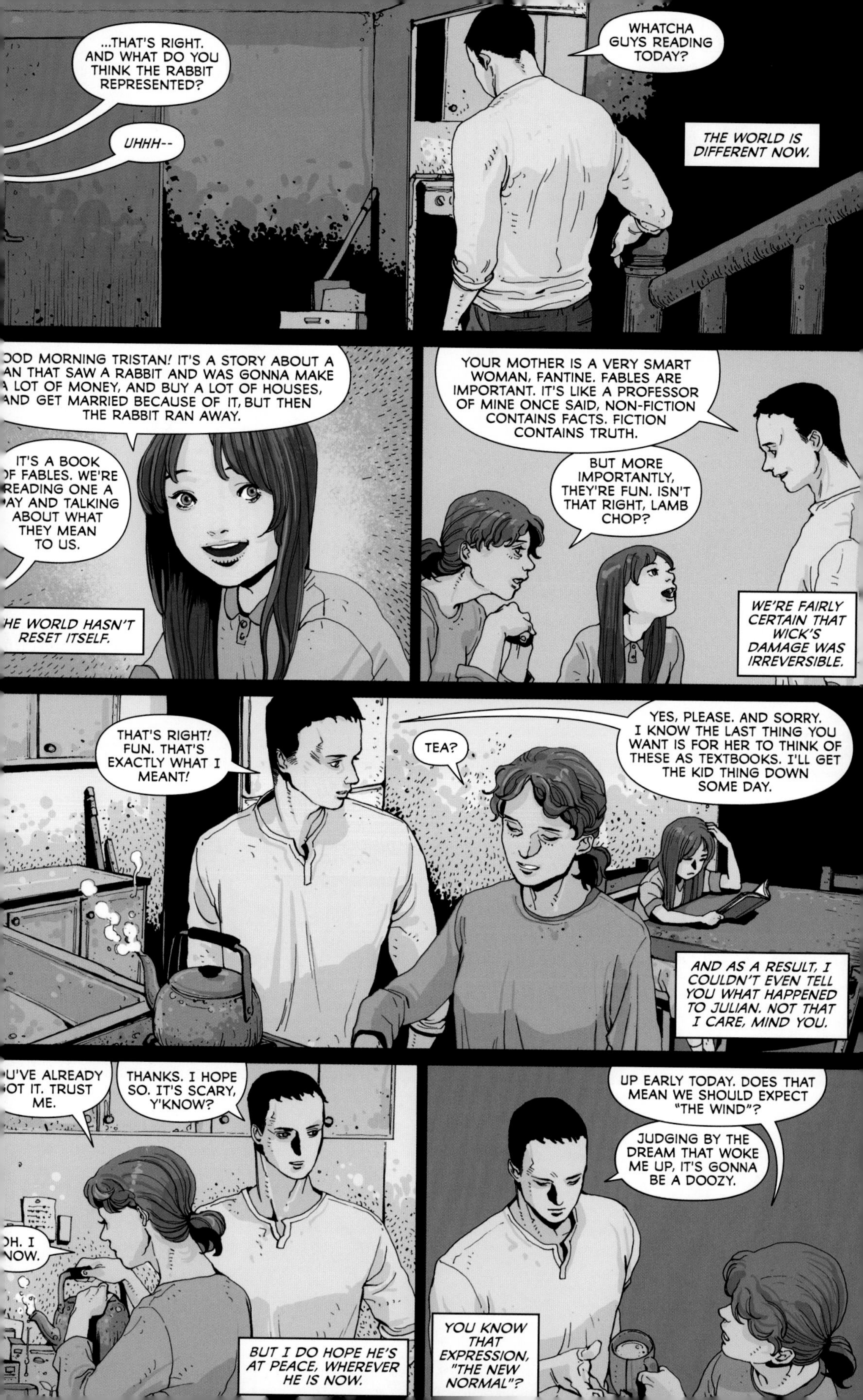

...THAT'S RIGHT. AND WHAT DO YOU THINK THE RABBIT REPRESENTED?
UHHH--
WHATCHA GUYS READING TODAY?
THE WORLD IS DIFFERENT NOW.
OOD MORNING TRISTAN! IT'S A STORY ABOUT A AN THAT SAW A RABBIT AND WAS GONNA MAKE A LOT OF MONEY, AND BUY A LOT OF HOUSES, AND GET MARRIED BECAUSE OF IT, BUT THEN THE RABBIT RAN AWAY.
IT'S A BOOK OF FABLES. WE'RE READING ONE A AY AND TALKING ABOUT WHAT THEY MEAN TO US.
HE WORLD HASN'T RESET ITSELF.
YOUR MOTHER IS A VERY SMART WOMAN, FANTINE. FABLES ARE IMPORTANT. IT'S LIKE A PROFESSOR OF MINE ONCE SAID, NON-FICTION CONTAINS FACTS. FICTION CONTAINS TRUTH.
BUT MORE IMPORTANTLY, THEY'RE FUN. ISN'T THAT RIGHT, LAMB CHOP?
WE'RE FAIRLY CERTAIN THAT WICK'S DAMAGE WAS IRREVERSIBLE.
THAT'S RIGHT! FUN. THAT'S EXACTLY WHAT I MEANT!
TEA?
YES, PLEASE. AND SORRY. I KNOW THE LAST THING YOU WANT IS FOR HER TO THINK OF THESE AS TEXTBOOKS. I'LL GET THE KID THING DOWN SOME DAY.
AND AS A RESULT, I COULDN'T EVEN TELL YOU WHAT HAPPENED TO JULIAN. NOT THAT I CARE, MIND YOU.
U'VE ALREADY OT IT. TRUST ME.
THANKS. I HOPE SO. IT'S SCARY, Y'KNOW?
OH. I NOW.
BUT I DO HOPE HE'S AT PEACE, WHEREVER HE IS NOW.
UP EARLY TODAY. DOES THAT MEAN WE SHOULD EXPECT "THE WIND"?
JUDGING BY THE DREAM THAT WOKE ME UP, IT'S GONNA BE A DOOZY.
YOU KNOW THAT EXPRESSION, "THE NEW NORMAL"?

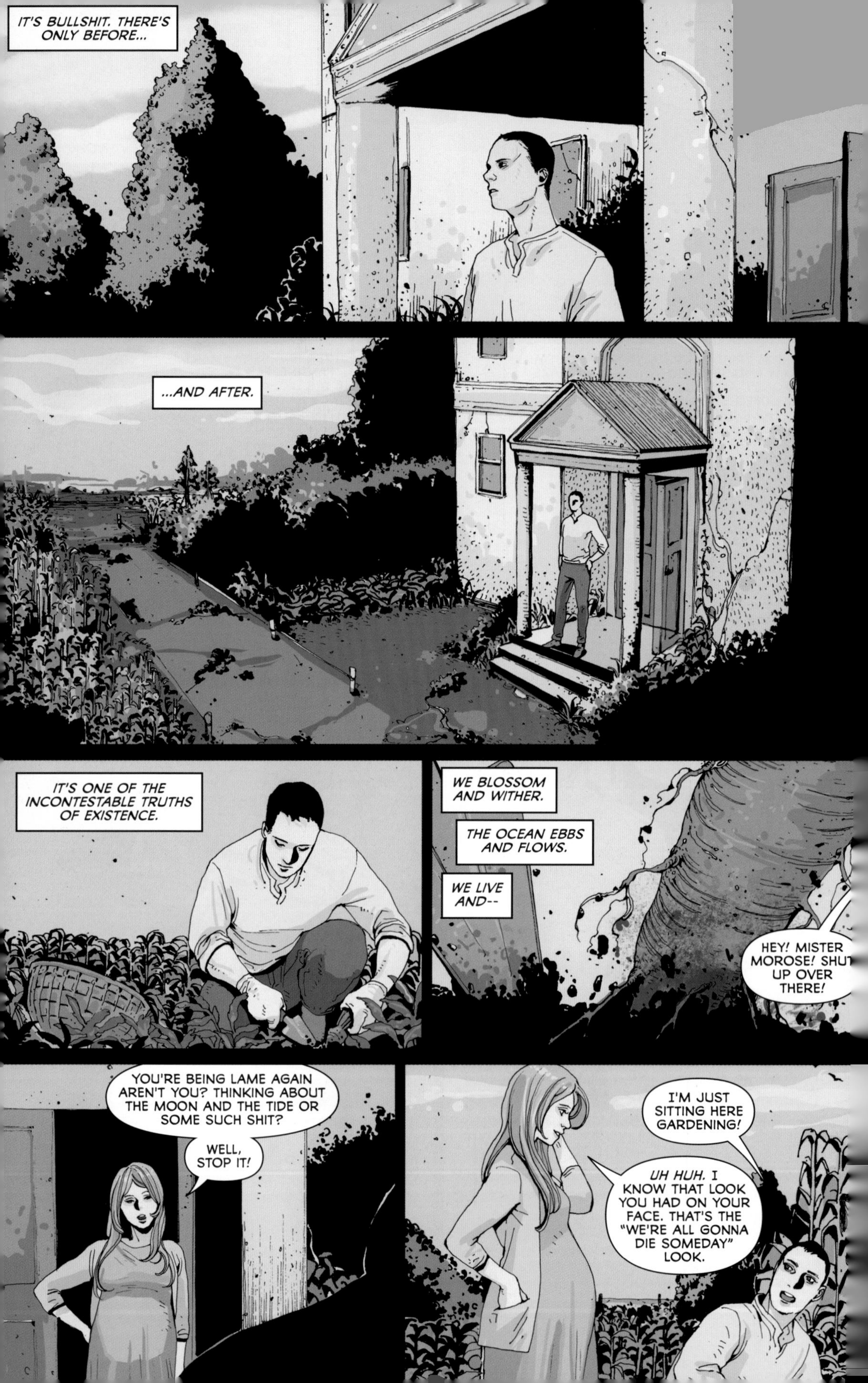
IT'S BULLSHIT. THERE'S ONLY BEFORE...
...AND AFTER.
IT'S ONE OF THE INCONTESTABLE TRUTHS OF EXISTENCE.
WE BLOSSOM AND WITHER.
THE OCEAN EBBS AND FLOWS.
WE LIVE AND--
HEY! MISTER MOROSE! SHUT UP OVER THERE!
YOU'RE BEING LAME AGAIN AREN'T YOU? THINKING ABOUT THE MOON AND THE TIDE OR SOME SUCH SHIT?
WELL, STOP IT!
I'M JUST SITTING HERE GARDENING!
UH HUH. I KNOW THAT LOOK YOU HAD ON YOUR FACE. THAT'S THE "WE'RE ALL GONNA DIE SOMEDAY" LOOK.

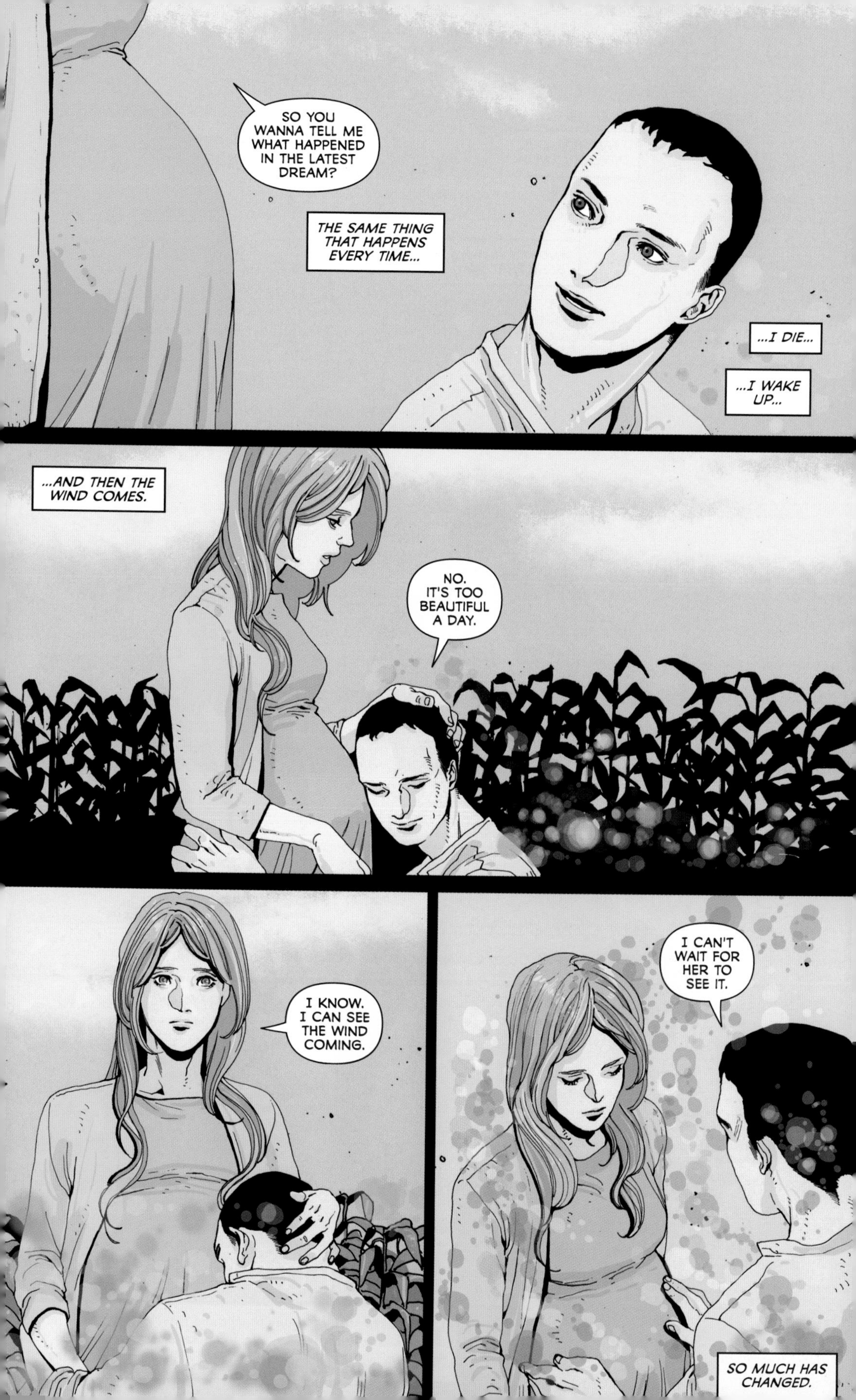
SO YOU WANNA TELL ME WHAT HAPPENED IN THE LATEST DREAM?
THE SAME THING THAT HAPPENS EVERY TIME...
...I DIE...
...I WAKE UP...
...AND THEN THE WIND COMES.
NO. IT'S TOO BEAUTIFUL A DAY.
I KNOW. I CAN SEE THE WIND COMING.
I CAN'T WAIT FOR HER TO SEE IT.
SO MUCH HAS CHANGED.

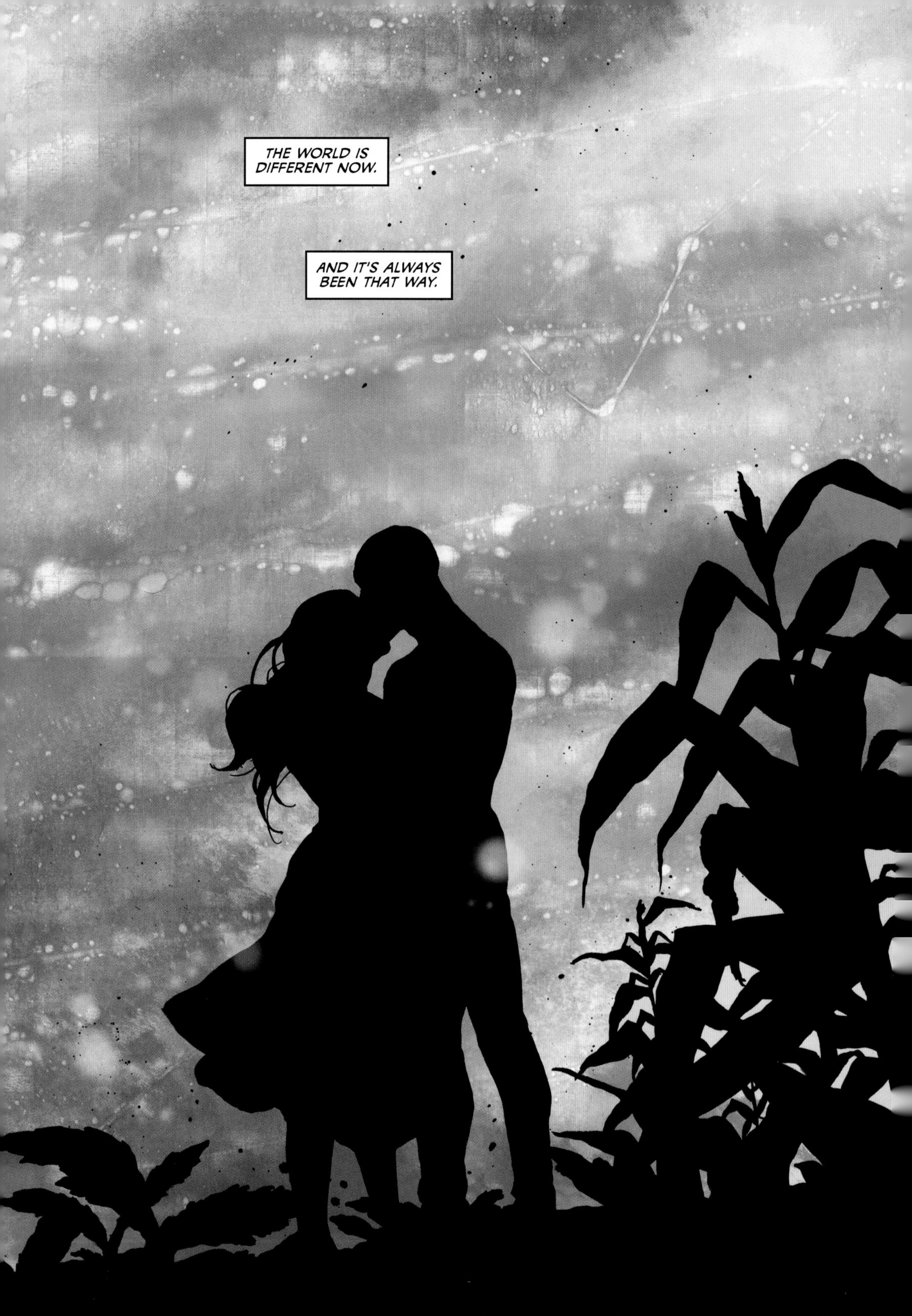
THE WORLD IS DIFFERENT NOW.
AND IT'S ALWAYS BEEN THAT WAY.

CHAPTER 12: GENESIS

"The One remains, the many change and pass, Heaven's light forever shines, Earth's shadows fly; Life, like a dome of many-coloured glass, Stains the white radiance of Eternity." —Percy Bysshe Shelley

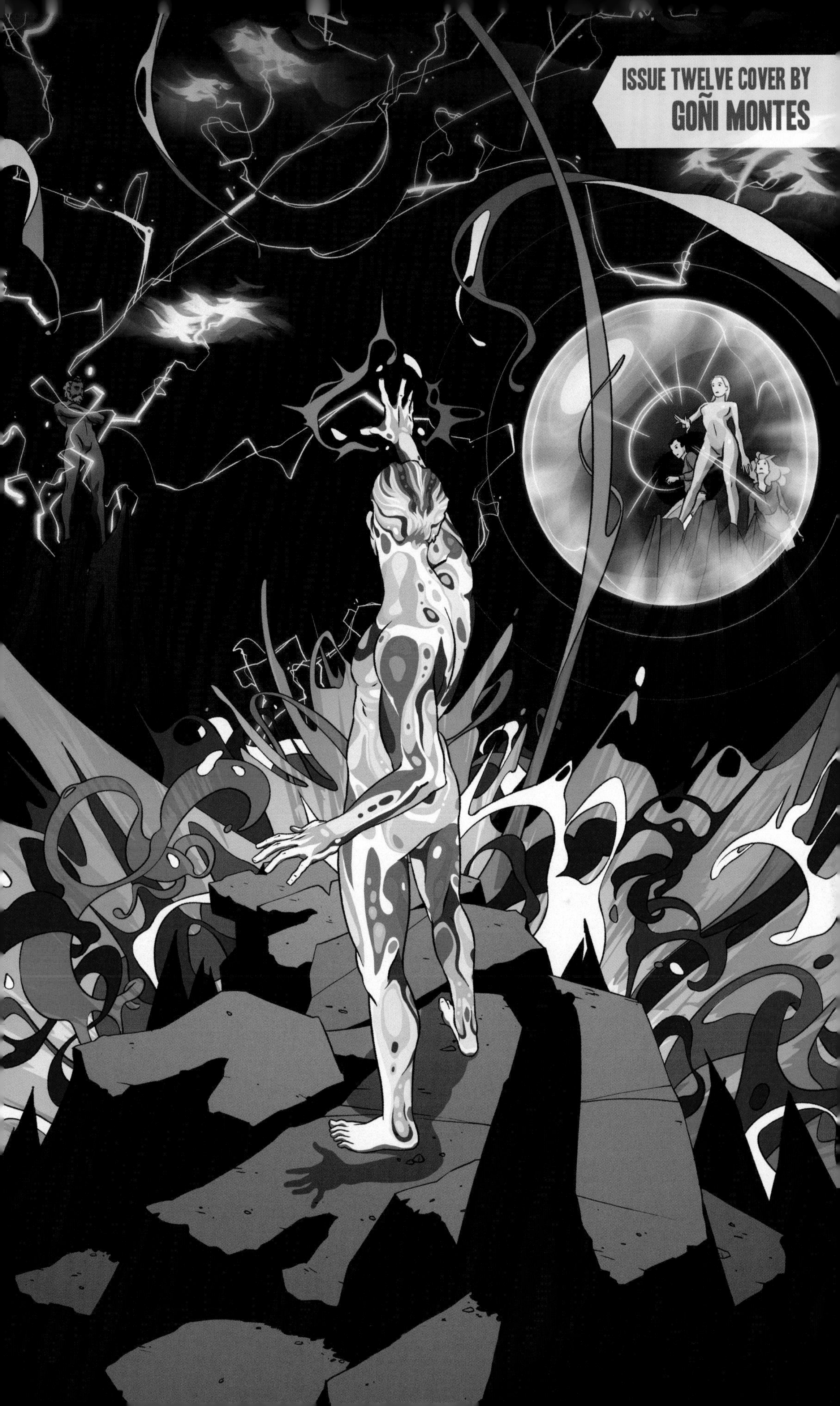

ISSUE TWELVE COVER BY
GOÑI MONTES

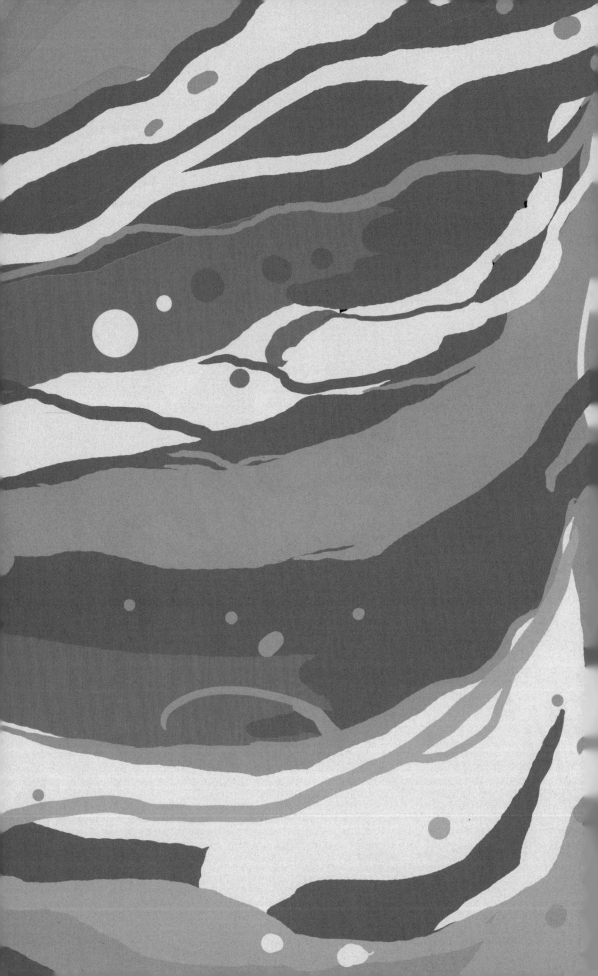

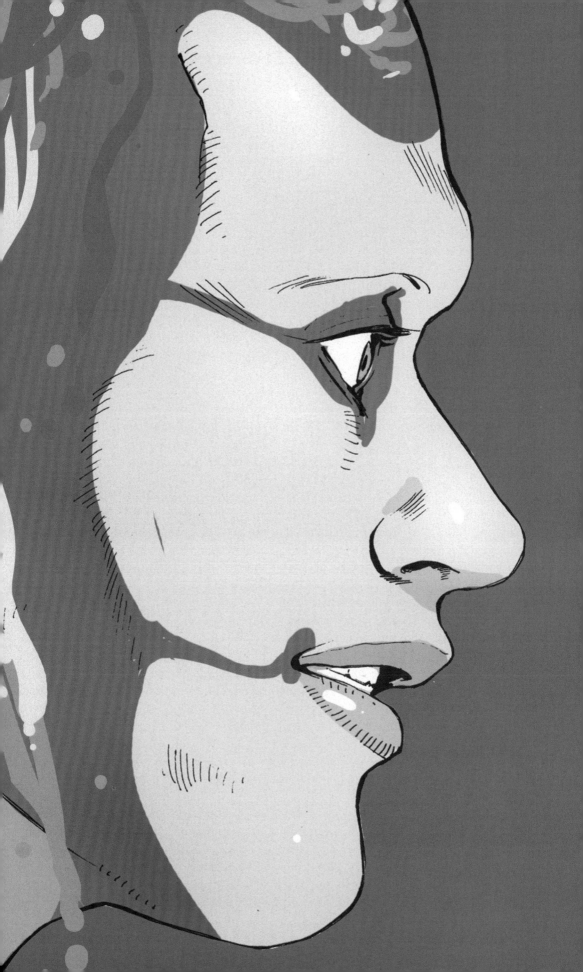

Afterword by Jonathan Maberry

In the beginning there was Clive.

For me, anyway.

Or maybe it was a new beginning.

For me. And for my love affair with horror and all things weird.

Let's start with prehistory. Again, for me. I was mostly raised by a spooky old grandmother who believed in absolutely everything. Werewolves, vampires, hinkypunks, redcaps. The works. She called it the "larger world." She was forty when she had my mother, and my mother was forty-one when I was born in 1958. My grandmother–we called her Nanny-was therefore born in the 1877. Yeah. I know. That's forever ago.

Nanny was born in Alsace-Lorraine, but her mother and grandparents were from Scotland. So, she was raised with rural French, German and Scottish folklore all around her. Or, as it was called then –beliefs. Folks in the villages believed in God and the Devil, and in all of the weird creatures of this larger world. She brought those beliefs with her when she married a Cockney cabinet-maker and emigrated to the United States.

When I came along in the Spring of '58, her beliefs were as strong, but by then she'd begun reading extensively about the beliefs here in the U.S. of A, and from other countries. She devoured stories of gods and monsters, of ghosts and spirits (which, she said, were not really the same thing), and all manner of other worlds.

My older brother and four sisters were all scared of her. She read tea leaves and tarot cards. She had visions, which she called her "sumthin's." As in "sumthin' tells me that you shouldn't go on that trip." She was right way too often to dismiss it out of hand.

I, on the other hand, found Nanny and her larger world endlessly fascinating. I learned how to read tarot cards. I began reading the strange books in her library. And eventually, or perhaps inevitably, I became interested in horror. Books, movies and comics. I started with an early edition of *I Am Legend* by Richard Matheson and was hooked. At ten years of age I snuck into the cavernous old Midway Theater in Philadelphia to see the world premier of *Night Of The Living Dead*. When Stephen King's novels hit the stores I devoured *Salem's Lot* and *The Shining*, and moved from there to Shirley Jackson, Peter Straub, August Derleth, and Lovecraft.

In 1978, Nanny passed at the venerable age of one hundred and one. She left me her books and some (not all) of her belief. I continued reading both the nonfiction and the fiction of the weird. When I became a magazine feature writer, I wrote articles for pop magazines and scholarly journals about supernatural beliefs. I even had a play produced that explored the concept of spooky other realities overlapping with our own world.

Then something happened.

By the early 1980s I was becoming deeply jaded about horror. Slasher films were on the rise and they were mostly cheap shock, devoid of genuine suspense or true horror. Many of the novels were attempts to copy Stephen King or copy Anne Rice. Sure, there were exceptions, but on the whole I wasn't reading much that jolted me. And I certainly wasn't reading anything that disturbed me, which shoved me out of complacency and into uncertainty. You see, for me, good horror, good fantasy and good science fiction must all open doorways to the possible even while telling an impossible tale. Matheson had done that with *I am Legend*. Shirley Jackson did it with *The Haunting of Hill House*. Peter Straub did it with *Ghost Story*. But the eighties were disappointing me. I found myself drifting from genre fiction.

Had that drift continued I would probably never have written my first novel, *Ghost Road Blues*. I wrote that in 2004 and it was published two years later. I'm currently writing my twenty-second novel.

What changed the course of my drift?

In 1985 my then girlfriend, Kate, went on a vacation with her mother. England, Ireland, and Scotland. I, being a lowly and underpaid college teacher, did not go with her. About a week after she landed in London, Kate sent me a letter saying that she found the perfect book for me. She knew that I was lamenting the decline of horror. She shared that view. She'd found, however, a book that she was certain would excite me, as it excited her. She promised to bring it home for me.

She did. Actually, she brought three books home with her. All written by the same author, each containing several short stories.

They were the first three volumes of *The Books of Blood* by someone I'd never heard of before.

Clive Barker.

Even with Kate's enthusiasm for the books, I read with great reluctance. Who wants to be disappointed again?

I remember that day. It was in the middle of October, which is a damn good time to read horror. So the setting was working on me. I took the book with me to work and read in on my lunch break, sitting on a bench with a coffee as the autumn winds blew past.
I was late for my next class. The coffee was abandoned untouched and cold.

During that lunch break I read one story, randomly picked. The last one in the book. *In The Hills, The Cities*.

Holy shit.

I mean, seriously. Who wrote like that?

No one.

If Lovecraft had not been a misogynist, racist and indifferent to dialogue he might have approached the fringes of this. But no closer than the fringes.

After work, I fled to my favorite open-all-night diner, drank endless cups of coffee, and read the rest of Volume One of the *Books Of Blood*.

The other stories were equally as powerful. But they were also completely different from each other. A lot of writers try for variety in their storytelling, particularly in their short works. Barker, apparently, doesn't have to try. This guy was clearly wired differently.

I gobbled up the other two volumes and was delighted to learn that Kate had already ordered the next three.
That was 1985.

That was a long time ago. The world has changed. I've changed. Kate died ten years after that autumn, alas. I'm no longer a college teacher. Now I live in southern California and I make my living writing novels and short stories and comics. People tell me I'm weird. People say I don't write like anyone else, that I have my own voice, and that my stories each have a voice of their own.

Nice.

Nowadays everyone knows who Clive Barker is. Everyone who doesn't, let's say, live in a cave. Horror has come alive again. He has a lot to do with that. Horror is interesting and there are many, many authors who felt empowered to write in their own voice rather than try to imitate Poe or Lovecraft, or King or Rice.

Nobody in their right minds tries to imitate Clive Barker.

Now Clive Barker is writing comics.

The comic, **Next Testament**, isn't like anything else.

Clive, and his writing partner Mark Miller, have tackled a trope that has long been in danger of being played out–let's call it deconstructionist religious storytelling. Sure, there have been some great entries in that genre. *Preacher* by Garth Ennis comes immediately to mind. But there have been a lot of comics in this genre that I'd begun to believe that there was nothing new to say. It was kind of how I was with horror back in 1985.

Then I saw the cover of issue #3 of Next Testament in my local comic shop. Loved the cover art by Goñi Montes. Then I spotted the names of the writers. Mark Miller and Clive Barker.

I knew Miller from his work on the **Hellraiser** comic, which spins off of Clive Barker's short novel *The Hellbound Heart*.

But here was Clive himself listed as co-writer. There had been a slew of adaptations of his stories, and others based on his ideas. As far as I knew this was the first time he was actually writing a comic.

I asked the guy behind the counter if they had the first two issues. He did, and I snatched up all three. Read them on a park bench. Yes, coffee was involved.

Once more I entered a version of the world as imagined by Clive Barker. Once more it was different than I expected. I admit to having some trepidations when I realized this was deconstructionist religious storytelling. As I said, I fell that genre hit a wall.

But I read it.

Holy shit.

Yes, that phrase is chosen with precision.

The story of a rich madman and legendary asshole Julian Demond who opens a hidden tomb and releases a powerful spirit that has been imprisoned there. The spirit–well, pretty much a worst-case scenario version of the Almighty. Wick, the Father of Color.

And then a lot of very weird, very violent, and very disturbing stuff happens.

There are good guys and more bad guys. They are other celestial beings.

There is a lot of violence.

And it never bloody well lets up.
From end to end Next Testament is a roller-coaster ride of dark fantasy, horror, piety, impiety, probably heresy, and ink-dark humor. There is even some warmth, heart, and hope sewn into the fabric. Issue by issue you need to buckle up because there's no real way to know where it's all going.

Having taken the whole ride, though, I can guarantee that the destination isn't on the map. Nope.

Clive Barker and Mark Miller are a seamless creative fit. And the art by Haemi Jang is fearless and inventive.

So, yeah…once again Clive threw the right bait into the water of creative ennui and reeled in something juicy, delicious and deeply strange.

But…it's Clive, so what the hell do you expect?

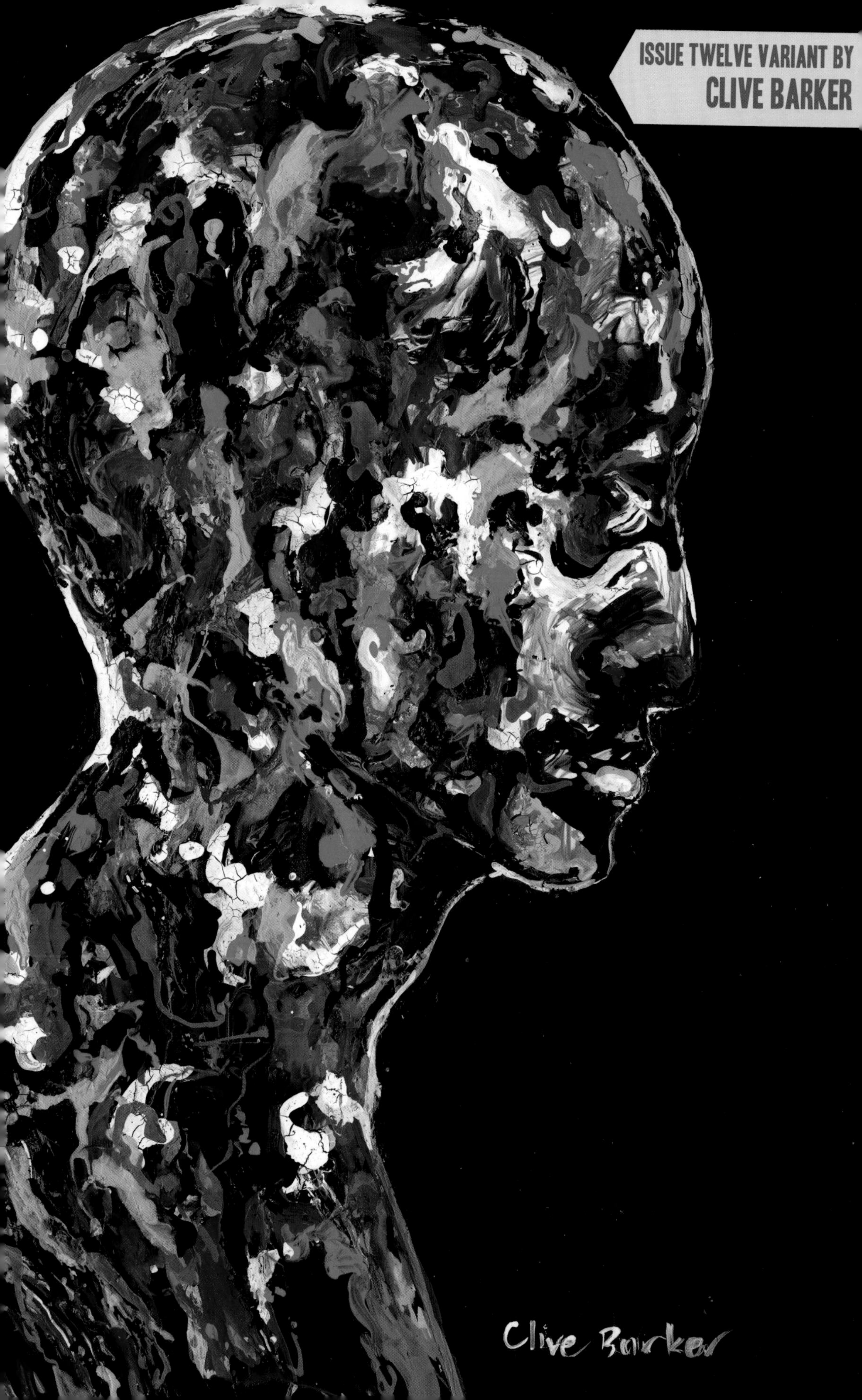
Clive Barker

ISSUE TWELVE VARIANT BY
CLIVE BARKER

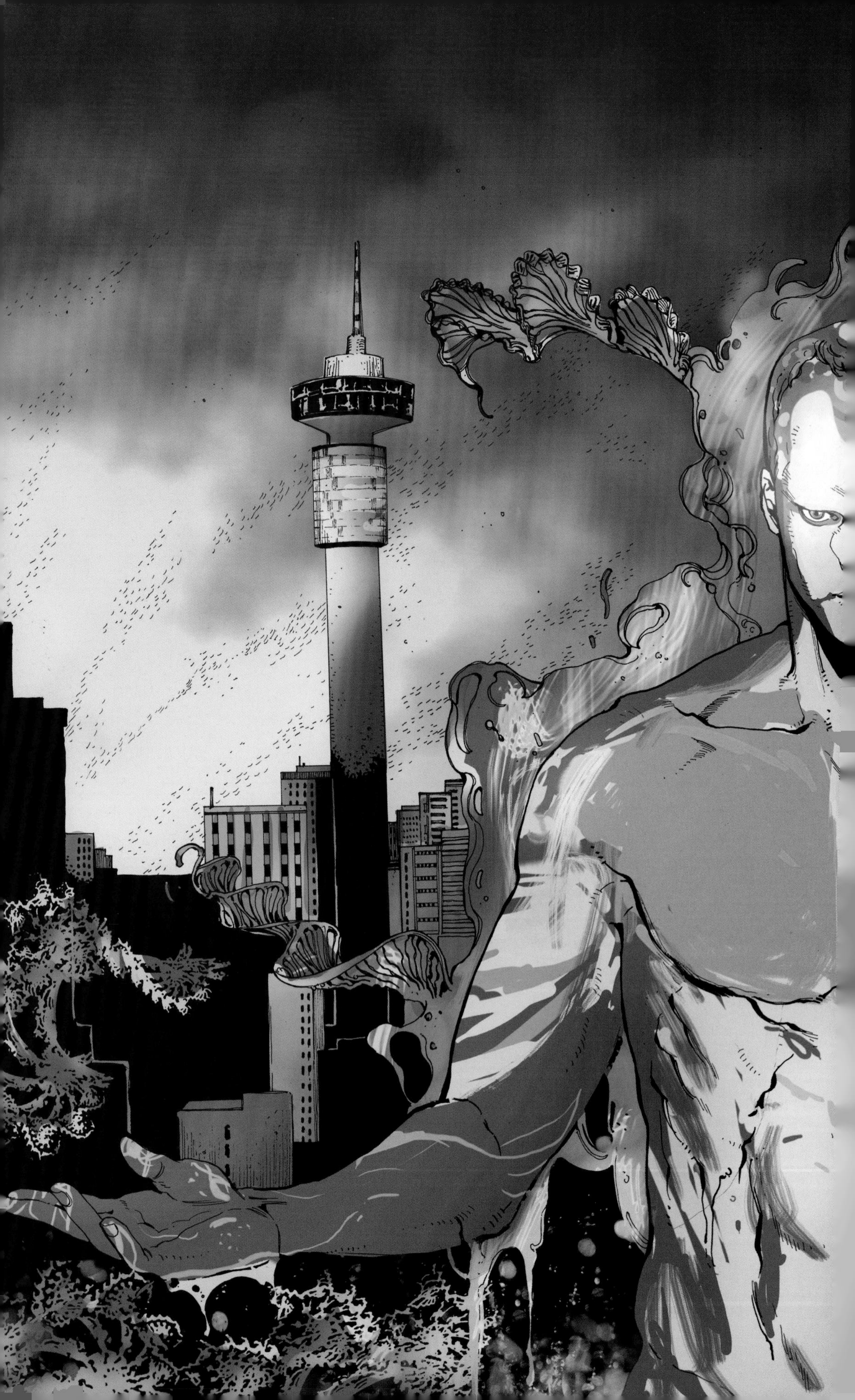

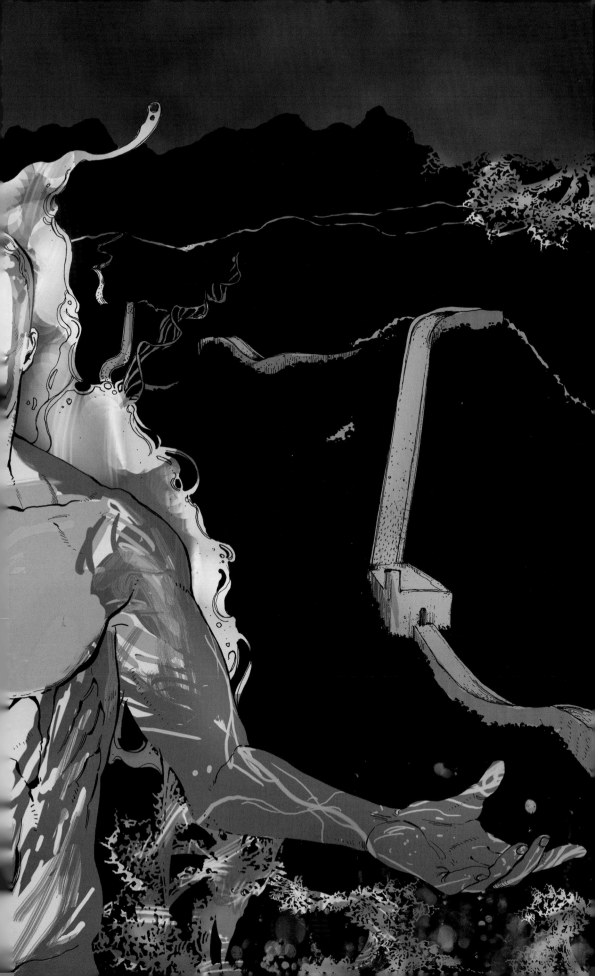

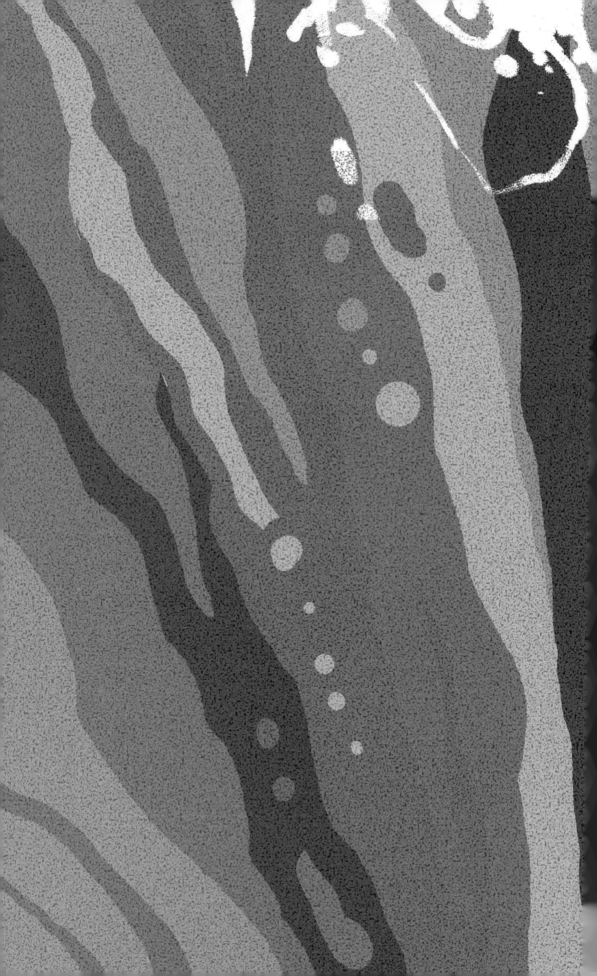